Githa Hariharan is the author of several acclaimed books, including the novels *The Thousand Faces of Night* (which won the Commonwealth Writers' Prize for Best First Book), *The Ghosts of Vasu Master*, *When Dreams Travel*, *In Times of Siege*, *Fugitive Histories* and *I Have Become the Tide*; the short story collection *The Art of Dying*; and the collection of essays *Almost Home, Cities and Other Places*. She has also edited an anthology of translated short fiction, *A Southern Harvest*, and the collection *From India to Palestine: Essays in Solidarity*.

Salim Yusufji was a schoolteacher for fifteen years, and has previously edited *Ambedkar: The Attendant Details*, a selection of reminiscences by people in close proximity to B.R. Ambedkar.

BATTLING FOR INDIA
A Citizen's Reader

Edited by

Githa Hariharan
Salim Yusufji

SPEAKING
TIGER

SPEAKING TIGER PUBLISHING PVT. LTD
4381/4, Ansari Road, Daryaganj
New Delhi 110002

Copyright © Indian Cultural Forum 2019

Copyright for individual pieces vests in the respective writers,
illustrators or the publications/sites

While every effort has been made to contact copyright holders and
obtain permission to reproduce material, this has not been possible in
every case. Any omission brought to the publisher's
notice shall be corrected in future editions.

ISBN: 978-93-88874-20-5
eISBN: 978-93-88874-19-9

10 9 8 7 6 5 4 3 2 1

Typeset in Minion Pro by SÜRYA, New Delhi

CONTENTS

INTRODUCTION

Here are some people, quite a few of them actually, that you and I should meet. Alivelamma, a woman farmer. Huchangi, Rohith, Ravan, poet, student, activist; all dalit. Sukalo, Rajkishor, Leelabati, activist, poet, singer; adivasis. Salima and Jaffruddin, who happen to be Muslim. Two workers; one a union member, the other home-based.

And there, not too far away, are journalists, writers, artists, teachers and many young people—some of them students, many of them looking for work.

What do all these people have in common? First, the crowded country where they all live, the nation called India. This nation is an idea too. Out of this idea grew a rights-based Constitution that steers the nation so all its people can live as equal citizens. But over the last few years, there has been a battle going on in this country. The battle began a while back, perhaps more than a decade back. But since 2014, it has reached a feverish pitch. We can now see two signposts as we enter the Indian nation. One reads: *Battling India*, and it knows only one language, of coercion and plunder. The other says, boldly, and in many voices that speak many languages: *Battling* for *India*; and this is the second thing the people we should meet have in common.

The Battling India Parivar, a many-headed beast, has both official and unofficial guides to take us around its dominion. It has its own police who shoot, lynch, bomb. It seeks to regulate what we think, write, sing; what we eat and wear; how we pray or whom we love. A versatile and busy force, this lot. The official guides (official because they are, for now, the government), smother us with cooked-up data and harangue us endlessly about development. They boast of making the GDP soar, crushing black money, and our eyes glaze over. To get our attention back, they try to scare us: there are enemies everywhere, across the border and within our borders. This is why they are building a sanctuary. Seeing this work in progress, we can tell that the inhabitants of the sanctuary will be mostly Hindu, preferably upper caste, ideally male and heterosexual. They will, of course, make room for their best friends, all of whom belong to a rich and exclusive gang of barons, company sharks and godmen.

Tired of all this exclusiveness, depleted by it, we seek some regular people so we can still recognise the India we used to call home. And we meet the Battling for India Republic.

Alivelamma, the farmer.

She is a 35-year-old widow. In 2013, her husband, also a farmer, committed suicide. The groundnuts he had sowed were not giving him returns; the debt was mounting; the moneylenders were chasing him. Alivelamma now works as a tenant farmer and takes care of her son who is studying at an industrial training institute. She wants a better life for her son and herself; but she also wants justice for her husband and others like him.*

The Parivar pretends to be deaf to her. It has more pressing (and more lucrative) matters to attend to than loan waivers, minimum support price, water as a fundamental right, piles of reports from commissions on farmers. It does have an accidental gift for farmers though: the cows it is supposedly protecting in its gaushalas stray into fields and destroy the crop.

Huchangi, Rohith, Ravan.

Huchangi is the son of a devadasi. He shows us the place he comes from and how his people live. They are forced to live outside the village in houses as small as ten square feet. They are landless. Many of the dalit women are dedicated to temples as devadasis and they survive "by begging during the day and doing sex work in the nights". Rohith is—was—a university student on a scholarship; bright, political, full of dreams. His fellowship is suspended; in a caste-ridden society, his birth is his "fatal accident". Ravan, or Chandrasekhar Azad, brings together a social movement, a Bhim Army to fight for bahujan rights.

---

*Rahul M. "Anantapur to Delhi: Alivelamma's Talsiman", PARI, November 30, 2018. See <<https://ruralindiaonline.org/articles/anantapur-to-delhi-alivelammas-talsiman>>.

The Parivar threatens Huchangi for writing poems about caste; it insists Rohith was not dalit; it charges Ravan under the National Security Act and keeps him imprisoned for a year. It garlands a portrait of Ambedkar, then sets loose its second and third cousins to flog dalits in Una, cut funds and scholarships, unleash cow vigilantes and destroy livelihood by banning cattle trade. As a postscript, it suggests the word *dalit* should not be used by officials or the media.

Sukalo, Rajkishor, Leelabati.

Sukalo is worried, like many adivasis, about being displaced if a dam is built on the Kanhar river, and about their water source being polluted. She joins protests against the Kanhar irrigation project. Rajkishor and his wife Leelabati can see what mining is doing to their ancestral lands in the Niyamgiri hills. But the authorities are not concerned; a multinational wants to mine the sacred hills for bauxite, used to make aluminium, and the government backs the multinational, not the people who live there. Rajkishor and Leelabati write songs about the injustice.

The police fire into the crowd and arrest Sukalo. Rajkishor and Leelabati also spend time in prison. The Parivar only talks about the fatherland and the motherland, not about the people's land. Like those who ruled before it, the Parivar too brings in many "development projects" with big companies, big miners, big dams, and bigger statues.

Salima and Jaffruddin.

Salima had a husband, Fazruddin. He was killed in a fake encounter; Salima was threatened and her home raided. Jaffruddin had a son, Salim. A mob of "cow vigilantes" killed him. The police exhumed his body—which traumatised the family further—but, strangely enough, they did not hand over a post mortem report.

The Parivar leaders are busy protecting and worshipping cows. They don't see Salima or Jaffruddin. But their ardent fans do. They spew venomous words; they pull out fists, knives, guns. They raise an axe. They are such specialists in hatred that some of them even record their words and acts of violence. The videos circulate freely. There is no fear they might be used as evidence.

Two workers; one a union member, the other home-based.

They have perfectly understandable demands, such as fair wages and good working conditions. How long will they work to fill the already bulging bags of the rich?

The Parivar responds by rolling out a plan of less and less rights. Then to ensure complete misery, its chosen leader demonetises every single worker, organised or unorganised; and for good measure, every ordinary person in sight.

Journalists, writers, artists, teachers and many young people.

Some of the youth are looking for work. Others are students, and they ask sharp questions; the teachers encourage them because how else will anyone learn? The journalists, writers and artists are simply doing what they must: chasing truth in their different ways.

The Parivar deals with the journalists, writers and artists quickly; they can be fired, trolled, hounded, their families threatened. As for the fearless, they can be taken care of by the unofficial side of the extended family—a network of assassins. The teachers and students can be branded seditious, anti-national, urban Naxal, and their universities starved of funds, even shut down. The unemployed youth can be taught to fry pakodas or join camps where they learn to be sevaks of a Hindu Rashtra. Women, whether young or old, student or farmer, can be reduced to bodies that can be shamed, threatened, stripped, raped. It helps of course if they are dalit or Muslim or adivasi or poor. Or politically awake.

We feel despair at the sight of this India, so shrunken that there's no room for most of its people. Is there something we are missing?

We look again. And we see that the people the Parivar and its associates have excluded from India do not suffer in silence or fade away. They get together to demand their share of dignity— of equality. They *include* themselves in India and lay claim to citizenship.

Alivelamma is in Delhi, at the Ramlila Maidan. Carrying a photo of her dead husband, she says: "We came here for justice, so that farmers don't commit suicide."* She is not alone. There are 180 farmer organisations that have given a call for farmers to march to Delhi. Earlier, 40,000 adivasi farmers, the poorest of farmers, walked a long march from Nashik to Mumbai with their demands.

Huchangi fights back; so does Ravan. There are Rohiths reborn with new names, to dream, and to fight to annihilate caste. In Una, after four cattle skinners are whipped by cow vigilantes, dalit protesters leave carcasses of cows outside a government office. It is as if they are saying, "If the cows are sacred, if they are your mothers, *you* deal with their corpses." Dalit organisations call for a Bharat Bandh. And there are brave new armies. There's a Bhim Army marching; there's a Safai Karmachari Andolan to insist that no woman or man should be a manual scavenger.

Sukalo, too, will not give up. She can continue to fight because it is not her fight alone, she is part of the union of forest-working people. Rajkishor and Leelabati travel from village to village, singing songs that spread the message of the movement against the destruction of the Niyamgiri hills. The poor people in the villages invite the couple into their homes and give them food and shelter.

Salima pursues justice for Fazruddin, supported by the Extra-Judicial Execution Victim Families Association (EEVFAM). Her fight is part of a larger campaign to confront the impunity of security forces and assert the rights and dignity of the people of Manipur. There are citizens from other parts of the country who travel to where she is, express their mohabbat and solidarity.

Workers across the country get together and strike in tea gardens, in the railways, in the states and the national capital. They raise powerful slogans. They declare a two-day industrial strike to protest job loss and demand better wages.

And students and teachers, writers and scientists, whatever their other identities, insist on their right to speak, to dissent. They strike a blow for everyone's freedom. Punjabi fiction writer

---

*Rahul M., PARI, 2018.

Dalip Kaur Tiwana returns her Padma Shri in protest against intolerance in 2015, saying, "In this land of Gautama Buddha and Guru Nanak Dev, the atrocities committed on the Sikhs in 1984 and on the Muslims recurrently because of communalism are an utter disgrace to our state and society. And to kill those who stand for truth and justice puts us to shame in the eyes of the world and God." A Class 11 student, Muddu Thirthahalli of Sahyadri High School, returns her Karnataka Sahitya Akademi award to protest the killing of scholar M.M. Kalburgi, saying, "There should be no curbs on free speech and writing." A veteran scientist, Pushpa Mittra Bhargava, returns his Padma Bhushan award to protest "the government's attack on rationalism, reasoning and science".

All these people who confront so many ways of being excluded from India, and who insist on being included—what are they saying, what are they *showing* us? That they are participating members of a political community. That they are citizens. The Constitution, which came out of a struggle for an independent country, belongs to them. When every institution, from the RBI to the mainstream media, appears to have buckled under pressure, they have held their ground. Their scattered groups look both vulnerable and mighty, exposed to the wrath of the state; but they are also aware that *they* remain the final arbiters of political destiny. We need to hear them, take heart from them, and be one with them, especially now, when the right-wing is tearing apart the diverse fabric of our collective home. In a time when the state and extra-state forces work hard to exclude more and more citizens from India, it is imperative that we battle for an inclusive India. That time is now.

*

It is from the varied voices of people who have asserted their citizenship—from the Battling for India Republic—that we got the idea of a citizen's reader. An Indian citizen's reader. We imagined a stage on which citizens speak. What might this be like? To begin with, there would be a cast of hundreds; thousands. There would be many languages, and many ways of speaking the same inclusive language. And there would be many matters that simply must be spoken about, and that must, at this very moment, be heard. That's the rough idea with which we began this modest book with an outsized ambition.

We heard voices we had not heard before, or not clearly enough. Only when we heard more and more conversations did we actually begin to re-learn the nature of citizenship, and the battle to claim it afresh. Hearing from our fellow citizens helped us enter into their stories; and that reaffirmed who we are and the India we make together, because citizens reside in the heart of the debates—and the battles—we are living through.

We have not called those battling for India "the Republic" without reason. In his address to the Constituent Assembly in 1948, B.R. Ambedkar said:

> In politics we will have equality and in social and economic life we will have inequality. In politics we will be recognising the principle of one man one vote and one vote one value. In our social and economic life, we shall, by reason of our social and economic structure, continue to deny the principle of one man one value. How long shall we continue to live this life of contradictions? How long shall we continue to deny equality in our social and economic life? If we continue to deny it for long, we will do so only by putting our political democracy in peril.*

What Ambedkar was making clear is that the Constitution should guarantee all citizens full rights to the nation. What he was making clear is that such a guarantee of political democracy would be meaningless without social and economic democracy. Social democracy—it meant that the age-old exclusion, caste, would not be dealt with only through support structures such as reservation, but also with a compact to annihilate it altogether;

---

*From B.R. Ambedkar's Address to the Constituent Assembly on November 25, 1949. See "Lessons for Today in Ambedkar's Last Address to the Constituent Assembly", *The Wire*, April 14, 2017.

that women, or minority communities, or adivasis, or people from neglected, brutalized regions of the country, would be included in a *lived* equality. Economic democracy—this meant freeing *all* Indians from poverty, famine, low life expectancy, illiteracy, unfair wages and unemployment; in effect, it meant a redistribution of resources. This was the rich and real democracy envisioned in 1948.

Seventy years later, such a democracy—a country with a *living* equality—can only be re-made, made afresh, by people who have laid claim to their citizenship despite all odds. M.M. Kalburgi, who was killed for what he thought and wrote, put a line into the mouth of an "untouchable" old man in one of his plays: "You can silence me, but you cannot silence the truth." The Indian people who have made themselves citizens—despite all attempts to silence them—know exactly what these words mean. This citizen's reader is for them; it is about them.

February 2019

GITHA HARIHARAN
SALIM YUSUFJI

PART ONE

FACING DOWN THE THOUGHT POLICE

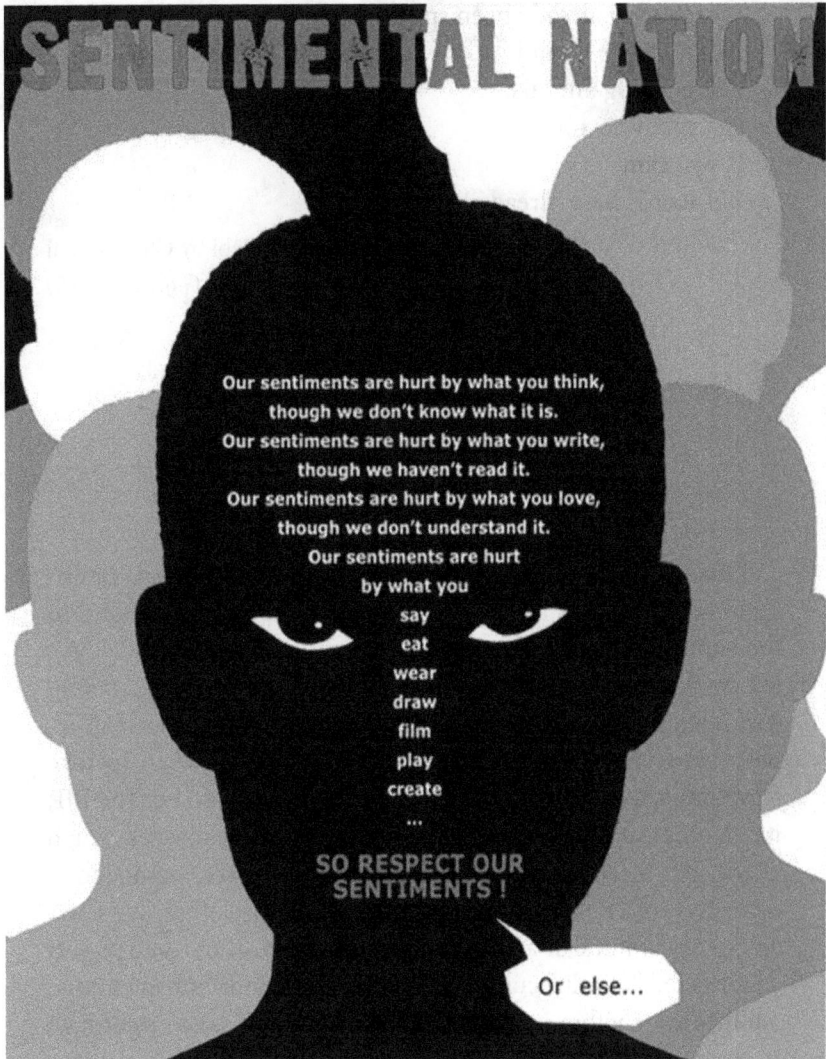

Orijit Sen, Indian Cultural Forum, 2015

WORDS

Lal Singh Dil

Words have already been spoken
much before us and
will be, long after us.
Cut off every tongue
If you can,
But words have already been spoken.

—Translated from Punjabi by Chaman Lal
(*Guftugu*, 2016)

DISSENT IN OCTOBER

Indian Cultural Forum

Culture in India has always been diverse, multilingual, multi-regional; and it has always been open to debate and dissent. In the summer of 2014, the National Democratic Alliance (NDA), led by the Bharatiya Janata Party (BJP), swept to power, taking 336 seats in the Lok Sabha. A new government was sworn in, with Narendra Modi as prime minister, and it began to take fresh interest in what "Indian culture" is and should be. The BJP, its ideological fountainhead, the Rashtriya Swayamsevak Sangh (RSS), and their cohorts stepped up their mission to homogenise diversity—of thought, idea, song, film, art, food, clothes, language; any sort of cultural or artistic practice and expression—and project a fabricated "Hindu" culture as synonymous with Indian culture. All means, whether insidious or violent, have become legitimate in the pursuit of this project. Writers, artists, intellectuals have been harassed, persecuted, attacked and assassinated.

In 2015, a large number of writers, writing in different

languages from different parts of the country, returned awards, given to them by state institutions, to protest against the rising culture of intolerance. This protest spread from literature to science to film, theatre and the arts. Writers, scientists, filmmakers, artists and theatre artistes returned awards, signed statements, held public meetings and rallies, and marched on the streets.

More than three years later, this unprecedented season of dissent can be seen as a part of a larger canvas of other protests in the country, whether in university campuses or among dalits, adivasis, minorities, women, farmers and students. It can also be seen as a beginning, or at the very least, a powerful milestone—when the cultural and scientific community, regardless of class or caste, language or region, spoke up in a resounding chorus against the "unmaking of India". This is the legacy of 2015 that lives on despite several attempts, then and now, to diminish its significance.

The following non-exhaustive diary re-lives the height of the resistance that October. It is a catalogue of events, a list of dates and names, plain and unembroidered, which speaks of the human spirit and solidarity more lyrically than a story.

*

February 2015: Govind Padharinath Pansare, a lawyer, trade unionist and communist leader, is shot outside his house in Kolhapur. Pansare passes away four days later. The police file a charge sheet naming a follower of the Goa-based Hindu right-wing organisation Sanatan Sanstha* as the perpetrator of the attack.

---

*The Sanatan Sanstha, registered as a charitable trust, was founded by "hypnotherapist" Jayant Balajai Athavale in 1999. On its website, its mission is described as imparting "spiritual knowledge to the curious in the society, inculcate religious behavior in the masses and providing personal guidance to seekers for their spiritual uplift". Persons owing allegiance to Sanatan Sanstha have been arrested in four bombings in Vashi, Thane, Panvel (all in 2007) and Goa (in 2009) and linked to the murders of Narendra Dabholkar, Govind Pansare, M.M. Kalburgi and Gauri Lankesh.

August 2015: Malleshappa Madivalappa Kalburgi, a leading scholar and writer in Kannada, is shot by two strangers in his home in Dharwad.

September 2015: Hindi writer Uday Prakash returns his Sahitya Akademi award, with the comment that free speech is endangered under the BJP government. He expresses his dismay at an Akademi that remains silent after the murder of M.M. Kalburgi, whose work the institution had celebrated with its award in 2006.

October 2015: As the silence of the Akademi grows louder in the succeeding days and weeks, Uday Prakash's gesture snowballs into the largest such protest by writers since Independence.

October 3: Kannada writers Veeranna Madiwalar, T. Satish Javare Gowda, Sangamesh Menasinakai, Hanumantha Haligeri, Shridevi V. Aloor and Chidananda Sali return their Kannada Sahitya Parishat awards in protest over the delay in the inquiry into M.M. Kalburgi's murder.

October 6: Nayantara Sahgal, writer in English, returns her Akademi award "in memory of the Indians who have been murdered, in support of all Indians who uphold the right to dissent, and of all dissenters who now live in fear and uncertainty". She says, in a statement entitled "Unmaking India":

India's culture of diversity and debate is now under vicious assault. Rationalists who question superstition, anyone who questions any aspect of the ugly and dangerous distortion of Hinduism known as Hindutva—whether in the intellectual or artistic sphere, or whether in terms of food habits and lifestyle— are being marginalised, persecuted, or murdered. A distinguished Kannada writer and Sahitya Akademi Award winner, M.M. Kalburgi, and two Maharashtrians, Narendra Dhabolkar and Govind Pansare, both anti-superstition activists, have all been killed by gun-toting motor-cyclists. Other dissenters have been warned they are next in line. Most recently, a village blacksmith, Mohammed Akhlaq, was dragged out of his home in Bisada

Village outside Delhi, and brutally lynched, on the supposed suspicion that beef was cooked in his home…*

In all these cases, justice drags its feet. The Prime Minister remains silent about this reign of terror. We must assume he dare not alienate evil-doers who support his ideology. It is a matter of sorrow that the Sahitya Akademi remains silent. The Akademis were set up as guardians of the creative imagination, and promoters of its finest products in art and literature, music and theatre.

October 7: Hindi poet Ashok Vajpeyi returns his Akademi award, saying "This is in solidarity with writers and intellectuals being murdered in broad daylight… [Nayantara] Sahgal was right. [Narendra Modi] is a very loquacious prime minister. Why doesn't he tell the nation that the pluralism of this country will be defended at every cost?"

October 8: The Prime Minister breaks his silence on the lynching of Mohammad Akhlaq in Dadri ten days after the killing. At an election rally in Nawada, Bihar, he says, "I have said it earlier too. Hindus should decide whether to fight Muslims or poverty. Muslims have to decide whether to fight Hindus or poverty. Both need to fight poverty together. The country has to stay united, only communal harmony and brotherhood will take the nation forward. People should ignore controversial statements made by politicians, as they are doing so for political gains."† Hindi writer Mridula Garg responds (on October 10): "If that is all [Modi] has to say and is not ready to be held accountable for the distortion of our so-called ancient culture and bashing of intellectuals in word and deed by his ministers and MPs, then I prefer him silent."

---

*The reference is to the public lynching on September 28, 2015, of Mohammed Akhlaq, at Bisada village, Dadri, Uttar Pradesh.

†"Modi breaks silence on Dadri lynching", *The Hindu*, October 8, 2015, https://www.thehindu.com/news/national/prime-minister-modi-breaks-silence-on-dadri-lynching-episode/article7738896.ece.

October 9: Urdu novelist Rahman Abbas returns his state Akademi award, calling on other Urdu writers to register their protest by doing the same. "It is high time," he says. "We cannot remain voiceless."

Carnatic vocalist, writer and social activist T.M. Krishna writes to the Prime Minister: "Words, strong and emotional words, come to you easily. So why do we need to shout and scream for a few sentences about a man who was lynched for allegedly consuming beef?"

October 10: The voices speaking up grow in number. The gestures of resistance—the return of awards, the resignations from the Sahtiya Aakdemi council and board—become multi-lingual and many-voiced. The protest is against "intolerance"—a code word for violence against minorities, and the clampdown on free speech and dissent.

Shashi Deshpande, writer in English, resigns from the Sahitya Akademi General Council, saying that in such a situation "silence is an abetment". Malayalam writer Sara Joseph returns her state Akademi award, saying, "There is a growing fear and lack of freedom under the present government…" Malayalam poet, critic and translator K. Satchidanandan resigns from the Executive Board and all other committees of the Sahitya Akademi. He writes to the Akademi: "I am sorry to find that you think this is a 'political issue'; to writers like me, this is an issue of our basic freedom to live, think and write." Malayalam writer P.K. Parakkadavu resigns from the General Council of the Sahitya Akademi, citing its failure to uphold freedom of expression. Keki Daruwalla, writer in English, writes to the Akademi President Vishwanath Prasad Tiwari: "What does it [your silence] say of the Akademi as an institution and of office bearers of this institution as upholders of our literary and cultural values?" Adil Jussawalla, poet in English, also writes to the Akademi President: "I believe this is the time for it [the Akademi] to boldly state that it unequivocally supports the rights of this nation's writers and condemns the violence used to suppress or destroy those rights."

October 11: Kannada poet Aravind Malagatti resigns from the Sahitya Akademi General Council. "I have resigned condemning the killing of Kalburgi and silence of [the] Akademi over the issue." Kannada writer Kumbar Veerabhadrappa (Kumvee) returns his Akademi award. "I'm doing this condemning the killings of Narendra Dabholkar, Govind Pansare and M.M. Kalburgi, and [the] Akademi's silence on the issue; also against [the] Dadri lynching... These incidents are an attempt to destroy the diversity of this country and it signals the entry of fascism into India."

Literary critic and activist G.N. Devy returns his Akademi award, saying: "Your moment of reckoning has come... I do this as an expression of my solidarity with several eminent writers who have recently returned their awards to highlight their concern and anxiety over the shrinking space for free expression and growing intolerance towards difference of opinion..."

Hindi writers Mangalesh Dabral and Rajesh Joshi return their Akademi awards. In a joint statement they say, "We clearly see a threat to our democracy, secularism and freedom. There have been attempts to curb free speech earlier also, but such trends have become more pronounced under the present government."

Four Punjabi writers—Gurbachan Singh Bhullar, Ajmer Singh Aulakh, Atamjit Singh, Waryam Sandhu—return their Akademi awards in a single day. Bhullar says he is perturbed by "...the attempts at disrupting the social fabric of the country, targeting particularly the area of literature and culture, under an orchestrated plan of action..." Aulakh says he is pained by the attacks on "progressive writers, leaders of the rational movement and the forcible saffronisation of education and culture...and the communal atmosphere being created in the country."

A federation of Kashmiri scholars, Adbee Markaz Kamraz, asks the top literary body to break its silence over the increasing "communal frenzy".

Kannada translator N. Ranganatha Rao returns his Akademi award, saying he was disturbed by the recent curbs on freedom of expression. D.N. Srinath, a fellow Kannada translator, announces he will return his translator's award.

Journalist and writer Aman Sethi returns his Yuva Puraskar: "The Akademi cannot draw its legitimacy by celebrating writers while shying clear of solidarity when they are targeted…"

October 12: Konkani writer N. Shivdas announces at a rally that he is returning his Akademi award, saying that no action had been taken against the Sanatan Sanstha, whose members were allegedly involved in the killing of rationalists Govind Pansare and Narendra Dabholkar.

Writer and founder of the Tarksheel (Rationalist) Society, Megh Raj Mitter, returns the Shiromani Lekhak, the Punjab government's highest award for writers.

Bilingual poet and critic E.V. Ramakrishnan resigns from the English Advisory Board of the Sahitya Akademi.

Critics and academics K.S. Ravikumar and C.R. Prasad resign from the Malayalam Advisory Board of the Akademi.

Oriya poet Rajendra Kishore Panda invokes the constitution of the Sahitya Akademi in his letter to the Akademi President, saying "one of its [the Akademi's] prime duties is to stand by writers and scholars expressing their thoughts…"

Novelist Salman Rushdie joins the protests against the spread of "communal poison" and "rising intolerance" in the country: "I support Nayantara Sahgal and the many other writers protesting to the Sahitya Akademi. Alarming times for free expression in India."

Kashmiri writer Ghulam Nabi Khayal says he is returning his award, adding: "The minorities in the country are feeling unsafe and threatened. They feel their future is bleak."

Translator and writer Gopalkrishna Gandhi says, "Writers returning Sahitya Akademi awards is a landmark moment… If writers and dissenters don't protest, who will?"

Theatre artist Maya Krishna Rao enlarges the stage of writers' protests by adding the voices of performing artists. Her protest, she says, is against the Dadri lynching and the rising intolerance in the country.

Kannada critic Rahamat Tarikere returns his Akademi award, protesting the recent increase in intolerance.

Four more writers from Punjab—Surjit Pattar, Baldev Singh Sadaknama, Jaswinder and Darshan Buttar—announce that they are returning their awards.

Gujarati poet and essayist Anil Joshi announces that he will return his Akademi award, saying, "People who are behind these killings don't have any respect for those holding different views and opinions. In that case, they would have killed Bhagat Singh, too, who did not believe in God, and Savarkar, who used to say that there is no need to worship cows…"

Professor and Punjabi writer Chaman Lal returns his Akademi translation prize.

October 13: It is no longer just Akademi awards being returned.

Punjabi fiction writer Dalip Kaur Tiwana announces that she will return her Padma Shri, adding, "In this land of Gautama Buddha and Guru Nanak Dev, the atrocities committed on the Sikhs in 1984 and on the Muslims recurrently because of communalism are an utter disgrace to our state and society. And to kill those who stand for truth and justice puts us to shame in the eyes of the world and God."

And filmmakers begin to express solidarity with the writers' cause; musicians, theatre persons and journalists begin to return awards. Filmmaker Govind Nihalani speaks out in support of the writers: "The situation of the days of *Tamas*, which saw the great divide and displacement of thousands, has not changed. In fact, the fissures in society have grown and the manipulation of the vulnerable has increased."

Bhai Baldeep Singh announces that he will return the Parman Patra conferred on him for his contributions to classical music and Gurbani sangeet, to protest "the lack of appropriate response to warn off those who have been perpetrating crimes against humanity".

Meena Alexander, poet in English, expresses solidarity with Indian writers and writes on the "Silenced Writer".

Marathi poet and fiction writer Pradnya Daya Pawar announces she is returning all her literary awards and the prize money to the Maharashtra state government to protest the "culture of intolerance" in the country. She adds, "We are living in an era of undeclared Emergency."

Assamese writer and journalist Homen Borgohain says he will return his Akademi award in protest against the Dadri incident, and attacks on minorities, liberal writers and rational thinkers. He also expresses his anguish over the growing fascist tendency in the country. Another Assamese writer, Nirupama Borgohain, announces she will return her Akademi award, saying, "Religious intolerance has reached extreme levels. But the leader of the country, Prime Minister Narendra Modi, has not assured us he will stop it and is remaining silent. It is as if he is encouraging fascism to grow…"

Bengali poet Mandakranta Sen announces that she will return her Young Writers' special award from the Akademi to protest against the Dadri lynching, and growing intolerance and communalism.

Marathi writers Harishchandra Thorat, Sanjay Bhaskar Joshi and Ganesh Visputay return their Maharashtra state government awards.

October 14: Individual protesters get together in public meetings and demonstrations; so do cultural groups. A hundred intellectuals write to the President. Constitutional experts speak up.

Keki Daruwalla, writer and poet in English, returns his Akademi award, saying "[I]n recent months it [the Akademi] has not stood up as boldly as it should for values that any literature stands for, namely freedom of expression against threat, upholding the rights of the marginalised, speaking up against superstitions and intolerance of any kind."

Expressing concern over rising communal polarisation and intolerance, 100 intellectuals from West Bengal write to President Pranab Mukherjee, saying that the Modi government should take a tough stand against fundamentalists. "The composite culture is the essence [of Indian society] but concerted efforts are on to destroy this. A dangerous game of communal polarisation is being played, the result of which are the murders of rationalist Narendra Dabholkar, leftist Govind Pansare and scholar M.M. Kalburgi." The 100 intellectuals and authors, including eminent poets Shankha Ghosh and Nabaneeta Dev Sen, add, "Be it the lynching in Dadri or cancelling [ghazal maestro] Ghulam Ali's concert or blackening senior journalist Sudheendra Kulkarni's face for hosting a book launch of [ex-Pakistani foreign minister] Khurshid Mahmud Kasuri, all are examples of this dangerous game of communal polarisation." "This is not the voice of a few authors or intellectuals but of the common people of our society who are now living in fear and apprehension," says Sahitya Akademi Award-winning author Nabaneeta Dev Sen. On October 15, another 63 intellectuals add their names to the letter.

The Goa Konkani Lekhak Sangh (GKLS) plans a series of demonstrations during the International Film Festival of India in Goa to condemn the murder of rationalists and writers in the country. Fifteen of the Konkani award winners, along with Padma Shri writer and academic Maria Couto, plan the protests to highlight their concerns before national and international delegates visiting the state for the 46th edition of the film festival. N. Shivdas, who had earlier announced that he would return his award, also plans to join the collective protest. "The trend of attacking people with creative temperament is not limited to a specific region but across the nation...he [Prime Minister Modi] should give us an assurance that such incidents will not recur and the killers will be brought to justice," adds Shivdas.

Punjabi writer Mohan Bhandari confirms his decision to return his Akademi award in solidarity with the nationwide protest by writers: "It pains me to see growing intolerance and communalism against which we writers have always raised a strong voice in our writings. Returning the award is a way of bringing attention to the disturbing conditions prevailing in the country today."

Forty Punjabi writers and theatre artists stage a protest in Chandigarh against the suppression of freedom of speech, and to express solidarity with those who have returned state awards.

The number of awards returned in Punjab is the highest in the country. The group of forty people includes Mohan Bhandari, Chaman Lal, Meg Raj Mitter, Hardev Chauhan, Dr Dharamvira Gandhi, and Harjinder Kaur, chairperson, Punjab Arts Council.

Noted constitutional expert Fali S. Nariman says it is high time Prime Minister Narendra Modi spoke against the "plague of intolerance spreading rapidly across the country" and those using "violent methods to stymie free speech and dissent" were brought to book.

October 15: Even schoolchildren begin to demand freedom of speech.

Class 11 student Muddu Thirthahalli of Sahyadri High School returns her Karnataka Sahitya Akademi award, received for a collection of essays in 2011. Saying it was to protest the killing of M.M. Kalburgi, she adds, "Curtailment of freedom of expression is bad. Literature is a medium to express one's opinions. There should be no curbs on free speech and writing."

Hardev Chauhan, who has returned an NCERT (National Council for Education, Research and Training) award for children's writing, says he will also return his Shiromani Bal Sahit Lekhak award.

Chikkappanahalli Shanmukha, principal correspondent with *Kannada Prabha* newspaper, announces in a Facebook post that he will return the Madhyama Academy award in protest against the delay in apprehending the assailants of M.M. Kalburgi.

Nand Bharadwaj, the noted Hindi writer from Rajasthan and former director of Doordarshan, announces that he will return his Akademi award, expressing his sadness at the silence of the Akademi amid the increasing attacks on writers.

Sahitya Akademi Award-winning novelists and poets from Goa, including Nagesh Karmali, Damodar Mauzo, Pundalik Naik, N. Shivdas, Datta Damodar Naik, Ramesh Veluskar, Meena Kakodkar, Hema Naik, Dilip Borkar, Gokuldas Prabhu, Mahabaleshwar Sail, Prakash Padgaonkar, Arun Sakhardande, Tukaram Seth, Maria Aurora Couto and Amitav Ghosh strongly condemn the rising trend of intolerance in the country, calling it a threat to the age-old liberal and all-encompassing philosophical traditions of the country. In a joint statement issued at a press conference, the writers declare, "During the last eighteen months in particular the rabid fundamentalist forces have torn apart the composite cultural mosaic of this country. If not contained, they will turn this country into a graveyard of creativity. This will kill scientific temperament and literary and cultural renaissance, ultimately stalling the economic progress of this nation."

October 16: Seventy-three sociologists at universities across India and around the world register their strong protest against "any attempt to impose a uniform belief or practice, on either individuals or communities" which is "antithetical to the freedom enshrined in the Constitution. It is the state's responsibility to ensure this freedom."

Telugu writer M. Bhoopal Reddy announces he will return his Akademi award. He will also return his Ugadi Puraskaram given by the Telangana Government to register his protest against the "indifference" of the state government to the growing number of farmer suicides: "They have increased since the new government came to power, but the government is more interested in spending money on building temples and other insignificant things."

October 17: Telugu writer Katyayani Vidmahe announces the return of her Akademi award in protest against "diminishing constitutional protection" for freedom of choice: "The violence that is being allowed by the Union government against beliefs of a particular section of the society [is] nothing but another form of state-supported violence… Remaining a mute spectator when the rights of some are being crushed is not possible."

In the following days, Urdu writer Munawwar Rana and Hindi writer Kashinath return their Akademi awards. They are joined by Danish Husain, who returns his Ustad Bismillah Khan Yuva Puraskar.

Thirteen writers and artists from Gujarat and ten from

Maharashtra add their names to the October 14 statement from Bengali intellectuals. By the end of the month, 250 distinguished academics from around the world have put their names to the October 16 protest letter of the sociologists.

In the opening days of November, writer Arundhati Roy and two dozen filmmakers—among them Kundan Shah, Saeed Mirza and Dibakar Banerjee—return their national film awards. The protest has now expanded to target the government's appointment of nondescript figures to head national institutions such as the Film and Television Institute of India (FTII) in Pune.

October 28: Adding new power to the ongoing resistance, scientists join in, saying that "the writers have shown the way with their protests", and that they "reject the destructive narrow view of India that seeks to dictate what people will wear, think, eat and who they will love."

A press statement from distinguished scientists across the country states:

> The scientific community is deeply concerned [about] the climate of intolerance and the ways in which science and reason are being eroded in the country.
>
> It is the same climate of intolerance, and rejection of reason, that has led to the lynching in Dadri of Mohammad Akhlaq Saifi and the assassinations of Prof. Kalburgi, Dr Narendra Dabholkar and Shri Govind Pansare. All three fought against superstition and obscurantism to build a scientific temper in our society. Prof. Kalburgi was a renowned scholar and an authority on the Vachana literature associated with the 12th-century reformer Basava, who opposed institutionalised religion, caste and gender discrimination. Similarly, Dr Dabholkar and Shri Pansare promoted scientific temper through their fight against superstition and blind faith.
>
> The Indian Constitution in Article 51 A (h) demands, as a part of the fundamental duties of the citizens, that we "...develop the scientific temper, humanism and the spirit of inquiry and reform". Unfortunately, what we are witnessing instead is the active promotion of irrational and sectarian thought by important functionaries of the government.

On the same day, veteran scientist Pushpa Mittra Bhargava announces that he will return his Padma Bhushan award to protest "the government's attack on rationalism, reasoning and science." He adds that the "Modi government is giving room for communalists and fringe groups to divide the country based on religion."

On 1st November veteran Hindi writer Krishna Sobti, then ninety years old, speaks at a public meeting called Pratirodh in Delhi:

In the long life bestowed upon me by the almighty, I have seen, lived and felt many historic turns of this great country in the deep corners of my heart. I have witnessed British rule and the battle for independence. The memory of revolutionaries walking with their heads held high resides in my heart. I have listened to the rallying cries of the soldiers of Azad Hind Fauj at Lahore's Gol Bagh. We were moved at that time by the notion that independence is our birthright and freedom was the most pious word of that era. It is not a film script but the reality of a narrow ideology, the same ideology that has forgotten Atalji and is trying again to impose its violent philosophy on this great country. Do we need these gestures of hatred in our society? No, we don't!

First Babri, then Dadri—in the name of Hindutva, they are showing bravery, an impotent bravery. If there is greed on one side of a hegemonic ideology and violence on the other, then you can only expect erosion of democratic values. The cultural pride that they claim to propagate belongs to the educated masses of this country. Even the illiterate [among us] can see through their designs. An attempt is being made to blur their wisdom through the allurement of money. I request the honourable Mr Prime Minister to please tell us who these people using derogatory terms like "gang" for people like us are. For writers who remain well within their discipline, I can say this with satisfaction, being a writer myself, that the distance between high-caste narrative and low-caste narrative of the society has narrowed down since independence. We can bridge this gap altogether. You will find such interwoven lives in Indian novels, forcing you to wonder [if] the narrative has flowed from the pen of India itself.

It is strange that we have ignored the rot within our society for so long, though we recognise it from the time Gandhi was killed after independence. Today, some people seek to replace history with mythology; superstition is being promoted at a time when technology is defining lives. They are trying to promote a new culture among people who will not take them seriously. This nation has never compromised with its values, and this time, too, the people will not lose sight of what is the right thing to do.

Friends, our nation is known for the strength of its social fabric, the resilience and depth of its intellectual tradition from the times of the Upanishads. We should take the deep human ethos enshrined in the concept of "unity in diversity" with utmost sincerity. This is a time fraught with danger; it is the time when a struggle is being imposed upon us. We bow our head to the President, who is reminding us of the values of universal brotherhood, integral to our traditional wisdom. This legacy has nourished the hearts and minds of Indians for ages. We hope that reactionary politics will not be able to erode it. What is the need to debate Muslim population in such a large nation, especially when you have an economic programme that can change the face of the world? Why are we at war with the values of this great Indian culture despite being a Hindu majority nation? What fear is prompting us to terrorise writers and derogate them with insinuations? I am ashamed that they have called the thinking class, the intellectuals, of this nation a "gang", and this is not the doing of just one man. I want to ask the Prime Minister: Who are these people in "Nagpuri organisations" who are vilifying us?

As the president has emphasised the value of tolerance, thrice in recent days…human values are part of our tradition.

Three years later

Overall, the October of dissent saw hundreds of writers, performing artists, filmmakers, academics, scientists, cultural groups and even schoolchildren speak up in one way or another. Throughout the weeks of awards being returned, statements, public meetings and marches on the streets, the gestures of resistance were described by right-wing voices as "publicity gimmicks" and "insults". They were asked a range of "whataboutery" questions, beginning with "Why now? Where were you when…" Finance Minister Arun Jaitley wrote on his blog, "A few questions to the protestors: How many of them courted arrest, protested or raised their voice against the dictatorship of Mrs. Indira Gandhi during the emergency? Did the writers speak against the Sikh killings of 1984 or the Bhagalpur riots of 1989? Was their conscience not shaken by the corruption involving lakhs of crores between 2004 and 2014?" The whataboutery helped him reach a convenient conclusion: "Is this protest real or a manufactured one? Is this not a case of ideological intolerance?… The manufactured revolt is a case of an ideological intolerance towards the BJP."*

At the time, no one took this patently absurd accusation seriously—considering that many of those returning awards had never heard of each other till the gesture was made by each; nor did many of them even share a common language. When scientists too joined the protest, and eminent scientist Pushpa Bhargava announced that he was returning his Padma Bhushan, Jaitley described those returning awards as "rabid anti-BJP elements". But two things were clear: the government and its official and unofficial spokespersons were rattled. And the protest did not abate; it only grew.

Indeed, though 2015 has come and gone, it is the BJP government and its right-wing friends who remember the collective voice of citizens well, and live in fear of it. In the run up to the Assembly elections in 2018, BJP President Amit Shah said, "BJP will win all elections despite Akhlaq killing and award wapsi."† Actually, they didn't. But the BJP has not given up, of course. Ahead of the 2019 elections, a new book on Narendra Modi has been published in "response to criticism". The book, entitled *Narendra Modi: Creative Disruptor—The Maker of New*

---

*Jaitley's blog post, entitled "A manufactured revolt—Politics by other means" is quoted in full in "Jaitley trashes 'paper rebellion', calls literary revolt a 'manufactured crisis' against PM Modi", *FirstPost*, October 15, 2015.

†News18, September 11, 2018.

India, is by R. Balashankar, former editor of the *Organiser* weekly and former convener of BJP's Intellectual Cell. One chapter is titled "Award Wapsi: Intolerance Care in India".

Drawn from the Indian Cultural Forum's record "Keeping Count of Dissenting Voices", October 19, 2015.

——————◆◆◆——————

WHY ARE WRITERS DANGEROUS?

Shanta Gokhale

Shanta Gokhale's wide-ranging involvement with creativity—as a critic, translator, novelist, playwright, journalist, and occasional actor—serves to illustrate her theme here: how the civic outlook of Indians has changed since Independence, from being a people who sought new answers to age-old problems in their society, to viewing newness as the problem and tradition as its answer. Gokhale's intellectual journey, with its broadening sympathies and horizons, is at once a counterpoint to the narrowing of the public mind space, and an acute barometer of this change.

For the last few years there has been a growing fear among us that if we write what we see and think, we might cause deep offence to some community or the other, and lay ourselves open to legal action. Public Interest Litigation (PIL) was originally created to help the powerless individual seek justice against the mighty State. It was a huge blessing then.* But more and more, it has become a curse for writers and artists. It seems as though anybody can run to the courts and file a PIL to seek redress in the name of caste, community and religion. Redress means gagging the writer and banning her work. Occasionally, hurt communities don't even

---

*This was in the aftermath of the Emergency. The term "Public Interest Litigation" was defined for the Indian context by the Supreme Court, in the *S.P. Gupta vs Union of India* case of 1981.

bother with the law. They use the old weapon of ostracism to make life unliveable for the artist. When I began to write some sixty years ago, we hadn't dreamt that a day would come when the newly born republic of hope would turn into a republic of fear for thinkers and writers. The world was full of iniquity and injustice even then. But identities hadn't been schooled into becoming these fragile, eggshell sensibilities. There was anger, gloom and frustration at shortages, unemployment and corruption. But we were allowed to express our views on them without fear. We evolved the navakatha, navakavya and navanatya to address these ills. We were doing our social duty by sweeping the old rosy romanticism out of the house to reveal its pitted walls and cobwebs. We, the educated, liberal middle-class, were doing our social duty. We were helping to build the nation. But we weren't connecting the dots. We did not see that the evils troubling us were an integral part of an entire system created expressly to benefit the few and deprive the many. Living through the seventies, we came to know better. A character in my 1988 play *Avinash* says that the depression his older brother suffers from may not entirely be the result of some inborn psychological tic. Its roots might also lie in economics, in the social structure and the political system. To this, the character's father retorts, "What has politics got to do with it? What you are is the result of your destiny."

What aroused us from our complacency was the Emergency. For the first time since Independence, the worm in the apple of democracy showed its ugly face. For the first time, we connected the dots. Shreeram Lagoo famously said we had been a generation of slumberers. But now we were wide awake. The Committee for the Protection of Democratic Rights (CPDR) was formed in Mumbai. Other civil liberties organisations were formed elsewhere. Earlier, in America, Woodward and Bernstein had investigated the Watergate scandal. The Emergency brought investigative journalism to our shores. Creative writers were called upon to stand up and be counted. G.P. Deshpande had already written his modern classic *Uddhwasta Dharmashala*, which I translated as *A Man in Dark Times*. In the play, a professor faces a university inquiry on the suspicion that he is a card-carrying Marxist. The play was inspired by the report of the House Committee on Un-American Activities whose work had wound up just a year before the Emergency was declared. Suddenly America and India were not too far apart. Of course, no inquiries were held during the Emergency. Political rivals were simply picked up, imprisoned and tortured. The police did their duty with dedication. And nobody was the wiser, since media was severely censored. Today the media does not need an external censor. Enough fear has been injected into its veins for it to censor itself.

The seventies were, altogether, an eye-opening decade for my generation. Two years before the Emergency, we had been knocked on the head by Namdeo Dhasal's collection of poems, *Golpitha*. That and the series of dalit autobiographies that followed, had tossed us right out of our soft beds into the open gutters running next door. Our navakatha and navanatya had been all about middle-class angst. Oh yes, we were angry, despondent about our dull routines, about the generation gap, even about corruption. We expressed these anxieties in well-chosen words. But did the English language have words to describe the life of rural dalits, forced to live a brutalised life on the outskirts of human society? It was a challenge for us translators to find those words. In the mid-eighties, when I was editing a literary section for the women's magazine *Femina*, I translated for it a chapter from the first autobiography written by a dalit woman in Marathi. This was Shantabai Kamble's *Majya Jalmachi Chittarkatha*.* I pored over half a dozen dictionaries chasing the word "chittarkatha". It was nowhere to be found. Finally, I translated the context rather than the word, rendering the title as *The Story of my Tattered Life*.

The third eye-opener in the seventies was feminism. Simone de Beauvoir had written *The Second Sex* in 1949. I had read it in my teens. But I had thought then that it was all about the West.

---

*First published as a book in 1986, Shantabai Kamble's autobiography had already been serialised for Marathi television in the early eighties.

Now I realised it was about us. All of us. My first novel, *Rita Welinkar* (1995), was born of this awareness. We were all victims of patriarchy, whoever we were, wife, other woman or sex worker, brahmin or dalit, Hindu, Christian or Muslim, right-wing or left-wing, at home or in the workplace.

In 1988 Salman Rushdie wrote *The Satanic Verses* and found himself at the receiving end of a fatwa calling for his death. The Indian government banned the book, but Indian writers and artists stood up against the ban in support of freedom of speech. We do that even today. But in the current social environment, to put this freedom into practice has become lethal. A sword hangs over the head of any writer who dares presume she has the right to speak out. As punishment the law will charge her with malicious intent to promote enmity between people of different religions, regions, languages or races.

I often think, wistfully, of Andersen's emperor who was tricked into wearing invisible clothes. Obedient courtiers and subjects marvelled at their colour and cut. It was a clear-eyed boy standing in the midst of this herd of adults who announced that the emperor was wearing no clothes. People saw the truth of the observation. So did the emperor. But he shut his eyes to it and walked on. He knew that, however foolish and vain he might appear to his subjects, they could do him no harm. Today's emperors know they are not safe. So, today's truth-tellers are arrested and imprisoned.

Fortunately, we are not, and I fervently hope never will be, in quite the same boat as writers in totalitarian states. But we are certainly in the same boat as Orhan Pamuk who was charged in 2006 with insulting Turkey's honour by referring to the killing of thousands of Armenians in Turkey during World War One as a genocide. Although the Istanbul court dropped charges against him under international pressure, the street court didn't spare him. He was abused, beaten, and pelted with eggs as he entered and left the court. And we are most certainly in the same boat as the Egyptian novelist Naguib Mahfouz who was stabbed, almost fatally, by an Islamist for writing novels that Islamist extremists considered blasphemous. The assault caused such extensive nerve damage that Mahfouz couldn't write for more than a few minutes per day. We know through our own experience that when political and religious powers feed people with self-serving, unitary definitions of culture, morality and nationalism, the man in the street feels empowered to lynch. In return, the state protects and occasionally even rewards him.

Fear has entered our lives like a pervasive miasma. In the cultural column I used to write till recently for *Mumbai Mirror*, I was often critical of political culture. In 2013, I wrote a satirical column about the then deputy chief minister of Maharashtra, Ajit Pawar, without raising an eyebrow. In 2015 I wrote in similar vein about the Prime Minister's theatrics in Shivaji Park, and had friends calling me to say, "Please be careful."

In 2016, Govind Nihalani asked me to write the script and dialogue for a Marathi film based on Manjula Padmanabhan's 1986 play *Lights Out*. The play didn't appeal to me as the basis for a film script. It was outdated. It didn't reflect the socio-political complexities of our times. It had a uni-dimensional plot that focused exclusively on the upper-middle-class habit of silence in the face of terrible things happening on its doorstep. It required fleshing out and layering.

I asked Govind for carte blanche to fill out the flat characters, introduce new ones and give the film a real-life context. In Manjula's play, girls were being raped, seemingly gratuitously, in the open, in an upper-middle-class neighbourhood. In my script they became trafficked girls. I replaced the silent maid of the original with a bright young tribal girl who realised what was happening next-door and feared for herself. I brought the fearful, silent protagonist of the film to an emotional point when she felt she had to call in the police. When they came, the "inquiry" they conducted made it clear they were hand-in-glove with the traffickers. However, I noticed that in the film as it was made, Nihalani had ironed out all hints of police complicity. I did not ask him why. I decided I knew. It struck me as ironic that *Ardh Satya*, Nihalani's 1983 hit film, had underlined the nexus among the police, the politician and the criminal. I happened to have played a two-minute part in it as a leftist activist who speaks out publicly against police atrocities. That kind of activist is now in trouble. Activists who are fighting for the rights of tribals and dalits are in worse trouble. Recently, five of them were labelled "Urban Naxals", whatever that might be, and arrested under the Unlawful Activities (Prevention) Act (UAPA).

Last year, dalit writer Urmila Pawar called me for advice. She had been invited to a seminar and was afraid she would have to face harassment if she said what she wanted to say. When she told me what it was, I advised subterfuge. I reminded her of Vijay Tendulkar's play *Ghashiram Kotwal*. It was written in the seventies, when he saw that the Congress in Maharashtra was creating a potential Frankenstein by nurturing the Shiv Sena as a counter to the Communist Party which had a hold over Bombay's mill workers. But how was he to fashion a play out of the situation? By the sheerest coincidence, he came upon a minor story about the time when the Peshwa minister, Nana Phadnavis, had appointed a Kanauji brahmin Ghashiram as the police chief of Pune city, to serve his own lascivious purposes. But Ghashiram, drunk on power, had incarcerated and tortured the Peshwa's most loyal subjects and supporters. I told Pawar that allegories make a clever and legitimate means for writers to point out truths without paying the price. We have a saying in Marathi: *Leki bole, sunelage.* A mother-in-law scolds her daughter for her daughter-in-law's misdeeds. The daughter-in-law gets the point but can't protest because the mother-in-law has not scolded her.

Mahasweta Devi, who has been an important point of reference in my life as a writer, was invited to speak about Indian culture at the Frankfurt Book Fair in 2012. She described Indian culture as "a tapestry of many weaves, many threads. Somewhere the cloth frays. Somewhere the threads tear. But still it holds." It would continue to hold as it has done for centuries, if only those who speak in the name of religion and culture would allow it to. A meticulously researched essay like A.K. Ramanujan's "Three Hundred Ramayanas" would not then be dropped from a university's history syllabus. Rather, students would be encouraged to feel proud that our culture had produced an epic of such rich possibilities that people across Southeast Asia had retold the story in 300 different ways and made it their own.

My personal experience of a young mind restricted by unitary ideas of culture, morality and nationalism came after my second novel *Tya Varshi (2008),* which I have translated into English as *Crowfall (2013),* was published. A young man who had just done his diploma in screenplay writing from Pune's Film and Television Institute came to ask me for permission to make a film based on it. He had read the novel twice over because the world it presented was so totally new to him. I was surprised. I hadn't written about some never-never land. It was the story of a year in the lives of a group of friends struggling with their creative processes against the background of politically engineered violence. The year the novel was set in was 2004 and the flashbacks were of the Mumbai riots of 1992–93. What the young screenplay writer couldn't get over was the warmth and mutual respect that the friends shared despite the community and caste differences that existed between them. After we had discussed the novel for two hours, the young man said, "I am confused. I haven't been brought up to live so freely. But I would love to live like that." It dawned on me then that, in being true to my ideas, I had been disruptive of his. In a very, very small way, it told me why writers are considered dangerous by those who desire to control young minds by not letting them think independently, doubt, question or dream.

In her speech at Frankfurt, Mahasweta Devi asserted that there could be no human growth without dreams. Speaking for herself, she quoted Tagore: "I dream of an India where there is no fear. Where knowledge is free. Where words come out of the depth of truth. Where tireless striving stretches its arms towards perfection. Where the clear stream of reason has not lost its way in the dreary sand of dead habit."

Let us say amen to that.

Edited text of a talk delivered at Ooty Literature Festival, 2018. Published in Indian Cultural Forum, September 17, 2018.

◆◆◆

THEY FEARED HIS WORDS:
A TRIBUTE TO M.M. KALBURGI

K. Satchidanandan

Malleshappa Madivalappa Kalburgi (1938–2015) applied the principles of secular, evidence-based scholarship to his study of Kannada folklore, epigraphy, and the Lingayat religious identity. While his prolific output won him literary and academic plaudits, it also drew threats and harassment from Lingayat temple-chiefs, amplified by organisations such as the Vishwa Hindu Parishad (VHP), Bajrang Dal and Sri Ram Sene.

On August 30, 2015, two young men entered Kalburgi's home under false pretences, claiming to be his students, and shot him dead. The assassination provoked writers Uday Prakash and Chandrashekhar Patil to return their Sahitya Akademi and Pampa awards, respectively, denouncing the state's failure to protect intellectual freedom. Their gesture would lead to a spate of award returns in protest.

"You fear words. Men who fear words exult in human blood. You can silence me, but you cannot silence truth. Truth and fire are ever inextinguishable. They will always keep burning somewhere. One spark is enough to create a conflagration."

These words, spoken by an "untouchable" old man in M.M. Kalburgi's play *Basaveshwara's Revolution*—when the brahmins shout and scream and ask the king to sentence Basaveshwara to death in exile, and King Bijjala promptly dismisses him from his post as the finance minister of his country—could well have been the playwright-scholar's own words addressed to the cowards who murdered him.

Yes, they feared his words of reason. They feared them as much as the brahmins of Basava's time feared Basava's dauntless speeches and scalding verses that condemned every form of religious hypocrisy and social hierarchy; and taught his people to dream of another world where all forms of discrimination based on caste, race and gender would vanish, and they would all just be what they are: human beings.

Kalburgi was not merely an academic who did revealing research on Basava's life and work, but an honest practitioner of Basava's thought. Examining folklore and the Vachana literature of the Veerashaivas, he had concluded that the 12th-century religious philosopher Channabasavanna (nephew and disciple of Basaveshwara) was a leather tanner (dohaara). He made his conclusion public in *Marga*, a landmark collection of his well-researched essays, which was to be the first volume of his collected essays, published when he had just turned fifty. A section of the Lingayats, who hold Channabasavanna in reverence and awe, and think of him as one of the pioneers of the cult, were offended by Kalburgi's proposition. They threatened to kill him. Kalburgi was even summoned to a Lingayat mutt in Dharwad and persuaded to recant his statement under threat to his life. That day he felt terrible—much like Perumal Murugan did when he had to tender an apology for his novel's reference to a temple ritual in his village.

But that was not to deter Kalburgi from his original research or his bold declarations of path-breaking discoveries. The 1938-born scholar, the most well-known authority on the history of Karnataka and its culture, literature and folklore, the author of eighty books, editor of several volumes of Vachana literature where for the first time he had presented hitherto unknown Vachana poets he had discovered, vice-chancellor of the Kannada University, Hampi, recipient of several prestigious honours like the Karnataka Sahitya Akademi Award, Karnataka Rajyotsava

Award and the Sahitya Akademi Award, continued to write and make statements that might have been provocative to some, but were always supported by meticulous research.

The claim that proved fatal to him was that the Lingayats were not Hindus, but had a distinct religious identity, and that this religion preceded Hinduism in Karnataka. He was also frankly critical of the Lingayat priests, a new "brahmin" class, whose very existence went against Basavanna's non-hierarchical and egalitarian social ideal. Kalburgi denounced the *Bhagavad Gita* publicly, and criticised idol worship and rituals that had crept into Lingayat practice. Kalburgi was not an atheist like Pansare or Dabholkar, murdered before him in similar circumstances; but his view of religion was quite radical, like that of Kabir, Namdev, or Basavanna himself. Kalburgi supported U.R. Ananthamurthy when the latter ridiculed idol worship at a seminar. Kalburgi's discovery of the positive aspects of Muslim rule in Karnataka, and his attempts to bring evidence by translating works in Persian and Urdu, and his stance against the celebration of Ganesh Chathurthi by Lingayats, irked the right-wing forces who had managed to penetrate into the Lingayat stronghold. He refused to be scared of fundamentalists, and said he was not afraid of death at the hands of those who had murdered Gandhi and Basava. That was why he refused state protection when it was offered to him.

Kalburgi belonged to a rare class of original thinkers and social critics who force society to look at itself critically, to change its old ways, and rewrite its history in the light of new discoveries. He will continue to speak to generations of men and women whose religion is truth, and who long to create a non-violent and just society.

First published in Indian Cultural Forum, October 21, 2015.

◆◆◆

BEEF

Chandramohan S

Since October 26, 2005, when the Supreme Court upheld the anti-cow slaughter laws enacted by state legislatures, such laws have grown more stringent, and their scope has increased. Today, in the states of Madhya Pradesh, Punjab, Haryana, Himachal Pradesh, Delhi, Chhattisgarh and Rajasthan, the burden of proof is placed on the accused—an anomalous principle in modern jurisprudence, but familiar enough from brahminical codes of law. On June 6, 2017, the Director General of Police (DGP) of Uttar Pradesh, Sulkhan Singh, instructed the state's police force to prosecute cattle smuggling and cow slaughter under the terms of the National Security Act and the Gangster Act. The result has been the outright negation of constitutional values and of the rule of law, whether through communal polarisation, unchecked majoritarianism, the rise of vigilante groups, lynch-mob violence, or assaults on the diet and livelihoods of the marginalised—Muslims, dalits and adivasis, among others.

My harvest of poems will be winnowed.
If done dexterously,
the lighter shallow stuff will be blown
away in the wind;
the heavier, meaty stuff
will fall back onto the tray,
become the fire in my belly.

First published in Indian Cultural Forum,
February 22, 2016.

"Bomb Squad", Unny, Guftugu, 2016

ELEGY FOR A LOST FRIEND:
GAURI LANKESH (1962–2017)

Pushpamala N.

Artist Pushpamala N. recaptures the many facets of Gauri Lankesh in a loving verbal portrait. What made Gauri such a force of nature, even more than her zest for life and fighting spirit, was her extraordinary integrity. She moved from English journalism to Kannada without altering her voice or message. Staying true to the journalistic values of her father, P. Lankesh, she ran her Patrike without advertisements, but also brought to it her own straight-talking style, wide-angle vision and open-hearted sympathies.

September 5, the day of her assassination, was a special day of remembrance for Gauri since she regarded her father as her teacher. It now becomes a day to remember her exceptional life.

I was preparing to leave Bangalore for three weeks when I got a call from a friend in Mumbai asking me to switch on the TV immediately, saying that Gauri had been shot. I thought Gauri had gone driving off on one of her trips and been shot at. She had always received threats since the time she took over the *Lankesh Patrike*. Within minutes of the news of her death, people from all over were sending messages and calling. Many of my friends, who had met her at my place, were also devastated. By the time we rushed to her house, journalists and other people had already reached there, and a crowd began to gather. In the sleepless nights after that evening, an absurd thought occurred again and again—of Gauri sitting at her desk at the office that night before the edition and calling out, "Stop press! Gauri Lankesh has just been killed, we have to cover that!"

Neither her family nor her friends had expected such a great public outpouring of grief and anger at her death, or that she would become a global icon of resistance. We had not thought that she was so powerful. With us, she was more vulnerable, speaking of her struggles and always good for an argument or a joke. We used to pop into each other's houses when we were depressed, to unwind. She could be brutally frank.

Gauri lived two streets away from my place, in a house built by her mother Indira, an astute businesswoman who owned a popular saree shop which had supported the family in lean times. Though we both grew up in Basavanagudi in south Bangalore, we only met when I moved into my newly built studio in Rajarajeshwari Nagar in 1996, after twenty years of having been away from the city. But I had known her father, P. Lankesh, since the early 1970s when, as a silly teenager just out of school, I used to hang around Central College with a disreputable bunch of older friends known as the "Chod" gang. The English department was famous. It had professors like the influential intellectual T.G. Vaidyanathan and P. Lankesh, the celebrated Navya (Modernist) Kannada writer, each with adoring groups around him. Later, becoming a new wave filmmaker himself, Lankesh had played the role of the rebel brahmin Naranappa in the first Kannada new wave film *Samskara* (1970), directed by Pattabhirama Reddy and based on the novel by U.R. Ananthamurthy, with Girish Karnad playing the good brahmin. It was a strong critique of caste, dealing particularly with the hypocrisy of the influential Madhava brahmin community (to which my family belongs). Though the censors had initially banned *Samskara*, the Union Ministry of Information and Broadcasting had revoked the ban. I do not remember much commotion from the brahmin community when it was released in 1970. My mother and her friends went off to see the film with a naughty air. I even acted in a play directed by Lankesh which had been staged in the Town Hall. It was the Kannada translation of Aristophanes' *Lysistrata*, a comedy about a woman, Lysistrata, who persuades the Greek women to boycott sex with their men to force them to end the Peloponnesian War. A family friend, member of the Swatantra party, wrote a strong letter to the *Deccan Herald* that the play was obscene. Though I was only in the crowd scenes, my father was furious and that was the end of my theatrical career.

Lankesh left his job and started the first Kannada tabloid *Lankesh Patrike* in 1980, to the disapproval of his literary friends who thought it would vulgarise his writing. He was probably inspired by the popular success of his political column in the Kannada newspaper *Prajavani*. Lankesh was a Lohiaite influenced by the charismatic Karnataka socialist leader Shanthaveri Gopala Gowda. I think his decision came out of a desire to "go to the people" after the tumultuous days of the 1970s, a decade marked by widespread movements for social justice and protests against the Emergency. Bangalore was the hub of the influential Navya literary movement, new wave cinema and new theatre dealing with social issues. Prasanna had founded the left-wing theatre group *Samudaya* just before the Emergency, and it had been performing political theatre all over Karnataka. The local paper *Deccan Herald* had also become a leading opposition after K.N. Harikumar came back from Jawaharlal Nehru University (JNU) and took over as editor in 1978. The actress Snehalatha Reddy, socialist and wife of Pattabhirama Reddy, who had played Naranappa's dalit lover Chandri in *Samskara,* was falsely accused in the Baroda Dynamite case and jailed and tortured during the Emergency.* She died soon after being released.

Based on Gandhi's *Harijan,* the *Lankesh Patrike* was a powerful anti-establishment voice for the oppressed and marginalised, running on readers' subscriptions with a strict policy against advertisements. It grew to have a huge readership. It was a mixture of political exposés and sensational tabloid writing mixed with a strong literary content, providing a platform to new voices. What Lankesh also did was to invent a new language, or maybe many languages, delightfully tweaking Kannada with the fluidity of a master. Film scholar Madhav Prasad says he used to wait to see the new edition in Kolkata for the sheer pleasure of reading the language. One cover had the title "Bam Gum Yuddha" (Bangarappa–Gundu Rao War). No one had used Kannada with such audacity.

When I moved to Rajarajeshwari Nagar, I was introduced to Gauri by our older friend, the ex-cricketer Balaji, a neighbour of the Lankeshes. His house had served as an intellectual adda in Basavanagudi where Lankesh used to go to play badminton every evening. Basavanagudi was the centre of Kannada literature and theatre. The Vidyarthi Bhavan café in Gandhi Bazaar had been the meeting place for two generations of writers. Prasanna used to have a running joke that the great Kannada Navodaya (Renaissance) writer Masti Venkatesha Iyengar was so lusty that he had not one, but "two-two dosas" every day.

When I first met Gauri, she was a journalist for the *Sunday* magazine edited by Vir Sanghvi. We used to meet often.

---

*The Baroda case, principally targeting George Fernandes but also some two dozen others, was launched by Indira Gandhi's government. The charge was that of "waging war against the state" by smuggling dynamite to blow up government facilities. Snehalatha Reddy was not named in the final charge-sheet but was nevertheless kept in prison for nearly a year, from May 2, 1976 to January 20, 1977.

Rajarajeshwari Nagar was lonely and scarcely populated. Gauri and her filmmaker sister Kavitha would talk in a racy, slangy Kannada that was delightfully new to me. We had completely different sets of friends and would throw large parties. My then husband Ashish Rajadhyaksha and our group of friends, all old Bangaloreans who had returned, had just started the Centre for the Study of Culture and Society—CSCS. Gauri had been married to journalist Chidanand Rajghatta, but they had broken up before we met. Lankesh and Ananthamurthy were the yin and yang of Navya literature and their children were good friends. But after Lankesh attacked Ananthamurthy in his paper, there was a rift. Gauri was loyal to her father and I never met the U.R.A. crowd at her place after that. I remember that at one of her parties, I was dancing on one foot because my other leg was encased in plaster after a bad scooter accident, when Prakash Belawadi (now a leading Modi bhakt) came up to me and bemoaned that people did not use their hands to dance. He demonstrated some fancy moves.

In 2000, when Lankesh suddenly died, there was a crisis and Gauri had to take over the paper as editor. The sisters adored their father. Though Kavitha had been Lankesh's favourite and Indrajit, the youngest son, was his pet, Gauri was the only journalist in the family. She had recently moved to Delhi and was enjoying working in the new ETV channel for the first time as a television journalist. After Lankesh's death, the family realised that the paper was broke and there were only a few thousand rupees—"just enough for his cards money"—in his bank account. The *Lankesh Patrike*, which had a readership of two lakhs in its heyday when Lankesh was known as a kingmaker, had lost out in the new era of 24/7 television. The family thought of shutting down the paper, but Gauri told me that if the paper had been shut down, the agents would not return the collections from the last issue and they would not be able to pay salaries. When her younger brother Indrajit was named proprietor, she chafed at the thought that she would have to work under him as the editor. Some years later, when they fell out over her activism, she began her own paper, the *Gauri Lankesh Patrike*.

Having been an English journalist, Gauri had to start from scratch and learn to think and edit and write in Kannada. She was belittled as a "convent educated" English journalist who was stepping into the shoes of a legend. For some years she disappeared from her friends' circle to immerse herself in her new world, working relentless hours till three or four in the morning every day. In Bangalore, many of us mix English words with Kannada, and the joke is that if you add an "u" sound to an English word it becomes Kannada—like table-u, chair-u. She had to stop thinking in English. Her writing would never have the literary magic of her father, but she followed his advice—that the secret of good writing was to express one's ideas simply and honestly. She had a naughty sense of humour and a sense of the absurd. There was a lot of palace intrigue in the paper when she joined. She laughed that her appointment was similar to that of the young Indira Gandhi, seen as a "dumb doll", being set up as president of the Congress by the old guard who thought that they could manipulate her. Soon, many of the experienced journalists left the paper. It was tough going. Towards the end she was practically writing the whole paper herself and continuing to run it without advertisements, trying to finance it with an examination guide and publishing section. She had recently talked to a friend about going digital. No one thought that her Kannada columns would someday be translated and published as important documents as they are being done today, or that she would win a major International award.*

Gauri never considered going back to a job in English journalism despite all her struggles in running the paper. She thought English journalism was frivolous and, if national in reach, had a scattered audience. As the editor of her own paper, she would have the freedom to take up her own causes and address a local but real constituency. (In fact, recently, when she was

---

*A month after her death, Gauri Lankesh was posthumously accorded the Anna Politkovskaya Award for 2017. The award was established in memory of the eponymous investigative journalist who was killed in Moscow in 2006.

invited to write for an English daily, her column was so hard-hitting that it was soon taken off on orders). The literary content went after a while, as that was not her forte. She soon realised that journalistic activism was not enough and she would have to plunge into activism on the ground to change things. Though her father was always a benchmark, she brought in her own radical politics, contemporary feminist sensibility and subjects such as LGBT rights, to the conservative Kannada readership. And in the middle of all this, bred in a literary milieu, she was also translating fictional works and essays.

The Kannada literary and journalistic world is extremely patriarchal and dominated by male chauvinists. Gauri was a rare being who was cosmopolitan, well-travelled, and very contemporary, while being deeply rooted in the regional. She must have been one of the few women in the state, if not nationally or even internationally, who owned and ran a political paper with a fearless voice. I would put her in a long and rarely recognised tradition of activist women journal owners and writers from the early nationalist period in India, like Nanjangud Thirumalamba and Belagere Janakamma from Karnataka.* Incidentally, Thirumalamba's writing was publicly dismissed by Masti Venkatesha Iyengar in an essay in the 1960s, resulting in her humiliation and disappearance from the Kannada literary scene. But Gauri was made of sterner stuff. One of our journalists wondered patronisingly why, Gauri, as a woman, did not stick to culture instead of getting into politics. He seems to have been unaware that cultural figures, from M.F. Husain to the "award wapsi" writers, have been the butt of attacks by our Hindutva forces. In fact, Gauri had started off at the *Times of India* covering the culture beat. She had several paintings gifted by artists from those days. I had given her a photograph from my *Phantom Lady*

---

*Nanjangud Thirumalamba (1887–1982) was the founder of the publishing house Sathi Hitaishini and the monthly magazine *Karnataka Nandini*. Belagere Janakamma (1912–66) is regarded as the first woman poet of the Navodaya period in Kannada writing.

series, which showed me jumping off a building in a masked
Zorro costume. Recently, when she had called us over to meet
dalit leader Jignesh Mevani, she introduced me as an artist and
dragged him by the arm to show him my work on the wall. Jignesh
was astonished and they both cackled with laughter.

One of the things we had discussed when we met Jignesh
was the number of threats to Gauri's life. I used to drop in at
her office for a chat and coffee when I was in Basavanagudi.
Once, in the early years, she showed me a pile of postcards on
her table and asked me to look at them. They were filled with
filthy sexual abuse and lewd bodily descriptions. Long before the
internet, the "chaddis" as her father had famously named them,
had discovered Gandhi's postcard to be an invaluable tool for
trolling.* And postcards were not subject to censorship. I asked
her how she could work facing this abuse day after day, and she
said she used to get upset at first but then decided to ignore it
and not be intimidated.

As women living alone in independent houses, we had, for
some years, a policeman on a yellow and black spotted bike
from the Cheetah force checking on us every night and signing
a notebook. Once, years ago, Gauri had attacked a powerful film
family and received threats on the phone. Late one night, I heard
some rustling sounds from the garden and found two policemen
peering through the living-room window like comic characters
from a Master Hirannaiah play. They said they had come to warn
me that they would be patrolling my house all night, asking me
to not to get alarmed. At my look of surprise, they asked me if
I wasn't Gauri Lankesh? I knew at once that they had come to
protect Gauri Lankesh, only they thought I was Gauri and Gauri
was Kavitha!

Only in crime films had I seen bodies lying askew in a pool of
blood. Dear Gauri. It is heart wrenching to think of your shock and

*The chaddis, P. Lankesh's preferred name for right-wing louts, was
inspired by the RSS, the Hindu chauvinist organization whose members,
till recently, wore khaki shorts.

pain. Gauri was smart, pretty, fun-loving, gutsy and independent. When she threw herself into Kannada journalism, she became an indomitable activist. Towards the end, she seemed to be moving away from all vanities, towards living an austere life. She "adopted" rising young leftist leaders such as Kanhaiya Kumar, Shehla Rashid and Jignesh, pampered them and organised meetings for them in Karnataka. Filmmaker Anand Patwardhan asked why Gauri was killed now, not before or later. Everyone agrees it is because of the elections.* The Lingayats form a strong voter bank; and Gauri, a Lingayat herself, strongly supported the demand for the status of a different religion for the Lingayats, a demand apparently researched thoroughly by Kalburgi. Gauri had recently published an edition covering this issue. Yet another friend is sure that the timing of the murder was linked with the fact that an important leader was visiting the city at the time. Gauri, a staunch rationalist who had become a nodal point for anti-fascist activism and an influential oppositional voice, had to go.

After those initial lonely years, Rajarajeshwari Nagar had grown and several good friends—all independent, like-minded, and vocal individuals—had moved here and we had a "gang". Gauri was complaining about our last meeting, saying that we went off for a night show at the local mall leaving her behind.

In our future gatherings we will miss, deeply, that most incorrigible member of the "gang", Gauri Lankesh who—hopelessly, carelessly, tragically—got herself *assassinated*.

First published in Indian Cultural Forum, November 8, 2017.

———◆◆◆———

---

*The Assembly election in Karnataka took place in May 2018.

THE WRITER'S SECOND LIFE

Githa Hariharan

Like M.M. Kalburgi before him, writer Perumal Murugan was
bullied into apologising for his words. As with Kalburgi, the coercion
did not relent after the apology. Since his tormentors had proved
to be literal-minded readers, unable to recognise fiction when they
saw it, Murugan mounted a breathtaking protest, publicly declaring
the death of his imagination. All of us, goons and bystanders alike,
were invited to this rhetorical event, joining him—the husk of the
dead artist—to witness the corpse of his creativity and take what
satisfaction we got out of it.

On January 12, 2015, the writer Perumal Murugan died. On July
5, 2016, the writer Perumal Murugan was resurrected.

This was no miracle, but a sad parable of Indian life today.

In January 2015, the writer died; but the teacher and citizen,
Perumal Murugan of Tiruchengode, Tamil Nadu, was still
alive. He announced his death himself. The cause of death was
his novel, *Madhorubhagan* (2010), translated from Tamil into
English as *One Part Woman* (2014) by Aniruddhan Vasudevan.
A young woman in this fiction is desperate to have a child. She
decides, as a last resort, to take part in a temple festival where for
one night, consensual sex is permissible between any man and
woman. The temple is dedicated to the one-part-woman god,
Ardhanareeswara. Actually, this fiction was only an excuse. The
cause of the writer's death was intimidation, a form of censorship
increasingly practised in India by individuals and groups. The
real cause was the ideological agenda behind the intimidation.

Four years after Murugan's novel was published, caste-based
groups, slow readers all, claimed the book "hurt" their religious
sentiments, and "defamed" women, the region and the community.
The BJP-RSS, on the lookout for allies, pulled out its familiar script:
mob censorship can divide people; division can court vote banks.
(It also destroys free speech and cultural well-being, but that can
be passed off as nationalism.)

Used to conflating history and fiction, the self-appointed censors put on their police uniforms. Instead of ignoring the thought police as aberrant haters of idea, imagination and word, the real police took them seriously. The writer was summoned for "peace talks". He was hounded into signing an apology and "withdrawing" his novel. He then took to Facebook to announce his death as a writer.

Between January 2015 and July 2016, the writer floated, dead and alive, in a menacing purgatory. In October 2015, he got an award, the Samanvay Bhasha Samman. His "shadow", the Tamil publisher, came to Delhi to receive the award. But there was a statement from the writer's "ghost". With heartbreaking logic, the ghost said, "The Samanvay Award for *Madhorubhagan* is a modern recognition given to Tamil, a classical language with a long and unbroken literary tradition. This recognition, bestowed on my language at an unfortunate moment, will, I hope, be a shining gem rather than an unsightly wart."

In July 2016, the writer was resurrected. The Madras High Court told him he could come back to life, think and imagine again, pick up his pen. Murugan the writer has accepted this offer of a second life: "It comforts a heart that had shrunk and wilted. I am trying to prop myself up holding on to the light of the last lines of the judgment: 'Let the author be resurrected to do what he is best at. Write.' I will get up."

Madhorubhagan has been described by Tamil critics as an imaginative effort to map the lore and ethos of the place Murugan comes from; to people it with characters who long for a reliable livelihood, marriage, children and acceptance by the community. But the point is not whether the novel is award-winning, or even good. The point is not whether a temple festival sanctioned a permissive night, or whether women wanting to conceive took advantage of this night. The real point is that the BJP-RSS and its casteist allies unmake India by depriving Indians of their rights, not only to write, but to read what they will. They insult their intelligence when they look to authority—whether the state, its "cultural" cohorts, the court, Batra-clones, Nihalani-doubles, or caste- and community-obsessed groups—to decide what we will read, write, paint, sing, see, or how we will live in our homes, classrooms and streets.*

The Madras High Court has bravely begun its judgement with Evelyn Beatrice Hall's encapsulation of Voltaire's outlook: "I may not agree with what you say, but will defend to the death, your right to say it." The court has performed its new job of bringing writers back to life, and it has done it reasonably well. Quite rightly, there is gratitude and jubilation among readers, writers and citizens partial to reason and imagination. But the judgement also forces us to confront the times we live in; what is happening to our home with its myriad riches. Literature, art, or a scientific breakthrough by an Indian Galileo, may challenge communities to look at the world afresh. Do we now look to the court to tell us what is worthy in art or science? Do we need the court, or anyone else, to allow us to tell stories?

These questions lead to an embarrassingly obvious point. But the obvious needs to be spelt out today, not just by the court or the eminent, but by the Indian people, every single one of them. We need, from childhood, to tell stories about ourselves and others. This need to imagine and recount is so powerful that it is inextinguishable. No law, no hurt sentiment, no official or unofficial censor, can destroy this yearning for different kinds of

---

*Dina Nath Batra is the right wing's resident expert on history, who counts Narendra Modi among his admirers. Modi has written the preface to one of Batra's books. Apart from an intense dislike of scholar and writer Wendy Doniger, Batra's views are animated by claims about modern scientific inventions anticipated by the technology of ancient India.

The Nihalani in question is Pahlaj, not to be confused with Govind Nihalani, director of *Ardh Satya*. Pahlaj Nihalani's Wikipedia entry reveals that he "considers Narendra Modi his action hero". His filmography includes a YouTube video made before the 2014 general elections, with the catchline: Har-har Modi, ghar-ghar Modi (All hail Modi. Modi in every home). Made chair of the censor board by a grateful government in 2015, he was removed from office in 2017.

truth. We know this from history and literature, and our essential knowledge of ourselves. History is replete with examples of resistance to the suppression of the imaginative idea, good, bad or indifferent.

We are besieged today by the BJP-RSS and its cynical gang who silence writers; prevent plays from being performed, films from being seen; art from pursuing what it must. Voices are muffled or silenced, whether they belong to women, the youth, or certain castes and communities. These voices need a second life like Perumal Murugan. But no government or court, no follower of identity politics is going to help. We have to resurrect the India we want to make with our own mass politics. We have to get this second life ourselves.

First published in The Indian Express, _July 9, 2016._

———◆•◆———

PARDON

K. Satchidanandan

This poem is dedicated to the Tamil writer Perumal Murugan who was forced into silence by anti-social communal outfits.

Pardon me
for what I have written,
for what I could not write,
for what I am likely to write
and for what I may never write.

Pardon me for the trees' flowering,
for the flowers' fruiting,
for having hoarded so much of
gold and water and spring
inside the earth.

Pardon me for the waning moon,
for the setting sun,
for the movement of the living,
for the stillness of the non-living.

Pardon me for filling the earth
with so much colour,
the blood with so much red,
the leaf with forest,
the rain with sky,
the sand with star
and my ink with dreams.

Pardon me for filling words
with so much meaning,
dates with so much history;
for having hidden today inside yesterday
and tomorrow inside today;
for creating the Creator
who fills gestures with dance
and nature with symbols.

Pardon me for the earthquake
and the tempest,
the wild fire and the raging sea.
The Earth is a damaged machine.
I am not someone who can repair it.
I am a king without a country,*
A god without a weapon,†
a life without a tongue.

---

*In the original "Perumal without a country". "Perumal" means "the Big Man", the king.

†In the original "Murugan without a vel". Murugan is Lord Subrahmanya who travels on a peacock and has a "vel"—a kind of spear—for his weapon. The two words together make the name of the writer.

Invent a god
Who doesn't ask for your head.
Invent the fearless man.

Invent
language,
invent
the alphabet.

Translated from Malayalam by the poet (Guftugu, October 30, 2015).

◆◆◆

CONVERSATION: MALAYALAM POET *KUREEPPUZHA* SREEKUMAR ON BEING ATTACKED BY THE RSS

Indian Cultural Forum

Malayalam poet Kureeppuzha Sreekumar was attacked by RSS and BJP activists on January 5, 2018, after a speech he delivered at the Kairali Library at Kottukkal in Kollam district, Kerala. Sreelakshmi of the Indian Cultural Forum spoke to the poet about the incident and about the increasing number of attacks against writers, artists and thinkers in the country.

Sreelakshmi (SL): On Monday, you were abused and physically assaulted by right-wing groups, allegedly in reaction to a speech that you delivered at the Kairali Library. Could you tell us what actually happened?

K Sreekumar (KS): The main issue here is not how I was attacked. Through my speech, I was trying to promote a certain kind of politics, a politics that is critical of rising religious fundamentalism.

It was an attack by the religious extremists on secular thinking and ideology. My speech dealt with the importance of preserving public land for future generations. Today, all the public lands are being occupied in the name of religion. Religious shrines are being built on common lands, with boards prohibiting the entry of people belonging to other castes and religions. I wanted people to wake up and open their eyes towards these issues. At the end of my lecture, I gave the recent example of Vadayampady in Ernakulam district. A specific piece of land in Vadayampady has been a public land for centuries; but, recently, this land was occupied by some fringe groups. Today, a "caste-wall" has emerged between the dalits and non-dalits. People should fight against such caste- and religion-based discrimination, regardless of their own religious beliefs. But it is only the Left forces who have chosen to take action against the developments in Vadayampady.

Recently, when the artist Ashanthan died, the local Shiva temple authorities near the Durbar Hall protested against the Lalitha Kala Akademi members keeping his body for public viewing. The temple was celebrating its annual festival at the time. Around twenty Congress supporters abused the Akademi members and tore the posters of Ashanthan's condolence meeting. The Akademi members were forced to remove the artist's body, which had been kept in the main hall, through the back door.

We need to speak up against such religious beliefs that forget humanity. Kerala does not belong to a single caste or religion. It is the land of social reformers like Sree Narayana Guru, Ayyankali, Sahodaran Ayyappan and Poykayil Appachan; and in a secular state like this, we need to raise our voice against such religious fundamentalism and extremism.

SL: After the attack, the BJP has become defensive about its action. BJP state secretary K. Surendran has accused you of having stirred this controversy for fame. How would you respond?

KS: I don't think there is any need for me to try and rake up such a controversy to gain popularity. Two years back, I had organised a march, along with my colleagues; the march lasted for fourteen days. The march went under the banner of "Beyond Secular and Cultural Practices" and stretched from Kasaragod to

Thiruvananthapuram. Besides, I have been a part of the literary circuit since my school days. I have been given enough awards, including awards from the Kerala University, the Kerala Sahitya Akademi Award and the Vyloppilli Yuva Kavi Award. My poem "Amma Malayalam" is recited by children in youth festivals. Another one of my poems, "Jessy", is sung by students in colleges even today. I don't think the BJP spokesperson, K. Surendran, has any knowledge of literary merit. I don't know what kind of poems he reads. I don't need controversies to become popular.

See, I don't believe in caste or religion. I became a rationalist at the age of sixteen and I am happy that I am not the only rationalist in the country. Vayalar Ramavarma, Thoppil Bhasi, N.N. Pillai, Ponkunnam Varkey, all of them stood for secular and rationalist thought. Vayalar, for instance, wrote, "Man created religions, religions created gods, man and religions and gods divided the land, divided minds." I have only reiterated what they said. My writings are appreciated by the people; my books are selling well. I don't need any further validation. I don't think I need to justify myself to groups that indulge in mob violence.

Translated from Malayalam by Sreelakshmi (Indian Cultural Forum, February 8, 2018)

———— ◆•◆ ————

WRITING THE AGE

Nayantara Sahgal

The political situation since 2014 has brought Nayantara Sahgal into greater engagement, public activity, and a more productive working life than ever. In a speech delivered at Panjab University, Chandigarh in March 2016, Sahgal explains how being a political writer united her imagination to her ethical values and convictions, in a creative exercise of citizenship. She urges her audience to stake such confidence on their own life experiences, their individual *points of view. True citizenship must be based on personal empowerment; it is a journey that enables truthful and fearless self-expression, the realisation of individual rights and diversity. In January 2019, Sahgal was invited to inaugurate and speak at the Akhil Bharatiya Marathi Sammelan in Nagpur. Following a threat from the Maharashtra Navnirman Sena (MNS), the organisers withdrew the invitation. In protest, various Marathi writers called for a boycott of the sammelan. Writers from other languages and cultural groups also expressed solidarity. The speech Nayantara Sahgal delivered in Chandigarh in 2016 needs to be read side by side with the one that she would have given in Nagpur in January 2019.**

The title for my talk—"Writing the Age"—was suggested to me and I thought it was appropriate because my writing seems to have been about the making of modern India. This was not a decision I made. As you know, writers don't choose their material. They use the material they have been given. My writing became politically oriented because I grew up in a family that was involved in the fight for freedom led by Mahatma Gandhi. Under a great and good leadership, a leadership that led by example, we achieved a first in human history—a non-violent fight for freedom. My novel *Lesser Breeds* (2003) was a recollection of that remarkable time. The high ideals that inspired that fight, and how those ideals declined and decayed, became the stuff of my writing. And some of the stories in my recent book of short stories are about what is happening in the country today. I suppose I should be thankful for the corruption that crept into national life, because it gave me the material for my novels, and also for my non-fiction—because I also wrote political commentary for the *Indian Express* and other papers for many years. But all writing is in a sense politically oriented. What we choose to write about, how we say it, what we choose not to say, are all political decisions. All writers are creatures of their times and we cannot but reflect the times we

---

*The speech can be read here: https://scroll.in/article/908496/what-nayantara-sahgal-was-not-allowed-to-say-at-marathi-literary-meet

live in. Engaging with one's times has made for a wide variety of unforgettable fiction. To name just a few that come to mind, we have the works of Brecht, of Pablo Neruda and other Latin American writers, of Chinua Achebe, Salman Rushdie and Faiz Ahmed Faiz. In India, writers such as Mahasweta Devi and Kiran Nagarkar, among others, have given us powerful political fiction. There is no getting away from politics since it is what makes for the atmosphere and conditions we live in.

Being as deeply involved as I have been in writing politically inspired literature, it is hard for me to separate the two at a time when [the] political atmosphere has launched an attack on literature and on all the creative arts. In this connection, since I am in Chandigarh, let me pay my respectful tribute to all the writers from Punjab and Haryana who have returned their Sahitya Akademi Awards in protest against the Akademi's long silence when the Kannada writer, Professor Kalburgi, was murdered, and before him, two Maharashtrian writers, Dabholkar and Pansare, both distinguished rationalists like Kalburgi who refused to kowtow to superstition. Now we are about a hundred writers who have returned our awards, and we have been supported by writers from 150 countries, showing that human rights are universal, and nationality is not a barrier wherever freedom of speech and thought are in danger. Let me also pay tribute to the professors of this university who have written against the destruction of our freedoms.

Our battle, as Indian writers, began as a demand for freedom of expression, but it became a much larger battle when the blacksmith Mohammed Akhlaq was dragged out of his house in Dadri village and brutally lynched on the excuse that he was a beef eater. The whole country was shocked and repelled by this incident. It raised the question of the very meaning of India, and of the rights guaranteed to us by our Constitution, which gives Indians the right to live as equals, to worship as they choose, and to eat what they like. Indian citizenship means a celebration of our diversity and differences, and its very meaning was undone by that hideous lynching of a poor man who had done no one any harm. By that time our premier institutions, starting with the Nehru Memorial Museum and Library, which attracts scholars from all over India and abroad, had already been under assault; their qualified heads were dismissed one by one, and replaced by obedient servants of the RSS, making it clear that disagreement with the ruling ideology or any questioning of it would not be tolerated. Going further, we see that dissent is now being treated as "anti-national". We have seen this happen in America when the notorious Senator McCarthy labelled Americans "un-American" if they did not fall in line with his anti-Communist fanaticism. Many distinguished men and women were persecuted and many careers were destroyed by McCarthy's hysteria against those whom he called "un-American".

Now we are watching this happen here—we who have a robust tradition of debate and dissent, we whose intellectual life as well as the aam admi's life have been enriched for centuries by our different ways of life and our different points of view, we who have kept the fresh air of different ideas flowing through our open society. And so, expectedly, there has been an outcry from scholars and thinkers from different disciplines against this campaign to shrink us into conformity. Historians and scientists, actors, filmmakers, students and academics have vigorously condemned the iron curtain coming down on freedom of thought. And obviously, assassinations, and other forms of criminal violence on those who refuse to fall in line with the ruling ideology, must revolt the conscience of every Indian. Historians and academics are rejecting the substitution of myths and superstition for historical research. Scientists are alarmed at the destruction of the scientific temper and the spirit of enquiry, without which no nation can all itself modern. A renowned scientist has returned his Padma Bhushan to the President, saying that "the direction in which today's government is driving my beloved country...will make the country a Hindu religious autocracy."

Dr Bhargava is, of course, a Hindu himself.* He says in his

---

*Dr Puspha Mittra Bhargava, founder-director of the Institute of Cellular and Molecular Biology, Hyderabad.

letter to the President that he has found the Hindutva ideology "divisive, unreasonable and unscientific". Another passionate protest has come from a retired Admiral of the Indian Navy, also a Hindu, who rejects the policy of turning India into a Hindu rashtra, and asserts his faith in a diverse and plural India.* The actor Saif Ali Khan has said in a public statement: "We are a blend, this great country of ours. It is our differences that make us who we are. I have prayed in church and attended Mass with my wife, Kareena, while she has bowed her head at dargahs and prayed in mosques. When we purified our home we had a havan and a Koran reading and a priest sprinkling holy water. The fabric of India is woven from many threads."

These are just three famous examples of a rebellion across the board, of Indians known and unknown who reject the falsehood of one religion, one ideology, one point of view; who refuse to identify religion with nation; and refuse to be divided, [refuse] an India belonging exclusively to Hindus, with all other Indians treated as second-class citizens. Hindutva is a perversion and distortion of Hinduism. In January, in a ten-minute inaugural talk to the Hyderabad Literary Festival, I suggested we reject Hindutva and embrace Hindustaniat and insaniyat instead. What is happening is that the doors to independent thinking, and our traditional openness to knowledge and research, are being shut down. This is ironic when Hinduism's most powerful prayer, the Gayatri Mantra, is a prayer for enlightenment. It is also ironic that Hindutva, which is raising a hue and cry against so-called "anti-nationals", is itself "anti-national" in its betrayal of our Constitution which created independent India as a secular democratic republic.

And now Hindutva has made a battleground of education, and it is for you—parents, teachers and students—to consider what this is doing to school textbooks, to the profession of teaching, and to the autonomy of universities, though the future of education is a matter of utmost concern to the entire country. What young

---

*Admiral (retd.) L. Ramdas.

people are going to be taught is a frightening thought, if the famous remarks that Ganesh's nose was grafted on him by Vedic surgery and airplanes flew in Vedic times are any indication.* Great teachers through the ages have opened up their students' minds to the world of ideas and have left their lasting and illuminating influence on them. Will teachers now be told what to teach? Last month it was reported that there has to be a "Bharatiya approach" to research and education, whatever that means. We might well ask, are we living in the 21st century or some fantasy-land that has no basis in fact or reason? Already many of our universities, starting with Hyderabad and JNU, are in ferment against this dangerous trend, with the RSS taking over all educational and cultural institutions and declaring that they must be purged of what they call "anti-national" elements. In this respect let me pay tribute to the courageous young men and women in universities across the land who have refused to be bullied and browbeaten by the ruling ideology, and for whom Kanhaiya Kumar† has set a shining example. The young are now in the forefront of the fight,

---

*The first claim was advanced by Prime Minister Narendra Modi, in his address to medical professionals at the inauguration of the renovated Sir HN–Reliance Hospital at Mumbai, on October 25, 2014. The information about airplanes in Vedic times was imparted to a gathering of the Indian Science Congress held at Mumbai, on January 4, 2015, by Capt. Anand J. Bodas, retired principal of a pilot training facility. Over 200 scientists had signed an online petition opposing his scheduled talk on "Ancient Indian Aviation Technology", to no avail. At the same conference, science and technology minister Harsh Vardhan claimed that ancient Indians had discovered the Pythagorean theorem but the Greeks had walked away with the credit for it.

†In February 2016, Kanhaiya Kumar, who was then the president of the Jawaharlal Nehru University Students' Union, was arrested and accused of sedition by the Delhi police for allegedly doing nothing to prevent the alleged raising of anti-India slogans during a student rally. Kumar denied the charges, and was released on interim bail on 2 March 2016 for lack of evidence. Upon his release, Kumar delivered a sensational speech in favour of freedom in India. As of February 2019, the Delhi police has not yet filed the charge sheet in the sedition case.

not only for the freedom of thought, but for the idea of India as conceived by our Constitution, and for all that still remains to be achieved in the way of justice and equality.

The print and electronic media have been talking about a climate of "intolerance". But is "intolerance" the word to describe the disappearing space for disagreement and dissent? It is certainly not the word to describe murder, or the violent attacks that are being made by thugs on whatever they disagree with—on books and book launches, movies, music concerts, exhibitions of paintings and the like. A gang of thugs turned up and hounded the Tamil writer Perumal Murugan out of his home and made him stop writing on pain of death. He has been forced to declare himself dead as a writer. Recently he was invited to Delhi to accept an award and he said he could not come because he was dead. In his place, I, too, would be terrified to be visible again, for fear of the harm that might come to me and my family. Another writer has been told his fingers will be broken if he goes on writing. Armed with threats, or sticks and stones, or black paint, or guns—but above all, with the knowledge that they have the protection of those in power—thugs are able to force the closure of whatever they disagree with. To date no one responsible for these crimes has been brought to justice, and the ruling power stays silent on these outrages. It has also targeted citizens like Teesta Setalvad and her husband who are working for the rights of the victims of the 2002 massacre in Gujarat. Arundhati Roy has been charged with contempt of court because she has written an article condemning the inhuman treatment of Professor Saibaba in jail. He is a man who is paralysed from the waist down and is in a wheelchair, and he has been confined to solitary imprisonment with no help of any kind.* Arundhati herself faces the possibility of a jail sentence. I have not even touched on Rohith Vemula's suicide…[that] tragedy

*Delhi University Professor Dr G N Saibaba, who lives with severe physical disabilities and uses a wheelchair, was arrested by the Maharashtra police in March 2014, for his alleged links to Maoists. The Gadchiroli sessions court sentenced him to life imprisonment in March 2017.

compounds so many other tragedies concerning the caste factor in universities; and also in Rohith's case, the role that Union ministers played in driving him to his death.

But now let me share with you my experience on the opening day of the Hyderabad Literary Festival. As I said earlier, I was invited to give a brief inaugural talk, and I spoke much the same as I am speaking now about matters of national concern, and the dangers we face in the climate we are now living in. The Governor of Telengana (and also of Andhra) was the chief guest on the occasion and he got up to speak after me. My speech had obviously upset and angered him because he set aside his own prepared address and angrily refuted all that I had said. Referring to me, he told the audience, "At the end of this festival she will realise that in THIS state we all live in harmony." A few days later came the news of Rohith Vemula's suicide at Hyderabad University. It made public his arbitrary suspension, along with four other dalit students. It revealed the whole grim and ugly political interference that had caused a brilliant young man, who aspired to be a science writer like Carl Sagan, to end his own life. The suicide letter he has left us is one of the most haunting and moving pieces of writing I have ever read, and the least we can do is to preserve it as a piece of literature. His death must remain a reminder to us all of the inhuman and unbearable discrimination that dalits face in our society. No, this was certainly no example of harmony in the state. But these are the platitudes we hear, and which we must separate from the realities we cannot ignore.

There is no question, then, that citizens must speak. Writers are doing so in every possible forum…

What the authorities have called a "manufactured" protest on the part of writers has, in fact, been nothing of the kind. It was neither planned nor organized. We writers live in different far-flung parts of this country. We don't speak each other's languages. We haven't read each other. We haven't met each other. We made individual decisions about returning or not returning our awards. That is the most remarkable fact about this protest. It has been a spontaneous upsurge and a matter of individual conscience. Nothing like it has happened in any other country. I was on an NDTV program where the usual accusation of a "manufactured" protest was made, saying that writers had protested because they were seeking importance. I had to correct my accuser and tell him that writers are not looking for importance, they are looking for publishers. The other remarkable fact is the way that the writers' protest has expanded—again spontaneously—into what we now see, where other voices from other disciplines have come into it—all of them for reasons directly affecting their own professions and institutions and their own rigorous standards of scholarship or artistic performance. We are under siege on many fronts and we are fighting back.

Religious fundamentalism is not religion. It is a disease, and it is women who suffer most from its dictates. We know what it is doing to women in countries around us, and now we see signs of this archaic mentality here in statements made by leading lights of Hindutva, statements that tell women they must be home before dark, that they must be housewives and must not take work outside the home, that they must bear a certain number of children, to increase the Hindu population, and other such uncivilised orders. It is for Indian women to reject such ideas as totally unacceptable, and for Indian men to support women in the continuing struggle against male domination, which is now getting a boost from the disease of religious fundamentalism.

I have said citizens must speak. At a time when we lack the leadership we need, the moral responsibility for making a stand rests on us, and that can be done in so many different, and always non-violent, ways. A story I like to tell is about a Canadian friend of mine who visited South Africa during the rule of apartheid. She got into a bus and sat down in the nearest available seat. The conductor came up to her and said, "Lady, these seats are for the blacks. The seats for Europeans are up front." My friend replied, "Oh, that's all right, I'm not European, I'm a Canadian," and she stayed where she was. And then, of course, there was the famous

Rosa Parks who started a civil rights movement in the USA by sitting in the white section of the bus and refusing to vacate it. Protest takes many forms, and one of these is by the words one puts on a page, what one writes about, and the way one writes. Pablo Neruda explained his transition from love poetry to political awareness in a poem called "Let Me Explain a Few Things": "You will ask: and where are the lilacs / and the metaphysics petalled with poppies / and the rain repeatedly spattering its words... / Come and see the blood in the streets / Come and see the blood in the streets...". But becoming politically aware did not prevent him from writing odes to red wine, or lyrics to the body of his beloved. His personal life and his politics were one and his writing reflected all of him.

I am here at your kind invitation because being here during these troubled times is also part of my role as a writer and all that I have written. Like other writers who have stepped into controversy, what I say, what I write, what I stand for, are a mixture of the personal and political. To end on a personal note, I am a child of Gandhi's India. I was a young girl when Nathuram Godse killed him. I was in the room in Birla House when Gandhiji breathed his last. Through my tears I remember promising myself, "I will never let him die." I hope I have kept that promise.

Published in Indian Cultural Forum, March 26, 2016.

*

From the speech Nayantara Sahgal was not allowed to make in Nagpur:

Today, we have a situation where diversity and opposition to the ruling ideology are under fierce attack.

Diversity is the very meaning of our civilisation. We have old literatures in many different languages. We eat different foods, we dress differently, we have different festivals, and we follow different religions. Inclusiveness has been our way of life and this ancient multicultural civilisation whose name is India is a most remarkable achievement that no other country has known. Today it is threatened by a policy to wipe out our religious and cultural differences and force us into a single identity. With one stroke, this policy wipes out the constitutional rights of millions of our countrymen and women who are not Hindus, and makes invaders outsiders and enemies of them. At Independence, our founding fathers rejected a religious identity and had the wisdom to declare India a secular democratic republic, not because they were against religion but because they understood that in our country of many religions, only a secular state would provide the overall umbrella of neutrality under which every Indian would have the right to live and worship according to his or her faith. The Constituent Assembly that took this decision was made up of a majority of Hindus, yet they drew up a Constitution whose preamble affirmed a life of liberty, equality and fraternity for all Indians.

This high ideal was inspired by Ambedkar, who was the chief architect of the Constitution and a great Maharashtrian, whose insistence that all human beings are equal started a revolution against caste. That high ideal has now been thrown aside. Minorities, and those who don't support the Hindu Rashtra agenda, have become targets for fanatics who roam the streets. We have recently seen five citizens falsely charged with conspiracy and arrested on grounds of sedition. These are men and women who have spent years of their lives working for tribal rights and forest rights, and for justice for the marginalised. Christian churches have been vandalised and Christians are feeling insecure. Lynch mobs are openly attacking and killing Muslims on invented rumours that they were killing cows and eating beef. We are watching all this lawlessness on TV. In Uttar Pradesh these mob attacks on the cow pretext have become common, while the authorities stand by and look on.

When terrorism of this kind becomes official, as it has in Uttar Pradesh, where can we look for justice?

Mob violence on defenceless people, backed by the state, goes on in many places and the guilty have not been convicted. In some cases victims have been charged with the crimes instead, and the criminals have been congratulated. The human cost of this tragic situation is that it is a time of fear and grief for many Indians who no longer feel safe living and worshipping as they have always done, and have a right to do. The poor and helpless among them—some of whom have been driven out of their villages and their homes and jobs—are living without work, or help, or hope.

...In this war that has been declared on diversity, dissent and debate, those who care about freedom have not stayed silent. There are marches and rallies against the destruction of our fundamental rights. There are protests by retired civil servants, students and academics, lawyers, historians and scientists, dalits and adivasis; [there is] the farmers' huge demand for their rights. The large numbers of farmer suicides in this area show the desperate situation they are no longer able to face. The Bhim Army, named after Dr Ambedkar, is making its voice heard, and we are reminded that it has an inheritance of dramatic revolt, when Ambedkar and E.V. Ramasamy Periyar publicly burned the *Manusmriti* in the 1920s for the insulting and objectionable laws it laid down for dalits in the caste system, condemning them to an inferior status. The singer T.M. Krishna and the historian Ramachandra Guha are among those who have made strong individual protests. Krishna's concert was cancelled and Guha received a death threat. Recently a great actor, Naseeruddin Shah, has spoken out against the war on Islam and how he fears for his children.

What can writers do in this situation? The answer is: we can write.

Powerful fiction has been the result of writers stepping into controversy and taking sides, but not as polemics or propaganda. Their plays, poems and novels have been about people, not ideas, written by authors who were deeply engaged with the times they were living in, and some are still living in. Writers don't live in ivory towers. Through our writing, we take sides between good and evil, right and wrong. Great literature worldwide, by writers of many nationalities, has done this. This is the literature that has touched chords in succeeding generations and stays alive. We show where we stand by the subjects we choose, the stories we write, and the way we write them. Whether we are writing about our grandmother's cooking, or the rain on the roof, or describing the body of our beloved, every word we write makes it clear where we stand. Writing, like all forms of creative art, is a powerful form of political activism, and it is a means of revolt. That is why dictators are so afraid of it and take steps to control it.

Extracts from "What Nayantara Sahgal Was Not Allowed to Say at Marathi Literary Meet", Scroll.in, January 7, 2019.

———— ◆◆◆ ————

BREAKING THE SILENCE

Shashi Deshpande

Shashi Deshpande, in her talk at the Goa Arts and Literature Festival in December 2018, spoke of the officially sanctioned bigotry that has gripped India, and she spoke about the backlash from the patriarchy that has followed the Sabarimala judgement and the #MeToo movement. Both point to a very real threat to the India promised by our Constitution, a threat that can only be confronted by disbanding old orders of segregation, and replacing them with civic egalitarianism.

When, decades back, I had to study the Constitution as a law student, it was in its infancy, scarcely a decade old. For us students, the chapter on fundamental rights mattered only because it was important for the exams. It took the Emergency for many of us to understand the real importance of these rights. Today, I look at the rights differently, perhaps with a greater understanding. Article 14, which promises all citizens equality before the law, seems remarkable when I think of what it meant to a people who, ruled by a foreign power, had been second-class citizens in their own country for two centuries. What it meant to a people who lived in a rigidly hierarchical society in which people could never even hope to be equal.

But before I talk of the right to equality, I will go back for a moment to an earlier, personal story. Many years ago, I was in Cambridge for a seminar on British literature. There were five of us from the subcontinent at that seminar: three Indians, one from Bangladesh and one from Pakistan. During a casual conversation, one of these two said to us Indians, "We envy you. You can stand in the middle of the street and criticise your prime minister." The other heartily concurred. I imagine we patted ourselves on the back then for being a mature democracy. We had the splendid example of the time when Indira Gandhi had attempted to subvert democracy and had been voted out of power. And the motley collection of parties and individuals who had formed a government after that had been voted out as well when it was clear they were totally unfit to govern. We felt good about ourselves. What made us feel even better was that we were not like our neighbours across the border. In fact, it gave us great pleasure to define ourselves as not-Pakistan.

Then, recently, I read an interview with Mohammed Hanif, the Pakistani writer, who writes so critically and courageously about the sad state of affairs in his country. During the course of the interview, the Indian journalist interviewing him referred to a poem written by a Pakistani poet, Fahmida Riaz, who sadly passed away a few days back. The journalist quoted a line from her poem, "*Tum bilkul hum jaise nikle*" [You turned out to be just like us].

Mohammed Hanif's response was, "How different could we be? We drink the same water, eat pretty much the same food, we breathe the same air..." And, finally, he added, "It's horrendous here, it's horrendous there."

It hurt to read this. It shocked me. However bad things were in our country, how could anyone say we had become another Pakistan? We had our courts, sentinels of our democracy. And a free and enormously alive press. But both Mohammad Hanif's words and Fahmida Riaz's poem were couched in tones of such regret that I thought we needed to take a long and hard look at our country. What I saw was not very reassuring; in fact, it filled me with dismay.

Era of mobs

After the 2014 elections gave the BJP a clear and strong mandate, for which many of us were thankful, because we were tired of corruption and coalitions and hoped to settle down to sensible governing, to the progress that had been promised. We were sadly disillusioned. We entered the Era of Mobs. Mobs came out of nowhere, it seemed—mobs who indulged in lynching, in barbaric killings in the name of the holy cow. Who turned into moral policemen in the name of "our culture". Mobs who attacked people in the name of patriotism and nationalism. Who imposed a kind of unofficial censorship, so that they decided whether a book, a film, a play, a painting exhibition or a musical performance was fit to enter the public domain. These mobs seemed to have some kind of a patronage, for very rarely were they punished for their crimes.

On an official level, there has been, apart from a clamping down on dissent and interference with institutions, a rewriting of history, an attempt to create a narrative of the past in tune with the ideology and desires of the ruling party.

Now, with elections approaching, we are back to vote banks and voter appeasement, which have always been the name of the game of politics in India. But the promises being made now—of a quick resolution of the Ram Janmabhoomi issue, in favour of Hindus of course; the construction of a Ram mandir; of a great statue of Shri Ram in Ayodhya, making it a symbol for the entire country—makes it clear that Hindutva, which was toned down in the 2014 elections in favour of development and progress, is to be a major issue in 2019.

Sadly, the Congress has jumped on the bandwagon, grasping for more Hindu votes. Though, one hopes that for the Congress it is just an election strategy. But for the ruling party, these slogans are in pursuance of their goal, which is the conversion of India into Bharat, a Hindu Rashtra. Something very hard to approve of for someone of my generation, we who accepted the mantra in which Pandit Nehru believed lay the magic of India: unity in diversity. This mantra, along with Pandit Nehru himself, has been consigned to the dustbin of history and the 2019 elections have become a crucial test for the country. Will India become a Hindu nation and will non-Hindus become second-class citizens in their own country? Will Article 14 of the Constitution apply only to some Indian citizens, not to all? This will have consequences that will change the shape of this country, indeed of the subcontinent, forever. And, therefore, something that should concern all of us deeply.

In all fairness, I have to ask myself whether those of us who have such fears are being unduly alarmist. Possibly none of these things will happen. It is to be hoped voters will reject the idea of an India of intolerance and hatred. I also think it will not be easy to convert India into a Hindu nation. Hinduism is, by its nature, not a religion that lends itself to becoming a monolithic dominating institution. And yet, when I see mobs inflamed by politicians demanding a Shri Ram temple, when I read of leaders exhorting the masses to agitate for the temple, I am frightened. One cannot but remember the post-Partition violence and carnage. What is more ominous is the polarisation that happened during the 2014 elections. Independent India has held many elections, but there has rarely or never been such open and ugly hatred between political parties and politicians. We have experienced the residue of the bitterness of the 2014 elections during the past four-and-a-half years. We have seen it in the way social media is used to troll enemies, in the shouting and ranting on TV, in the way abuses are traded, wild personal charges that should never be part of a political debate are made, and so on.

The polarisation that happened after 2014 meant that not only the country, not just politicians, but even families were divided by a sharp clean line. I know for a fact how much bitterness developed between friends, within families. There never was a midway meeting ground; the general understanding was that "if you are not with us you are against us". This has left its mark on the country and I fear it will be worse after the coming elections. My great anxiety is: will we be able to come together again? Will we be able to live in harmony as we once did, each religion, each culture having its own place in society, none threatening the other? Once the elections are over, will we be able to forget the hatred, the seeds of which have been sown so generously? Or, will the nation continue to be divided by a most dangerous divide—a divide based on religion. Politicians in India have consistently followed a policy of dividing people, but the divide seems alarming and threatening as never before.

Sabarimala and #MeToo

For me, as a writer and a person who has been keenly alive to the injustice women have had to suffer, almost, perhaps, since time began, there is another matter of great concern. I am referring to the issue of women's entry into the Sabarimala temple. I have to wonder why at such a time, in the 21st century, when it should [be] impossible to deny women their constitutional rights, the entry of women between ten and fifty [years of age] is being so fiercely resisted? Why, day after day, mobs surround the temple and chant, not with devotion but with a kind of ferocious frenzy to keep women away. Why they behave as if the temple is under attack. I am mystified that women themselves are part of this opposition. In fact, at times, they are fiercer than the men. And I have to ask myself whether they have been so conditioned by society that the idea of entering the temple fills them with a superstitious fear. And how can they regard menstruation as something unclean, not a normal physiological process? Simone de Beauvoir, in her book *The Second Sex*, speaks of menstruation as life constructing a cradle in the body every month. A beautiful concept and a truth. Yet, people are so determined to keep women out of the temple on the basis of the fact of menstruation that they defy a Supreme Court judgement.

Talk of tradition, of a god who does not want women of reproductive age near him, rouses a suspicion that the men are imposing their own misogyny on god. So is it merely anti-women? Or, is it what it has now undoubtedly become—a part of the political game politicians always play, both the major national parties brazenly disregarding the Supreme Court judgement and backing the traditional stand so as not to lose any votes?

Whatever it is, it seems both unbelievable and sad that at a time when women have been steadily making headway in their struggle to assert themselves as an equal half of the human race, they should be regarded as lesser beings. In fact, looking at the unrelenting opposition, a suspicion dogs me: is the anti-women campaign in Sabarimala connected to the #MeToo movement, is it a backlash to that movement? I get a hint of how the #MeToo movement is regarded in the words of a famous and popular actor in Kerala, a man who is obviously not constrained by political correctness. He calls the movement a fad, a fashion, which will soon die out. These words for a movement in which women are trying to reclaim their right to their own bodies.

Breaking the silence

More than thirty years ago, I wrote a novel, *That Long Silence,* which was about the breaking of women's silences. To me, the breaking of silences is the beginning of revolution. And now, here are women breaking their silence about something that had remained secret and unspoken for centuries—sexual assault. I am very pleased that this has happened, I am pleased that the world is listening to women's voices and taking them seriously. I am pleased that whatever the outcome, one thing is true: men will now be apprehensive about forcing their attentions on a reluctant woman, even if the woman is in their power. Hopefully, no man will ever be able to exploit any woman and get away with it. Above all, I am pleased that, finally, shame has gone back to where it belongs—to the perpetrator of the wrong. The strangest thing about crimes against women was that, unlike all other crimes, shame was attached to the victim. And therefore the silence. No longer, I hope.

Yet, I have some anxieties. Will the movement percolate down to women in small jobs, women who face harassment almost daily in their working lives? Women for whom their job is of such vital importance that to speak out would be to endanger that job and make life harder for themselves and their families. And once again my great fear is, will the #MeToo movement make the two genders always suspicious and fearful of each other? Will there be another polarisation, and will we have to live in a world of men against women? Will men and women be able to live together in love and harmony after women have asserted their right to be equal under the law? I think that the answer to this can only come from men. The ball is in their court.

One of the questions asked of the women who named men who had sexually harassed them was: why were you silent all this time, all these years? In reply, I give a quote from Caroline Norton, an Englishwoman who lived in the 19th century, at a time when married women had no rights at all. She fought a bitter legal battle with her abusive husband for the custody of her children—which she lost—in the course of which she wrote a letter to Queen Victoria in which she quoted these words: "History teaches that in all cases of great injustice among men, there comes a culminating point after which that injustice is not to be borne."

I believe that the culminating point for women has come.

The great danger

Behind all these exclusions and divisions looms a bigger danger, a threat to the shining promise of equality before the law given to all citizens by the Constitution. The Sabarimala issue is an indicator that women still have to fight for that right. And the threat to all non-Hindu citizens of becoming second-class citizens now appears a dreadful possibility. A country in which some citizens live with fear is a failed state. I am hopeful that the gender divide will not become a festering issue, because, a cynical thought, we need each other. But the divide caused by religion is more dangerous; we have only to look at the various bloody civil wars being fought in the world to see what can happen. All those who want a Hindu state must think of the consequences of establishing it. Perhaps we need to go back to Rabindranath Tagore's well-known poem and think of the "heaven of freedom" that he prayed for, which we can enter only when all of us, whatever our religion or caste, our class, gender or language, are equal. Considering the human track record, this seems almost impossible. But the fact that so many of us continue to love, support and cherish the people in our lives should give us hope. All that we need to do is what Arjuna did on the eve of the battle of Kurukshetra—we only have to expand the range of the words "my people" to embrace all Indians.

This is the edited text of the keynote address delivered by Shashi Deshpande at the ninth edition of the Goa Arts and Literature Festival in December 2018. The original text was first published in Scroll.in, December 11, 2018.

———◆◆◆———

CONVERSATION: GHANSHYAM SHAH ON HIGHER EDUCATION IN GUJARAT

Indian Cultural Forum

Over the last few years, Indian education has become something of a battlefield. Appointments are made based on the sole qualification of loyalty to the government's (Hindutva) ideology. Debate, dissent and freedom of expression are suppressed on campuses around the country. Texts are banned through coercion by individuals and groups, often based on "hurt sentiments" or other non-academic reasons. Institutions built over the years are being saffronised, and are losing their autonomy.

Perhaps it is not unexpected that Gujarat, often viewed as "a *laboratory" for the Hindutvavadis, passed a bill that will further erode the idea of a university in the state. The bill proposes a "Gujarat State Higher Education Council" headed not by academics, but by the Chief Minister.* The Council will have sweeping powers to overrule university decisions and insist on compliance with its directives. The government will be able to interfere in all day-to-day matters at universities. Will the process of learning and research survive such a move?*

The Indian Cultural Forum (ICF) spoke to well-known sociologist Ghanshyam Shah about the bill. Professor Shah is the author of numerous books, including Social Movements in India (2009), and has taught at several universities, including JNU in New Delhi. He was a national fellow at the Indian Council of Social Science Research, affiliated to the Centre for Social Studies, Surat.

Indian Cultural Forum (ICF): What are the dangers of this bill for universities in Gujarat? How is it going to affect the quality of learning, teaching and research?

Ghanshyam Shah (GS): Although the number of state-sponsored universities in Gujarat has increased in the last two decades, the quality of education has declined considerably. Grants to universities have been reduced. The government does not even permit the filling up of vacant positions, leave alone creating new posts. One of the reasons for the poor state of higher education is the excessive power the Government of Gujarat is exercising in the academic sphere. The present bill further increases these powers. It will further bureaucratise and politicise the already stifled institutions of higher education in the state.

ICF: How is the council this bill proposes to set up different from similar councils in five other states?

---

*"On March 31 [2016], the last day of its Budget session, the Gujarat House passed a law giving sweeping powers to the government to ensure the 'planned and coordinated development' of universities, striking a blow to their autonomy, and drastically cutting the powers of Vice-Chancellors. The Bill [...] was passed in the absence of Opposition MLAs who had been suspended by the Speaker a day earlier." *The Indian Express*, April 27, 2016.

GS: The government has consolidated its powers through this bill. It legitimises the government's power to give any directive to the council, and it is obligatory for the council to implement such directives. The bill proposes the chief minister as chairperson, the education minister as vice-chairperson and the education secretary as secretary of the council. It has no provision for teacher or student representatives.

Moreover, no one is allowed to file any criminal case against any action of any member of the council or its officers. So they are above the law.

There is also the question of how the bill was passed. In a democratic society, all important bills are first placed before the public, inviting comments from the stake-holders. Here, this was not done. Moreover, the bill was passed in the state assembly in the absence of the opposition party, without discussion.

ICF: The Gujarat government also recently announced a list of eighty-two topics for doctoral theses, at least five of which must form the subject of a PhD student's research, including "Comparative study of Sardar Patel Awas Yojana and Indira Awas Yojana" and "Education of Minorities—a Critical Study". Would you comment on this move?

GS: It is a disgusting and anti-intellectual idea to feed students and teachers with the subjects on which they are required to do or guide PhDs. I can only say that those who have floated this proposal do not know what harm they are doing to the creative, intellectual life of Gujarat. They assume teachers and students do not have the capacity to think of what to study and what to write.

First published in Indian Cultural Forum, May 1, 2016.

◆•◆

DISCIPLINING THE CHERRY ORCHARD:
CAMPUS TALES FROM DELHI

Somok Roy

The rites of spring at Delhi University have assumed a dire character in the past few years, as Somok Roy, a student of Delhi University's Ramjas College, explains in this piece written in 2018.

For the past two years, the country's premier universities take to the streets every spring, in defence of our constitutional rights, walking past tree-lined avenues with sagging semal branches, singing songs of resistance and freedom, ushering in the march of spring in an otherwise ujda dayaar, ruined wilderness. The Leviathan of authority fears being reduced to a paper tiger, and every year, in a fit of skittishness, ends up de-legitimising its existence. Trapped in the turbid waters of insecurity, the whale tries to destabilise the sea—causing a shipwreck or two—but in vain. The seafarers' spirit has managed to survive all orchestrated assaults and attacks.

In February 2016, the Jawaharlal Nehru University (JNU) was declared the greatest threat to the nation, the nation that is Bharat Mata, the "mother" adorned with a regalia of barbed wire and reduced to an exploitable resource-base for her favoured sons. The mere act of being a "citizen" of this democratic nation, as opposed to a "subject", can earn you the dreaded tag of being an "anti-national". For, citizenship entails the freedom to think, ask, critique, sing, and read, sans censor; to dance, eat the food of your choice, "solidarise", resist; and most importantly, to love—to unite in love. The imagined community of subjects, in contrast, must define itself against other imagined communities and perpetuate its existence by creating borders. Any transgression of these borders, even in the realm of ideas, rattles the Leviathan. When such transgressions translate into performances of resistance, the state unleashes its brute force (and, unwittingly, helps in demystifying power for the people).

On March 23, 2018, a march organised by the Jawaharlal Nehru University Teachers' Association (JNUTA) and the Jawaharlal Nehru University Students' Union (JNUSU) was supposed to cover a distance of around 13 kilometres, from the University's north gate to the Parliament. The call, issued by JNUSU, made an "appeal to the JNU community" and the "citizens of Delhi" to join the long march "…to ensure that the continuing injustices in JNU and across universities are put to a halt". The leaflet announcing the march listed gender justice, social justice, academic freedom, accessible and equitable education as some of its prime agendas. It also addressed the topical issue of the state's brazen agenda to curtail the autonomy of universities. This concerned the unprecedented move—dubbed as "historic" by the Central government—of March 20, when the University Grants Commission (UGC) granted "autonomy" to fifty-two universities and eight colleges, a great leap towards privatisation and self-financing, ringing the death knell of a public education system which, in accordance with the ideals of the Constitution, made education relatively accessible to people from diverse socio-economic backgrounds in an otherwise stratified society. The UGC notification had one leitmotif recurring in almost every clause—the "condition" that the initiatives of these universities "shall have to be paid from their own revenue sources and not from Commission or Government funds". So "autonomy" only meant pushing the institutions to raise the money they needed on their own, mainly by charging exorbitant fees and throwing open the door for private entities.

The police stopped the JNUTA-JNUSU march near the INA market, attacked the protesters by using water cannon, and finally resorted to that reliable fall-back of brute force—a lathi-charge. I was alerted to this brutality by a friend, who, like me, couldn't join the foot-soldiers from JNU. We frantically started calling people to check if they were fine. Apparently, twenty-three people were detained by the police, and several others beaten up. This did not surprise people who had witnessed the events of February

2016 in JNU. Or of February 2017 in Ramjas College, when the police remained comfortably numb and passively facilitated the siege of the campus by the goons of the Akhil Bharatiya Vidyarthi Parishad (ABVP)*.

Qestioning the "autonomous status" granted by the UGC to select institutions, and deeming it an "abandonment" on the part of the government, implies a refusal to buy the state's narrative, and this is an embarrassing failure for the ideological apparatus of the state. Hence, it becomes imperative for the state to invoke what Althusser called the Repressive State Apparatus (RSA)—the army, the police, the court, the administration, and the prisons, all of which "function by violence".

The police atrocities at the march left people injured, bruised and unconscious. But such violence is not merely inflicted on the corporeal, and it is not frozen in a specific temporal moment. The visual image of a protester being brutally beaten with a lathi and the presence of water cannon to disperse dissenting individuals construct a political iconography of "fear, reverence, terror", in the words of Carlo Ginzburg. Meant to serve collectively as a deterrent, the success of these images depends on the perfomativity of our memory.

It is the same ideology of 'fear, reverence, terror' that is behind the proposal to install an army tank in JNU—a classic example of the use of iconography to militarise an academic space, to discipline citizens "visually".

And for the instruction of the student body, the administration at Ramjas is benevolently recreating the perfect setting for the study of Michel Foucault's seminal text, *Discipline and Punish: The Birth of the Prison*. In January 2018, a week before the acting principal was impeached for embezzlement, his office, in an unprecedented feat of shamelessness, issued warning boards reading, "You are under surveillance", "Loitering in the corridors

---

*The right-wing student organisation affiliated to the RSS. It functions as the BJP's student wing, though officially neither the ABVP nor the BJP acknowledge this.

is prohibited", "CCTV camera", and so on. Yes, we were being watched. As a member of Wordcraft, the infamous literary society that curated "Cultures of Protest" in February 2017, I know how impossible it has become to conduct open-air sessions in the college without being subjected to the administrative gaze.* It hardly matters if the CCTV cameras are inoperative; that they are there and that you *could* be observed from a higher pedestal in the power hierarchy serves the purposes of the administration...

At Ramjas, students have held their ground, and quite literally so. "Reclaiming spaces" is more than a slogan. The amphitheatre and its rear facing the ECA room—ECA stands for Extra Curricular Activities, a retrograde phrase—is one of the most vibrant spaces in the college, and it has witnessed innumerable conversations, fearless and passionate, on topics ranging from war poetry to how different Lucknow's khana is from Delhi's. The administration fears this part of the college, because it is here that people question, sing, dance, read, and love. Deploying the usual neo-liberal artifice, the college authorities invited two private food chains to set up counters near the amphitheatre. Besides being a source of revenue, the eateries were meant to de-politicise the space. Sadly for the authorities, students know how to savour burgers without falling prey to the oh-so-seductive-American-dream! On an almost giddy spree, the authorities got instructive boards installed at the ECA, appointed two guards to "monitor" them, and issued a couple of notifications on attendance.

Social geographer Doreen Massey studied space as a product of social relations, which comes into existence as a result of acceptance or refusal of relations. The refusal to accept the authority's paternalistic patronage, the refusal to be infantilised by the administration, the refusal to choose the "normative" over

---

*The event, scheduled for February 22, 2017, and organised by the English Department and the Literary Society, was to feature a session with filmmaker Sanjay Kak, JNU professor Bimol Akoijam and the student leader Umar Khalid. However, the ABVP decided to disrupt the session, and proceeded to do so—with slogans of "Bharat Mata ki jai" and "Vande Mataram" and with stones and heckling.

the "democratic", is what keeps alive the amphitheatre at Ramjas. Just as similar spaces are kept alive at JNU. It is the informed subversion of a megalomaniac authority that makes the freedom square in JNU a spatial manifestation of democracy. As Mukul Manglik said in one of his recent speeches at JNU, we, the students, "...are doing for the survival of democracy what spring does for the survival of the cherry tree."

First published in Indian Cultural Forum, March 26, 2018.

❖

SEDITION AND THE STATUS OF SUBVERSIVE SPEECH IN INDIA

Lawrence Liang

In this piece on sedition and free speech in India, Lawrence Liang is clear that freedom of expression cannot be held hostage to narrow ideas of what constitutes "anti-national" speech. This piece was written in 2016, soon after JNU students including Kanhaiya Kumar were arrested for, allegedly, raising anti-national and seditious slogans.

Let's be absolutely clear: the final arbiters of what constitutes sedition are not a zealous nationalist public, it is not the media, it is not the police and, finally, it is not even common sense. The mere declaration by a group of someone's speech as sedition or even the filing of a case against someone under section 124A of the Indian Penal Code (IPC) does not make the speech seditious. There have been hundreds of cases filed before and these, when tested in courts of law, have led to the adoption of tests and doctrinal standards that determine what the law of sedition in India is.

It is unfortunate that despite the relatively high standards laid down by the Supreme Court of what actually constitutes sedition, the police and the lower judiciary have continued to ignore precedent. One reason for this is abundantly clear—in politically motivated cases there is no real interest in seeking the conviction of the accused. Given the nature of the criminal justice system, the process is the punishment. The second is that in the age of instant media spin, these arrests serve as "profitable obfuscation" where the arrest and the charge are used as the pretext for whipping up frenzied, ill-informed, opinions on the seditious character of the offending speech act. It may therefore be useful to remind ourselves of what the law actually states and how it has evolved over the years.

The law of sedition was introduced by Section 124A of the IPC in 1870 as a draconian measure to counter anti-colonial sentiments, and most major leaders of the independence movement—including Gandhi and Tilak—were tried under this provision. Gandhi famously described Sec. 124A as the "prince among the political sections of the Indian Penal Code designed to suppress the liberty of the citizen".

When the constituent assembly deliberated on the scope and extent of restrictions that could be placed on free speech, the prominent exclusion from what eventually became Article 19(2) was the word sedition. In the original draft that was up for discussion, the word sedition had been included as one of the grounds for restriction on speech. A number of the constituent assembly members took objection to this and reminded the assembly that Indians had suffered greatly through the misuse of sedition laws. T.T. Krishnamachari argued that the word sedition was anathema to Indians given their experience of it and he suggested that the only instance where it was valid was when the entire state itself is sought to be overthrown or undermined by force or otherwise, leading to public disorder.

Public order and sedition

The question of how much criticism a government can tolerate is indicative of the self-confidence of a democracy. On that count,

India presents a mixed picture, where we regularly see the use of sedition laws to curtail political criticism even as we find legal precedents that provide a wide ambit to political expression.

At the heart of the debate on subversive speech is the question of how the law imagines the relationship between speech and action. In thinking of the scope of free speech in relation to public order in Art. 19(2) and sedition in Sec. 124A of the IPC, a key question has been how courts conceptualise the relation between speech and effect. Is someone who advocates the use of violence to overthrow the government entitled to protection under Art. 19(1)(a)? Does a harsh criticism of the government amount to an act that undermines the security of the state or a disruption of public order? It will be useful to maintain a comparative frame to examine the evolution of different standards in two constitutional traditions, the US and India.

In the United States, the initial test applied to speech that criticised the government (especially during war) was the "bad tendency" test, which did not protect any speech that had a tendency to cause any illegal action. In *Schenk*, Justice Holmes and others added a new dimension even as they accepted the bad tendency test. Holmes asked "whether the words used are used in such circumstances and are of such a nature as to create a clear and present danger that they will bring about the substantive evils that Congress has a right to prevent." A doctrinal shift begins with the Abrams case, where the majority reiterated the bad tendency test, but Holmes dissented. He relied on his own formulation of "clear and present danger" in *Schenk*, and clarified its scope to create a rupture between speech and consequence, arguing that it was only the present danger of immediate evil, or an intent to bring it about, that justified limitations on speech.

The "clear and present" danger test remained the prevailing standard till the 1960s when the Ku Klux Klan case (i.e. *Brandenburg vs Ohio*) held that while the test may even have some value in times of emergency, in ordinary times it had no place in assisting the interpretation of the first amendment. According to the court, "The constitutional guarantees of free speech and free press do not permit a state to forbid or proscribe advocacy of the use of force or law violation [i.e., subversive advocacy] except where [1] such advocacy is directed to inciting or producing imminent lawless action and [2] is likely to incite or produce such action." The two-step Brandenburg test currently stands as the prevailing standard to determine protectable speech.

Let us turn now to the Indian position on the relationship between free speech and subversive speech. Indian courts explicitly rejected the "clear and present danger" test, arguing that the doctrine cannot be imported into the Indian Constitution because fundamental rights guaranteed under Art. 19(1) of the Constitution are not absolute rights and subject to the restrictions placed in the subsequent clauses of Art. 19. The rejection of American standards by itself does not solve the problem of where the line between speech and action while interpreting Art. 19(2) is drawn. Unlike the relatively straight line that can be drawn to trace the doctrinal development of subversive speech and action in the US, in India it emerges more as a criss-crossing set of lines that move between different standards and across different forms of speech.

If the "bad tendency" test established a loose nexus between speech and effect, and the "clear and present danger" test demanded a closer proximity between speech and consequence, in India we find a slightly different spectrum which runs between "bad feelings", "bad tendency" and the standards of "clear and present danger". The interpretation of sedition during the colonial period tended towards a narrower space for any subversive speech and in that sense the *Romesh Thapar* and *Brij Bhushan* decisions of 1950 were rather remarkable for their ability to distinguish between different levels of threat and impact in assessing speech in a postcolonial context.

Wrestling with the problem

The first major case after the first amendment to the Indian Constitution in 1951 was *Ramji Lal Modi vs The State of U.P.* This was not a sedition case but it was the first to examine the scope of the words "in the interest of" and "public disorder" in Art. 19(2). The question in this case was whether Sec. 295A of the IPC was protected by Art. 19(2). The petitioners argued that 295A sought to punish any speech which insulted a religion or the religious beliefs of a community but not all insults necessarily lead to public disorder and since the provision covers speech that does not create public disorder, it should be held to be unconstitutional. The Supreme Court disagreed with this interpretation and held that the phrase "in the interests of" has a much wider connotation than "for maintenance of" public order. Thus, if certain activities have a tendency to cause public disorder, then a law penalising such activities as an offence cannot but be held to be a law imposing reasonable restriction "in the interests of public order" even if those activities may not actually lead to a breach of public order. The court also held that 295A does not penalise every act of insult, it penalises only those acts of insult which are perpetrated with the deliberate and malicious intention of outraging the religious feelings of a class. The court introduced two tests—"aggravated form", which defines the criteria for what counts as an insult, and the "calculated tendency" of the insult to disrupt the public order. This is a confusing standard, for, while interpreting the words "in the interest of", the court comes close to the bad tendency test with no requirement of any actual proximity between speech and consequence, at the same time it qualifies the bad tendency test with "calculated tendency".

The next major case to deal with these issues was *Superintendent, Central Prison vs Ram Manohar Lohia* in 1960. The court discussed the idea of public order and observed that under Art. 19(2), the wide concept of "public order" is split up under different heads (security of the state, friendly relations with foreign states, public order, decency or morality, etc.) and they argued that while all the grounds mentioned can be brought under the general head "public order" in its most comprehensive sense, it was important that "public order" be demarcated from the others. In their understanding, "public order" was synonymous with public peace, safety and tranquillity. In their discussion of *Ramji Lal Modi*, the judges say the distinction between "in the interest of" and "for the maintenance of" does not ignore the necessity for an intimate connection between the law and the public order sought to be maintained by the law. They added that after the word "reasonable" had been added to 19(2) it was imperative that restrictions have a reasonable relation to the object which the legislation seeks to achieve and must not go in excess of that object. The restriction made in the interests of "public order" must have a reasonable relation to the object to be achieved, i.e., the public order. If the restriction has no proximate relationship to the achievement of public order, it fails the reasonableness test.

The judges approvingly cited the Federal Court in *Rex vs Basudeva*, which established the proximity test where a restriction has to have a proximate connection or nexus with public order, but not one far-fetched, hypothetical or problematical, or too remote in the chain of its relation with public order. *Lohia* therefore introduces a double test—"proximity and proportionality", which Gautam Bhatia argues is the introduction of an additional moral dimension to the public order exception. Bhatia describes the consequences of this as "introducing an 'inbuilt autonomy-respecting limitation' by which the chain of causation (and, by extension, responsibility) between speech and public order disruption is broken when the actions of autonomous, rational individuals intervene".

The Supreme Court had an opportunity to clarify the scope of public order in *Kedar Nath Singh vs State of Bihar*, a 1961 case which challenged the constitutional validity of Sec. 124A (i.e. sedition). The court in *Kedar Nath*, after examining the conflict in standards in the colonial decisions (between "bad feelings" and "bad tendency") observed that since sedition was not included in Art. 19(2) it implied that a more liberal understanding was needed in the context of a democracy. They made a distinction between a strong criticism of the government and words which excite with the inclination to cause public disorder and violence. They also distinguished between "the government established by law" and "persons for the time being engaged in carrying on the administration". The court then held that "strong words used to express disapprobation of the measures of government with a view to their improvement or alteration by lawful means would not come within the section. Similarly, comments, however strongly worded, expressing disapprobation of actions of the government, without exciting those feelings which generate the inclination to cause public disorder by acts of violence, would not be penal."

They argued that what is forbidden are "words, written or spoken, etc., which have the pernicious tendency or intention of creating public disorder or disturbance of law and order". So if *Ramji Lal Modi* introduced the idea of "calculated tendency", in *Kedar Nath* we have the phrase "pernicious tendency". Does this effectively bring us back to the bad tendency test? It appears that part of the confusion in *Kedar Nath* emerges from the eagerness of the court to save Sec. 124A from being invalidated and towards such end acknowledge that if sedition were interpreted to mean disaffection in the sense of creating bad feelings alone, it would be invalid on the basis of exceeding Art. 19(2). It is only by drawing a nexus between speech and consequence in a manner consistent with Art. 19(2) that the provision is saved. While *Kedar Nath* cites *Ramji Lal Modi*, it completely ignores *Ram Manohar Lohia* which had reinterpreted *Ramji Lal Modi* to develop a strict test of proximity.

Squaring the circle

One of the most significant tests that have emerged after *Lohia* and *Kedar Nath* is the analogy of "spark in a powder keg" in the *Rangarajan* case. In a crucial paragraph in *Rangarajan*, the court explicitly holds that while there has to be a balance between free speech and restrictions for special interest, the two cannot be balanced as though they were of equal weight. One can infer that the courts are making it clear that exceptions have to be construed precisely as deviations from the norm that free speech should prevail, except in exceptional circumstances. And what is it that the court considers an exceptional circumstance?

Our commitment to freedom of expression demands that it cannot be suppressed unless the situations created by allowing the freedom are pressing and the community interest is endangered. The anticipated danger should not be remote, conjectural or far-fetched. It should have proximate and direct nexus with the expression. The expression of thought should be intrinsically dangerous to the public interest. In other words, the expression should be inseparably locked up with the action contemplated, like the equivalent of a "spark in a powder keg".

The court in this paragraph lays down in no uncertain terms the standard that has to be met in alleging a relation between speech and effect. The analogy of a spark in a powder keg brings in a temporal dimension of immediacy where the speech should be immediately dangerous to public interest. In other words, it must have the force of a perlocutionary speech act in which there is no temporal disjuncture between word and effect. A cumulative reading of the cases on public order and sedition suggest that as far as subversive speech targeted at the state is concerned, one can infer that even if there is no absolute consistency in the doctrinal tests, there is a consistency in the outer frame, namely that democracy demands the satisfaction of high standards of speech and effect if speech is to be curtailed.

Therefore, advocating revolution, or advocating even violent overthrow of the state, does not amount to sedition unless there is incitement to violence, and more importantly, the incitement is to "imminent" violence. Thus, in *Balwant Singh vs State of Punjab*, the Supreme Court overturned the convictions for "sedition" (124A, IPC) and "promoting enmity between different groups on grounds of religion, race etc." (153A, IPC), and acquitted persons who had shouted, "*Khalistan zindabaad, Raj Karega Khalsa*," ("Long live Khalistan; the Khalsa shall rule") and "*Hinduan Nun Punjab Chon Kadh Ke Chhadange, Hun Mauka Aya Hai Raj Kayam Karan*

Da" ("We'll drive Hindustan out of Punjab; the time has come to establish our own rule"), late evening on October 31, 1984—a few hours after Indira Gandhi's assassination—outside a cinema in a market frequented by Hindus and Sikhs in Chandigarh.

And finally the Supreme Court in *Arup Bhuyan vs State of Assam* has incorporated the Brandenburg standards into Indian law. After citing the Brandenburg test, the Court explicitly stated the following: "We respectfully agree with the above decisions, and are of the opinion that they apply to India too, as our fundamental rights are similar to the Bill of Rights in the U.S. Constitution."

It is abundantly clear, then, that freedom of speech and expression within the Indian legal tradition includes within its ambit any form of criticism, dissent and protest. It cannot be held hostage to narrow ideas of what constitutes "anti-national" speech and we hope that the courts will step in not merely to defend free speech but also pass strictures on those who abuse the legal process to create a chilling effect on constitutional rights. This is particularly important in the context of the ongoing case against the students of Jawaharlal Nehru University, because if free speech and thought is curtailed within universities, we run the risk of endangering one of the most crucial spaces of political freedom in the country.

First published in TheWire.in, *February 14, 2016.*

●◆●

"IN MY 40 YEARS AS A JOURNALIST, I HAVE NEVER WITNESSED SUCH A TOXIC ATMOSPHERE"

Nikhil Wagle

Speaking at a convention in New Delhi after a spate of attacks against journalists, senior journalist Nikhil Wagle recounts his experience of the changing techniques of coercion used against the media. Amid the convergent anti-democratic goals of Hindutva and crony capitalism, he notes a qualitative change in the strong-arm tactics deployed against free expression—especially with the simultaneous rise of Modi and the social media.

I started my career as a journalist in 1978. There is nothing new about threats, abuse is not new, even the risk to life is not new. I was first attacked in 1979, then in 1991, then again after the demolition of the Babri Masjid in 1993. I was again attacked in my office in 2009, when I was editor at IBN Lokmat. But in my forty years as a journalist, never before have I known such a foul, toxic atmosphere as we see today.

I'd say this began post-2010; that's when I joined social media. Before 2010 we [journalists] did receive abuse and threats. People would get worked up about what we wrote, and even break into our offices to beat us up. After 2010, when social media took off, all this started gaining legitimacy. Except that you don't need to thrash anyone these days. You start with character assassination; and if journalists still don't back down, you assassinate them. This is the strategy. Look around you and you'll find this is what is playing out.

Some of you have spoken of Modi. I accept that he's been the worst prime minister we have had. He has played a major role in vitiating the atmosphere in our country. But I also want to speak of the rise of several "Modis" in my state, and in different parties, as well as among those who belong to no party, or who run terrorist organisations unaffiliated to any party.

In the last five years, there has been a lot of talk about the murders of Dabholkar, Pansare, Kalburgi and Lankesh. Gauri Lankesh was a journalist; she was one of us. My first experience of trolling, threats and abuse by the Sanatan Sanstha, the organisation behind these murders, was in 2012. Before that time, it was mostly our friends in the Shiv Sena who were given to assaults and such. When I was with IBN Lokmat, I had a daily show. Dr Dabholkar was alive then. He used to be a regular on my show; so were members of the Sanatan Sanstha, and they would get into arguments. Once, the Sanstha members began to say something wrong. It is the duty of the anchor to make sure no one says anything unacceptable. If anyone veers off the subject, he has to be brought back on track. So I stopped the Sanstha spokespersons. They took offence and stormed off the set.

The next day I was trolled for the first time, but not on social media. The organisation's mouthpiece *Sanatan Prabhat* is a newspaper that publishes third-rate, vile stuff every day, and the government never acts against them. They published my number there and I began receiving abusive phone calls and SMSes all day. This went on for an entire month. So it's not just political parties that are given to trolling. A terrorist organisation like the Sanatan Sanstha can troll just as well as the BJP.

One day, I saw a tweet from a handle that seemed to be mine as it bore my name and face. The tweet had me declaring that I would walk around naked if Narendra Modi won the elections. I had never tweeted such a thing and it alarmed me. Then I saw that this fake handle had been cleverly created by joining two v's to look like the "w" in Wagle. This fake tweet still shows up on social media each time I criticise the BJP or Modi.

Later, another tweet said I had molested a woman at my workplace. However fearless you may be, charges like molestation and rape will get to you and make you fearful. This is character assassination. We journalists have no credentials but our honesty and character. We have not been bought by anybody. All we want to do is our job: telling the truth to people and society. A look at the social media accounts of the people who spread such stories will help you figure out their party affiliations. I have seen that the Congress has its trolls, just as the BJP has. Let me repeat: the most vicious and venomous party is the BJP; but you will get trolled if you criticise Sonia Gandhi or Rahul Gandhi. You will be trolled even if you criticise Anna Hazare or Arvind Kejriwal. The difference is in the way the BJP slanders you, not sparing even members of your family. If the trolling doesn't affect you, they will write about your wife. That's the political culture they have created to silence journalists. Once, someone tweeted—it embarrasses me to admit this—that my wife was having an affair. I couldn't even bring myself to show her this. But somebody tagged her in that tweet, so she came to me and asked what was going on. She told me to stop retweeting her because when I do that, she gets trolled.

Whether it is the BJP or Sanatan Sanstha, the plan is clear. For one, they do not believe in democracy; their power works only when democracy is dead. To kill democracy, they need to silence journalists who question the government, seek the truth, or criticise. I have criticised every party and government. Before 2014, we would criticise the Congress every day. The BJP was very happy to see the Congress put on the mat on issues such as the 2G scam or the coal scam. But when the harsh spotlight was turned on the BJP and its extended family, it was a different story. I want to tell you that this culture of threats, intimidation and trolling came into its own from 2013 onwards, ever since the BJP declared Narendra Modi as their prime ministerial candidate. Now our prime minister has become the biggest troll of all.*

---

*In her book *I Am a Troll: Inside the Secret World* of the BJP's Digital Army (2016), journalist Swati Chaturvedi recounts the BJP's early lead in establishing an electronic presence for itself, with the launch of the party's website in 1995; whereas the Congress did not set up its website till 2005. From 2001 onwards, the RSS began conducting shakhas for IT professionals. When Narendra Modi joined Twitter in 2009, not only did he find the field clear (Rahul Gandhi's account was not created till 2015) but a formidable machine was in place to amplify his message and overwhelm any opponents. In 2016, Modi had 21.6 million followers on

I was the editor of IBN Lokmat from 2007 to 2014. In the period 2007–13, my managing director never wrote an email to the staff. The first time this happened was in 2013, when Raghav Bahl, our managing director, wrote me an email saying that I should be careful when I tweeted about the RSS and Modi. Yes, let the record show who was up to what in those days. The editor-in-chief of the network was Rajdeep Sardesai. He would see my tweets every day but never said anything about them to me. But media owners such as Raghav Bahl began trolling their own journalists in day-to-day life.*

Even before Modi became prime minister, news stories against him began to be censored and suppressed. This was the case with our network [IBN] as well. At the time of the bhoomipujan for the Sardar Patel statue in 2013, the residents of the area held a protest against the project. But there was no news about it in the national media. I had sent a reporter to Gujarat and we did a story about the people and NGOs protesting against the construction of the statue. My own channel, CNN-IBN, would not air this story. So these things didn't start after Narendra Modi became prime minister. The unholy alliance between Modi, his crony capitalists and the media dates from the time before he took office.

Trolling is almost a business model now, a honed technique. If people do not get afraid, then threaten them; and if that doesn't work, kill them. Having seen so many attacks, I have no faith in the police. It is the done thing to say that we have faith in democracy. Well, I have been attacked many times since 1979. The perpetrators

---

Twitter, while he followed 1375 people (officially described as yoddhas or "warriors" by the BJP and its IT Cell). In this select group, Chaturvedi notes twenty-six accounts that "routinely sexually harass, make death threats and abuse politicians from other parties and journalists, with special attention given to women, minorities and dalits." This concentration of bigots is made all the more striking by Modi's decision not to "un-follow" any of these accounts.

*On October 12, 2018, Raghav Bahl joined the ranks of news barons and their organisations in disfavour with the government, when an income-tax raid took place on his premises.

have not been sentenced in a single case—they may be arrested but they get bail soon after. The party in power through much of this time was the Congress, not the BJP. The issue we should be talking about is this undemocratic political culture.

If the perpetrator is never punished—whether in the case of the people who lynched Akhlaq, or someone who attacks a journalist—what message goes out to the people? The government has given legitimacy to this gang. Modi follows them on Twitter, as do many cabinet ministers of the BJP. They also re-tweet messages from people who are involved in spreading filth and lies, and who incite murderous violence.

Someone said to me: our time is up. This does seem to be the case. The police certainly can't save us. When news broke that my name was on the Sanatan Sanstha's hitlist, the police visited my home. A senior police officer called me and said that I should get protection, but I said that would not solve the problem. I had no faith in the police since they simply made themselves scarce all the previous times I had been assaulted. The officer pointed out that it was the Shiv Sena that had attacked me before. Bear in mind, he said, that they are a political party, whereas the Sanatan Sanstha is a cult; they are capable of anything.

If a terrorist cult is capable of doing anything to anyone in this country, then do we have a Constitution? Do we have laws? This is my question. Will the person who is stationed with me for my protection be able to save me? We have to create an atmosphere in which all the citizens of the country feel safe. Dabholkar, Pansare, Lankesh and Kalburgi were murdered; tomorrow anybody could be murdered. They have arrested many people but I can't say for sure that those implicated in the murders will be sentenced and punished. The police could well sabotage their own case in the collection of evidence, and let the perpetrators go scot free. I don't have faith in this system.

So, what is to be done now? This is the last thing I want to talk about today. I want to thank the organisers of this convention, which is a first of its kind. Earlier, we only gathered when an attack took place, in the aftermath of the attack. You have convened this gathering before the next attack happens. This is a head start.

I want that a system should be created so that journalists feel safe. Today, if someone reports an attack, the police even fail to register an FIR. There is no follow-up, and eventually the matter has to be taken to court. Defamation cases have become a weapon of choice. The Sanatan Sanstha filed three defamation cases against me last year. They file a defamation case after every article. The cases are filed in Goa, because that is where their headquarters are. Their aim is to harass you by using the law, because you will have to travel to Goa for every hearing. This is torture; an abuse of the system. But that's what these people do: they deploy the law to harass journalists. They have a dedicated organisation of lawyers for this, lawyers who believe in Hindutva.

I am of the opinion that we should come together in response. Once upon a time there used to be unions of journalists, like the Bombay Union of Journalists, which took to the streets, for example, when the Bihar Press Bill was passed.* Today, there are no such unions left. The Editors' Guild does nothing. Every time there is an outrage, the Editors' Guild has to be prodded by us on Twitter before it comes out with a statement. I believe your organisations, the Committee Against Assault on Journalists (CAAJ) and the Committee to Protect Journalists (CPJ), can do something about this together. If there are such cases in the future—whether an attack or a murder—we can come together to help the journalists who are victimised. We are city-based journalists—I am based out of Mumbai, and there are others from Delhi here—but the worst condition is that of journalists in the villages. They don't even have permanent employment. Most of

---

*In 1982, Chief Minister Jagannath Mishra pushed through the Bihar legislature a bill with penalties for the publication of "grossly indecent" and "scurrilous" matter, as also material "intended for blackmail". The first offence could land a journalist in jail for two years. Thousands of publications across the country shut down in protest and the Bihar Press Bill was withdrawn after a year.

them are freelancers, stringers. The liquor mafia is killing them, so
are the sugar mafia and the sand mafia—in Mumbai alone there
are more than fifty such cases. When journalists are killed in the
villages, the police refuse to register FIRs because the local mafia
is run by the political leader of one party or another. We need to
unite and help journalists from the villages. We in the cities can
do something about this, not least because such people come out
in support of us when we need it.

I won't deny that I am afraid of being killed—you can get shot
anytime, forget about being abused. But this threat is precisely the
reason we must not be afraid. Because our journalism is a way to
seek the truth. And in this search, we are ready to sacrifice even
our lives. You may kill us, but there will be another journalist in
our place doing the same thing. As a community, we are not afraid
of trolls, we are not afraid of threats, we are not afraid of attacks.
We care about just one thing—that the ones who are doing good
journalism should not die.

Transcribed and translated from Hindi by Ishita Mehta from a video on
Newsclick, September 24, 2018.

P. Mahamud, Indian Cultural Forum,
2018

MURDER

Uday Prakash

After he dies,
he thinks
nothing.

After he dies,
he speaks
nothing.

When he does not
think or speak,
he dies.

Translated from Hindi by Akhil Katyal
(*Guftugu*, February 2016).

PART TWO

THE NUCLEUS OF STRUGGLE

ROHITH VEMULA

"I LOVED SCIENCE, STARS, NATURE, BUT THEN I LOVED PEOPLE WITHOUT KNOWING THAT PEOPLE HAVE LONG SINCE DIVORCED FROM NATURE..."

Orijit Sen, 2017

DEATH OF A YOUNG DALIT

Meena Alexander

In Memory of Rohith Vemula (1989–2016)

Trees are hoisted by their own shadows
Air pours in from the north, cold air, stacks of it
The room is struck into a green fever
Stained bed, book, scratched window pane.
A twenty-six-year-old man, plump boy face
Sets pen to paper—*My birth*
Is my fatal accident. I can never recover
From my childhood loneliness.
Dark body once cupped in a mother's arms
Now in a house of dust. Not cipher, not scheme
For others to throttle and parse
(Those hucksters and swindlers,
Purveyors of hot hate, casting him out).
Seeing stardust, throat first, he leapt
Then hung spread-eagled in air:
The trees of January bore witness.
Did he hear the chirp
From a billion light years away,
Perpetual disturbance at the core?
There is a door each soul must go through,
A swinging door—
I have to get seven months of my fellowship,
One lakh and seventy thousand rupees.
Please see to it that my family is paid that.
She comes to him, girl in a cotton sari,
Holding out both her hands.
Once she loosened her blouse for him
In a garden of milk and sweat,
Where all who are born go down into dark,
Where the arnica, star flower no one planted

Thrives, so too the wild rose and heliotrope.
Her scrap of blue puckers and soars into a flag
As he rappels down the rock face
Into our lives,
We who dare to call him by his name—
Giddy spirit, become
Fire that consumes things both dry and moist,
Ruined wall, grass, river stone,
Thrusts free the winter trees
From their own crookedness, strikes
Us from the fierce compact of silence,
Igniting red roots, riotous tongues.

Writing this Elegy

When I was twenty-four, I lived in Hyderabad. There was a neem tree in the garden of The Golden Threshold, once the home of the poet Sarojini Naidu. It is now the site of the new Central University. When time permitted, I would sit in the shade of that tree, shut my eyes and dream. Then, as now, images came to me, and I tried to craft a few lines of poetry.

I returned to the city several times. In early January 2016 I attended the literary festival there. I met Nayantara Sahgal after a gap of many years. As I listened to her give the keynote address at the festival, I was inspired by her courage. I was learning afresh what it means to live in a time of difficulty, what it means to bear witness. Later that month, news came that a dalit student at the university had killed himself—a tragic act of protest that resonated throughout the country. He left a haunting letter for us to read. I have included lines from his letter, and set them in italics in my poem.

Night after night as I worked on this elegy, the wind and winter chill comingled with the memory of rocks and stones and trees in a city I loved. I was consumed by the tumultuous hope and the very real despair of a young man I had never met.

First published in Guftugu, April 7, 2017

THEY CHOSE DEATH OVER HUMILIATION

Vidhya and Tilak Tewari

On January 17, 2016, death knocked on the doors of Hyderabad University. Rohith Vemula, a PhD scholar two weeks shy of his twenty-seventh birthday, chose death over a life of humiliation. "My birth is my fatal accident", he said in a note that exposed an unequal society. His death woke us from our slumber of complacency, laid bare our complicity in silence and tore down the walls of privilege. This privilege has been strengthened by years of denial. Vemula reminds us that we have failed to create a democratic society.

Let us look at each life lost, each family devastated, each history erased in the struggle against discrimination. Let us not rest till we achieve a truly democratic, caste-less society. For every life that refused to remain, in Vemula's words, "a vote, a number, a thing"; for every young mind that was snuffed out too soon; for every voice that confronted brahminism, imperialism, feudalism, patriarchy and fascism—we remember them. We unite and fight for every Rohith.

For a dalit scholar who died fighting against an institution that was set to fail him

Senthil Kumar belonged to a sub-caste of the dalits named 'panniyandi', known for pig rearing, and was a student of Hyderabad Central University. He was one of the first to pursue a doctorate from his community. However, because he was from a reserved category, Senthil faced severe discrimination, to the extent that he wasn't even allotted a supervisor. The minimum pass mark for course work examinations was intentionally raised for dalit students so that they failed and abandoned their studies in distress, said S. Thennarasu, a research student, studying in the same university. In February 2008, the twenty-seven-year-old's dead body was found in his room. The institution initially claimed the cause of death was a heart attack, but in reality it was because of poisoning. This raised the question of institutional discrimination on the basis of caste. Although the committee that was set up eventually absolved the authorities in its final findings, the report highlighted the severity of institutionalised caste discrimination on campus.

For a bright mind that refused a life of half-existence

On March 3, 2010, twenty-four-year-old Bal Mukund Bharti succeeded in killing himself. A final year student of MBBS in the All India Institute of Medical Sciences (AIIMS), Bal Mukund had attempted suicide three days earlier but was saved by his friends. He was from Tikamgarh in Bundelkhand, Madhya Pradesh. He repeatedly faced casteist prejudice from the faculty members in AIIMS. Bharti came from a poor family, and his parents had taken heavy loans so that he could pursue higher education. He had cleared the entrance for AIIMS, IIT and the CPMT exam in the same year, but he chose a career in medicine with the hope of moving out of the shadow of his caste. Instead, he faced a hostile environment in AIIMS. This hostility came not just from his department but even his hostel. The principal openly claimed that "harijans" and adivasis did not have the brains for medicine. When he asked questions in class, the teachers did not find them worthy of any response. He was asked to sit at the back of the class. He was graded down in his practical exams by the instructors. He was even asked to move from his allotted hostel room to another one with other SC/ST students. Despite this, a few days before he killed himself, he had purchased books worth thousands of rupees hoping to complete his education and leave the country that discriminated against him because of his caste. In the end, the harassment and humiliation proved too much for this bright mind and he chose death over what can only be described as a life of half-existence.

*For an adivasi boy who reached AIIMS but found himself alone
in a sea of privilege*

Anil Meena belonged to a tribal family of agriculturists, and had
cleared the entrance exam for the prestigious AIIMS. However,
within two years of his stay, in March 2012, he committed
suicide at the age of twenty-two. Students like Anil Meena were
deliberately neglected by the teachers and authorities in AIIMS
because they belonged to the reserved category. Anil Meena was
not allowed to write his exams as he was short on attendance.
Interestingly, only students belonging to the SC/ST category were
not allowed to write the exams due to low attendance, whereas
other students belonging to the General category were allowed
to sit.

In 2007, the Indian government constituted a three-member
inquiry committee under the chairmanship of Professor S.K.
Thorat, the then UGC chairperson, to look into the complaints of
dalit and adivasi students of AIIMS. The systematic segregation
on caste lines in hostels, with SC/ST students being forced to shift
to the two top floors of Hostels 4 and 5, after sustained pressure,
humiliation, abuse and even violence by 'upper' caste students,
should be a matter of great shame for a premier institution like
AIIMS. "Being a doctor is not just being in a profession, what
comes with it is also cultural capital, and a denting of traditional
caste roles," says Gurinder Singh Azad, a student coordinator.

*For the minor dalit girl found raped and killed in a water tank
in Rajasthan*

Delta Meghwal, a seventeen-year-old girl from Barmer in
Rajasthan, pursuing a teachers' training course in Nokha in
Bikaner, was quite a prodigy. At the age of seven, she was awarded
by the government of Rajasthan for her artwork. Her last days were
spent in the hostel of the Jain Adarsh Teacher Training Institute for
Girls. Under the instruction of the hostel warden, Priya Shukla, she
was forced to clean the hostel premises and regularly faced casteist
slurs from the authorities. On the evening of March 28, 2016,

she was asked by the warden to go to her PT instructor Vijendra Kumar's room in order to clean it. There were only three other girls in the hostel at the time. Most hadn't returned after the Holi vacations. In Vijendra Kumar's room she was sexually abused for hours. Late at night, when the others in the hostel went looking for her, the warden knocked on the door of the PT instructors' room. When he answered, it was apparent that Delta, a minor who was still in his room, had been raped. Instead of addressing this, the officials of the institution arranged for both the PT instructor and Delta to write a maafinama (letter of apology) wherein they were made to claim that the physical relationship was consensual. The next day, a worker of the school found Delta's body in the water tank of the hostel. The police was informed and two constables arrived and arranged for her body to be removed from the tank. They ignored the established procedure and removed her body in a municipal garbage disposal truck, without a 'panchnama' or any documentation of the process on video. An FIR was filed a day after her body was found. On the insistence of Delta's parents, the FIR named the warden, her husband, the PT instructor and the principal of the institution responsible for the death of their daughter. After an outcry from across the country, the warden, PT teacher, and principal were booked for her death.

For the twenty-nine-year-old dalit law student raped and killed in Kerala

Jisha, a law student at the Government Law College in Ernakulam in Kerala, was raped and killed on April 28, 2016 by a migrant labourer in Perumbavoor. She was brutally hacked to death. Raped, killed using sharp objects, then stabbed over thirty times, Jisha's body was severely mutilated when found by her mother Rajeshwari. The mother and daughter lived in a small home on purampokku land (land liable to be submerged when the canal is full) in an area surrounded by palatial homes belonging to Nairs and Christians. The duo were ostracised by the neighbourhood, citing the mother's "unusual" behaviour over the years. On closer inspection, it was found that this family of two living in a shack next to a canal did not even have basic utilities in their house. Living out of little boxes, without a toilet or a bathroom, and estranged from their extended family, they kept to themselves.

A quick glimpse at the history of the family in the area reminds us that Rajeswari, the mother, had strived to protect her daughter through thick and thin. In the past, when Jisha was harassed, injured, attacked or their home pelted with stones, Rajeshwari had filed police complaints several times. Jisha, on her part, strove to complete her education. She hoped to save enough money to purchase land and build a pukka home for the two of them. Early in her life, Jisha's father abandoned the family. When Jisha's elder sister Deepa moved away from the family to marry, Jisha and Rajeshwari were left to fend for themselves. The wealthy, "high" caste neighbours wanted nothing to do with the family, they had no idea of the way the mother and daughter survived and vehemently denied having discriminated against them over the years. Only after Jisha's classmates in the Government Law College and human rights activists raised the issue did her brutal murder come to light. Following an outcry from across the state, the Kerala police nabbed the man who had killed Jisha.

For a man disqualified for his caste

Dr Jaspreet Singh committed suicide in 2008 because of harassment. He failed to clear his exams because of the casteist behaviour of one professor who taught him in his fourth year in Government Medical College, Chandigarh. He was a dalit student from a very humble background. A school topper, the twenty-two-year-old had successfully cleared all papers without a hiccup until his fourth year, when he was placed under a professor whose criterion of assessment was Jaspreet's caste rather than his academic performance. The professor humiliated him on caste lines and threatened to continually fail him in his papers. "Do whatever you can do, I will make you do your MBBS all over again", taunted Prof N.K. Goel, Head of Department, Community

Medicine. Jaspreet left a suicide note in the library where he hanged himself, naming the professor and revealing his casteist behaviour. The exam in which the professor had failed Jaspreet Singh was later sent for re-evaluation, and he was given a passing mark.

For a dalit harassed by the University for being 'chamar'

Manish Kumar Guddolian, studying in the Department of Computer Science and Technology of IIT Rourkee, committed suicide at the age of twenty in 2011. Both IIT Roorkee and Roorkee police attributed his death to his inability to cope with academic pressure. However, the truth is that he was unable to tolerate caste-based assaults against him by his own classmates, and the insensitive attitude of the hostel warden, who had forced him to live outside the IIT campus. The institution also made his father sign a false statement saying that he did not want an inquiry into the death. Manish's parents have alleged that he faced caste-based harassment throughout his stay at IIT. Their testimony has been recorded on camera by Insight Foundation, an activist group which aims to protect the rights of SC/ST students. The recording is part of a documentary series which has already documented two other cases of suicide of dalit students in medical colleges. Manish's mother, Bhanmati, has said in the documentary: "They used to call him a chamar and asked insulting questions like 'Do chamars have the capacity to study?'" Manish had to shift outside the hostel, undergo psychiatric treatment, drop a semester, and rejoin the course. And then, after years of marginalisation and humiliation, he killed himself.

For a mother without a son, the dream of IIT stopped short because of caste

Aniket Ambhore, twenty-two, was a dalit student in IIT Bombay who committed suicide in 2014, on account of being discriminated against on the basis of caste. His parents had submitted a ten-page testimony to the Director of IIT Bombay, elaborating the kind of caste discrimination he faced in his life. An inquiry committee was eventually set up. However, its findings were never made public. Ambhore's mother said, "Students' agitation is the only hope remaining. Perhaps only the students will be able to wake up the system. We are waiting to find some solace for the pain suffered by Rohith's family and the dalit society."

For three dalit girls driven to suicide after being pressured to pay excess fees

Three girls—V. Priyanka and E. Saranya who were eighteen, and T. Monisha, a nineteen-year-old—studying Naturopathy in SVS Yoga Medical College in Kallakurichi, near Villupuram, committed suicide in January 2016. They did so to escape the torture they faced at the hands of the college chairperson Vasuki Subramaniam. They were aware that their decision to kill themselves could bring to light the excesses of the chairperson. They felt cheated by an institution that was determined to extract money without providing education. Their suicide note pre-empts the attempts that would be made by this chairperson to discredit their account by calling these girls 'characterless'. Yet, in their death, they hoped that this act would expose the extortionist institution and force the authorities to take action against the chairperson. Their suicide was preceded by a long series of protests by students of the college demanding basic facilities like adequate teachers, bills for each payment made, and a stop to the hiking of fees. Instead of addressing the concerns of the students raised over several years, including suicide attempts by students in 2015, the authorities, including the state government, turned a blind eye to the violations of the management.

First published in Indian Cultural Forum, January 17, 2017

CHILDREN OF GOD

Huchangi Prasad

In 2014, Huchangi Prasad was twenty-two and a journalism student in Davanagere, Central Karnataka, when he published a collection of prose and poems called Odala Kicchu (The Fire Within)—*which describes the lives of dalits, and issues a challenge to the continuing violence and day-to-day discrimination against them. After his book was published, Prasad was attacked by Hindutva goons.* They said, "Why are you connecting being a dalit or devadasi to Hinduism?" They threatened to cut off his fingers if he wrote another word. *Prasad managed to escape, mainly because his attackers were drunk. Later, he would say, with great courage, that he would continue to write about and against caste.*

On January 20, 2016, at a panel discussion on Caste, Religion and Lived Experience organised by the Indian Writers' Forum at Ambedkar University, Prasad began his talk with a poignant tribute to Rohith Vemula who had died three days earlier on January 17. When he was struggling to stand up to the right-wing goons, Prasad said, it was Rohith who constantly encouraged him on the phone, "teaching [me] courage". Prasad then went on to speak about his own life, and read one of his poems in Kannada, which was translated for the audience as "The Children of God".

…[This] is where I come from, this is how my people live. We are forced to stay outside the villages in houses as small as ten to twenty square feet. All of us are landless. Illiteracy is rampant; caste plays a dominant role in our society. The devadasi system is still prevalent in our village—dalit women are dedicated to the temples as slaves of the deity. The women dedicated as devadasis are expected to sleep with the upper-caste men in the village. This brahminical practice ensures that the lower castes remain oppressed. Our village has many such women and they live by begging during the day and doing sex work in the nights. Many of them are HIV-infected…

I too am the son of a devadasi. My mother is Yashodamma.

We cannot be sure who my father is, but since the school records demand the father's name, a certain Chitrappa was named as my father. When I was nine years old, I began working as a bonded labourer in the fields of an upper-caste landlord. I would earn a meagre seven hundred rupees a year. I would wake up at five in the morning, graze the cows, and do whatever else I was asked to do. We were not allowed to enter the landlord's house. We would eat off disposable plastic plates and drink water from coconut shells.

I must share one of the many incidents from this time, because this one has left a permanent mark on my life. One day, I was asked by the landlord's wife to look in the toilet, into the pot there, put in my hand and take out her daughter's chain. I had no choice; I had to do it. I put my head in the toilet, I put my hand inside the pot and tried to find the chain. But I couldn't. The landlord's wife called me a liar. She smashed my head against the pot. I can never forget this.

It's the plight of my people that got me to start asking questions about why we are treated the way we are. This is what led me to education. The Karnataka government had then started work to abolish child labour. Some teachers who found me grazing cattle shifted me out to Chennagiri Taluk and helped me enrol in a school. I began my studies in Chennagiri with the desire to make sure future generations born into my caste do not go through what I had been through.

Transcribed and translated from Kannada by Yogesh S.

*

Children of God

We perished, one after the other,
in the furnace of exploitation,
we fell as mere words
in mythology and history.
And it seems someone said we are the children of God.

We were ordered to build tanks,
we became the foundation
of temples, mosques, minarets.
And it seems someone said we are the children of God,
the children of God.

We sold ourselves
to the fire of hunger,
we surrendered our arms and backs
to the master's cane.
And it seems someone said we are the children of God,
the children of God.

We roamed naked
though we grew cotton,
We died
searching for a morsel of food.
And it seems someone said we are the children of God,
the children of God.

We lost our limbs
to the blows of a hammer,
we were charred, withered
by the strike of lightning:
And it seems some great soul said we are the children of God,
the children of God.

Translated from Kannada by Chandan Gowda

STRUCTURAL DISCRIMINATION IN
INSTITUTIONS OF HIGHER EDUCATION

Vidhya

"Today, equality and humanity are both denied to lives like those of Muthu and Rohith when we fail to see the root of the structure that perpetuates this violence," writes Vidhya in this essay. The supposedly meritocratic system in place at India's institutions of higher learning is neither caste-blind nor caste-neutral, as dalit students regularly learn, at the cost of their self-esteem and even their lives.

On March 13, 2017, Muthukrishnan Jeevanandham, aka Rajini Krish, was found hanging from a ceiling fan in a friend's room in Munirka, a locality of Delhi that houses hundreds of students besides middle-class families. He was dead by then. He belonged to the reputed university near Munirka, Jawaharlal Nehru University. Just a year after the death of his friend and fellow student in the University of Hyderabad, Rohith Vemula, Muthu opted out—a path frequently taken by the 'lower' castes and classes in this country. Both Rohith and Muthu were twenty-seven-year-old dalit scholars, and belonged to poor households in the southern states of Andhra Pradesh and Tamil Nadu, respectively. They had travelled great distances to continue their higher education in central universities with the hope of ridding themselves of the historic burden thrust on them by a caste-based society.

Muthu joined JNU in October 2016, and attempted to make himself at home in a university known for its vibrant environment of debates, discussion and critical thinking. The young man found himself feeling alienated in this space as well. His inability to converse in English, the lingua-franca of research, left him alone in the midst of endless chatter. His friends at the University of Hyderabad remember a vibrant Muthu, known to his friends as Krish, a lover of Rajinikanth movies, food and the company of friends. In Delhi, he appears to have had several acquaintances but few friends. Neither his mentors at the Centre for Historical Studies (CHS) in JNU nor his peers in the university knew him well; this was evident at the series of condolence meetings organised in the university after his passing. He had found his voice on social media where he spoke of the need to implement provisions meant for students like him, like the Thorat Committee Recommendations. The recommendations, released in 2011, spoke against policies that deprived students from marginalised communities of their chance to do well in higher education. But now, such policies have been renewed instead. For instance, with the restrictive policy of admission based only on a viva voce for MPhil and PhD, following the University Gazette Notification in 2016, which students have been resisting ever since; and the lack of mechanisms to address cases of structural discrimination built into higher education, revealed in the wake of Rohith Vemula's death in 2016.*

No government, present or past, has made efforts to address these concerns, let alone implement policies that would benefit young minds like those of Rohith and Muthu. Acting swiftly after a Delhi High Court order of March 16, 2017, the JNU administration restricted the number of students a faculty member can mentor for higher research, further curtailing the chances of students like Rohith and Muthu to reach the exalted spaces of knowledge and critical thinking in this country. In April 2017, the Vice-Chancellor (appointed after the present BJP-led government came to power) announced that JNU would be reducing its intake of research scholars by 82.8 per cent, offering a mere 242 admissions against the 1408 approved by the Academic Council.

---

*The weaponisation of the viva voce against SC/ST candidates goes back to the dawn of Independence. In the very first UPSC examination held in 1950, a dalit candidate and alumnus of Calcutta University, Achyutananda Das, scored the highest marks in the written examination but stood second in the final result, on account of having received the lowest score in the interview. In 1954, the first ST candidate to join the IAS, Nampui Jam Chonga from Assam, had a similar experience.

The announcement also ended the system of 'deprivation points' awarded by JNU to students from marginalised communities in research courses.

Meanwhile, the government and its agents were busy defending their actions, which have repeatedly led to students dropping out of universities, failing to complete their courses, or committing suicide out of sheer frustration at the innumerable hurdles placed in their path. In response to Muthu's suicide, Union Minister Pon Radhakrishnan callously claimed, "[These] incidents have been happening at many places for the last 60 years... I will not accept [the accusation] that this [death] has happened because of the BJP coming to power." The remark was made during the minister's visit to Salem, ostensibly to pay his "last respects" to the dead student's remains that had been brought from Delhi. Another Union Minister, Nirmala Sitharaman, promised to provide adequate compensation for the death of the student and consider jobs for his sisters—in a cold-blooded recognition of death as an occupational hazard of student life. The magnanimity of those in power extends only as far as floral tributes, cash dole-outs and opportune publicity photos. Muthu, in a Facebook post days before he decided to end his life, clearly states, "When equality is denied, everything is denied." Today, equality and humanity both are denied to those like Muthu and Rohith when we fail to see the root of the structure that perpetuates this violence.

The Delhi Police, in its characteristic style, tried portraying this death as a case of suicide due to "depression" and "personal reasons". Several well-known scholars, intellectuals and commentators displayed extraordinary keenness to probe the personal life of Muthu, his relationship with his friends, his interests and even his intellect. Besides insinuations of a possible failed affair, rumours spread of an alleged charge of sexual harassment against Muthu. The salacious details implied by such presumptions about the deceased student reached such a pitch that the Gender Sensitising Committee Against Sexual Harassment (GSCASH) in JNU issued a statement refuting these claims.

Meanwhile, Makarand Paranjape, a professor at JNU, wrote an op-ed insinuating that the lack of rational thinking and intellect leads to such deaths. "One of the problems is that many disadvantaged students are fed on ideological myths, rather than encouraged to develop real competence in their chosen fields of study," he said in his reading of the situation. In the midst of all this, the Vice-Chancellor and drumbeating autocrat of JNU, Jagadesh Mamidala, condescendingly tweeted regret at the death of a student in the institution that he heads. The Centre of Historical Studies (CHS), to which Muthu belonged, scrambled to come to terms with his death. Students remain shocked and in rage, the teachers are grief-stricken, while Muthu's father is at a loss to explain what he could have done to save his son.

It becomes our responsibility to revisit the ways in which this situation can be read and addressed. For this, the Thorat Committee Recommendations help articulate what we have known for generations. In 2007, the United Progressive Alliance (UPA) government had constituted a committee headed by Professor Sukhadeo K. Thorat to look into allegations of differential treatment of SC/ST students in the All-India Institute for Medical Sciences (AIIMS), a fully-funded institution directly under the Central government. After interviewing students, teachers and staff, the committee report, tabled in 2011, says, "Given the relational nature of such experiences it is often difficult to capture the nature of discrimination. The self-reported experiences of SC/ST students indicate that discrimination takes the form of avoidance, contempt, non-cooperation, and discouragement and differential treatment by teachers towards these students."*

---

*Examining the living and academic conditions for SC/ST students at AIIMS, Delhi, the Thorat Committee found rife institutional and cultural discrimination. With respect to the examination system, where 50 per cent of the outcome depends on internal assessment, 76 per cent of the respondents disclosed that the examiner had enquired explicitly about their caste identity, while 84 per cent said that their caste had been directly or indirectly probed. It is noteworthy that, while maintaining a viva voce component to the examination, the AIIMS had not arranged for any

The report, an archive of cases of discrimination, goes on to say, "Subjectivity apart, the problem seems to be deep rooted. This relates to the very attitude of some high-caste teachers, if not all, who carry with them the attitude of non-cooperation, and at times of contempt, which results in differential treatment towards SC/ST students. From the self-experience of the students it seems clear that SC/ST students live with a feeling that the teachers don't treat them on par with other students, that they are not equally supported by teachers, that they face differential treatment from the teachers... This created a feeling of insecurity, frustration, psychological problems leading to withdrawal and helplessness. All of this resulted in social isolation and ultimately failure in examinations."

Suggesting pro-active measures to address this discrimination built into the structure of [AIIMS], the committee recommended: "The educational institutions are required to undertake remedial coaching for SC and ST students to improve their language skill and also remedial courses in the basic courses so that they are able to cope up with the regular course." Recognising that it is difficult to capture caste bias as it is embedded in social relations and behaviour, the committee recommended that the institution undertake measures to make the faculty more sensitive towards the problems faced by SC/ST students. The steps suggested to fight caste bias included an increase in objective evaluation and more transparency in practical and viva evaluations.

The UGC's circular dated March 1, 2016, on "Prevention of Caste-based Discrimination in Higher Educational Institutions", regulates that faculty members should desist from discrimination

---

remedial assistance with language skills for students from disadvantaged backgrounds. Unsurprisingly, 88 per cent of these students reported social isolation as well: the Report noted that SC/ST students were concentrated in the top floors of two out of the five campus hostels, 76 per cent of SC/ST students mentioned restriction from membership of private messes (distinct from the general dining facility), and 32 per cent had had no participation at all in the annual students' festival, PULSE.

on the basis of caste, provide a mechanism so complaints may be registered on a page on the institution's website, and be sensitive while dealing with such cases of discrimination, especially in the case of ragging, where it is clearly stated that "complaints...must be recorded properly and dealt with promptly". The question that needs to be raised here is how far are these regulations being followed? When will the Thorat Committee Recommendations be implemented? And when will we dare to accept that discrimination exists, and recognise that we need to call it out before yet another life is snuffed out?

First published in Indian Cultural Forum, March 17, 2017

CONVERSATION: CHINNAIAH JANGAM ON DALIT MEMORY, IMAGINATION AND THE NATIONALIST NARRATIVE

Indian Cultural Forum

The Indian Cultural Forum spoke to Chinnaiah Jangam, author of Dalits and the Making of Modern India *(2017) and a historian specialising in modern South Asian social and intellectual history. In this wide-ranging conversation, he speaks on the nature of dalit traditions of coping with and resisting caste discrimination and oppression. He insists on the inclusion of the dalit narrative in the history of Indian nationalism, and contextualises Bhima Koregaon in this narrative. He also exposes the appropriation of Ambedkar and Gandhi by the Hindu right wing, as a mask for their real intentions.*

Indian Cultural Forum (ICF): You speak of the strong cultural memory of the dalit community in the past. We recall writer Bama talking about the dalit relationship with the land serving as a bond in the rural areas. What sort of "memories" replace these—if they do—among dalits in urban areas?

Chinnaiah Jangam (CJ): Historically, dalits have been denied access to a writing culture. The only way they could retain their culture and identity was through memory—of individual experience and, collectively, as social memory. For dalits, memory acts like a protective layer, and it manifests itself in two ways.

First, individual dalits have to withstand and overcome loathsome, casteist, brahminical assaults, both physical and mental. They share individual experiences with their brethren and extended families to work out the means to cope with humiliation, oppression and living in dehumanising conditions. As part of this strategy they weave humorous and rebellious songs, sign language, music and fables, which expose the deceptive and hypocritical character of their oppressors.

Second, the collective memory is narrated and performed by the satellite castes—for instance, the chindus, a "dependent caste" of the madigas in Telangana. All dalit castes have dependent satellite castes, and their primary duty is to narrate and perform the history of the patron caste. Satellite castes narrate alternative histories of dalits, countering demeaning brahminical renderings. They challenge caste hierarchy and discrimination; they illustrate the degeneration of human lives due to brahminism. They trace the roots of dalits to non-brahminical anti-caste egalitarian pasts. Dalit histories in the form of oral traditions, folk narratives and performances subvert the dominant brahminical puranas, as also the brahminical renderings of the *Mahabharata* and *Ramayana*. In dalit Ramayanas, Ravana emerges as the hero from the perspective of the oppressed. So, through individual and collective memory, the dalit imagination creates a tradition of being anti-caste and non-brahminical.

Urban dalits are, generally, migrants from rural villages. Their memory of discrimination continues to haunt them. The everyday sufferings of extended families in the rural areas act as an impetus for their activism. Moreover, caste prejudice and subtle humiliations in urban settings seems to be invisible to the non-dalits, but for a dalit it is an everyday presence, and a source of everyday anxiety.

ICF: The Bhima Koregaon anniversary complicates the "nationalist" narrative—in this instance, it's the battle against the Peshwas that holds meaning, not the mainstream narrative of the battle against the British.* Your comments?

CJ: This is where my book, *Dalits and the Making of Modern India,* makes a contribution. It challenges and complicates the singular narrative of nationalism in India—we have to see nationalism as a plural narrative. The danger with the singular narrative is that it plays into the hands of right-wing conservative caste Hindu elites. That is why the recent rise of the Hindu right in India is able to capture the imagination of ordinary people by using the rhetoric of nationalism, even though it has made the least contribution—by way of either ideas or participation—to actual anti-colonial nationalism.

I argue that mainstream nationalism as articulated by caste Hindus is imbued with Hindu brahminical consciousness, and that dalit intellectuals and activists deciphered that contradiction. Anti-caste thinkers such as Jotiba Phule, Ambedkar and others across British India pointed out the collusion between colonialism and brahminism. For them, both colonial state and the caste Hindu elites represented the same structures of oppression. From the dalit perspective, the denial of material wealth and mental freedom precedes colonialism; but colonialism embraced brahminical structures and was able to rule by assimilating caste Hindu elites in its project. But the social reality of caste and untouchability led to an ethical crisis for colonialism, given its "civilising ideals" (Christian ethic and liberal philosophy). Since the ideas of the civilising mission were used as ideological weapons

---

*Fought on January 1, 1818, the Battle of Bhima Koregaon saw the English East India Company's forces successfully defend their position against a much larger force fielded by Peshwa Baji Rao II. A cenotaph at the site commemorates the Company's soldiers killed in battle that day. Of the forty-nine names inscribed there, twenty-two are identified as distinctively mahar. Before Independence, the Mahar Regiment's crest featured the obelisk that stands at this site.

to justify colonialism, it had to acknowledge the injustice faced by dalits. The project of colonialism was not humanitarian, it was a purely an economic power relationship in which dalits figured in the margins; but still, it had to address dalit subjugation. Intended and unintended consequences of colonialism included the percolation of education down to the lowest sections of society, such as dalits. Access to education provided new employment opportunities, away from caste occupations and towards the language of rights. Based on the platform of colonial modernity, dalits organized themselves politically, and altered the meaning of colonialism and nationalism. The meaning of colonialism is very different for the oppressed dalits compared to their caste Hindu counterparts. It is in this context that Bhima Koregaon represents dalit experience—their fight against the oppressive brahminical Peshwas under whom they lived as sub-humans. It is in this way that the meaning of colonialism has to be complicated, through the optics of caste experience, which provides an alternative social history of colonialism.

ICF: The irony of excluding the dalit contribution to anti-colonial nationalism seems particularly sharp in times when the right-wing nationalist narrative is on the ascendant. Would you agree?

CJ: It is true that with the rise of Hindu nationalism, the socialisation and imaginative powers of dalits are being violently contained. But during anti-colonial nationalism, the Hindu right's nationalist imagination was a marginal force. The dominant nationalist imagination, articulated by caste Hindu elites, was imbued with brahminical consciousness; but it stood for a secular and inclusive nation with egalitarian values. They were more receptive and responded to dalit critiques of nationalist politics, and accepted the dalit imagination as central to the very idea of India. Otherwise how can we understand the role of Ambedkar in drafting the Constitution using anti-caste ethic and liberal philosophy? The Hindu right, with its covert brahminical agenda, is now trying to subvert and delegitimise Ambedkar's ideas, and obliterate dalit subjectivity and their role in the making of modern India.

ICF: Would you comment on the various re-readings—including "appropriations"—of Ambedkar today?

CJ: Ethically, conservative philosophy stands on empty rhetoric rather than substance. Because of its moral emptiness, it preys on all available ideas and opportunities to further its agenda. No wonder the Hindu right in its political avatar is trying to appropriate two seminal figures, B.R. Ambedkar and M.K. Gandhi. The appropriation of Ambedkar is ironic because Ambedkar, as an anti-caste philosopher, argued that the annihilation of caste is possible only by destroying the religious and ideological foundations of Hinduism. In principle and practice Ambedkar is not amenable to appropriation by the Hindu right. As the recent protests and articulations by dalits across India demonstrated, the Hindu right might have temporary inroads but in the long run it always stands against dalit welfare and existence.

In his attempts to appropriate Gandhi, Prime Minister Narendra Modi humiliates Gandhi's ethical principles of inclusion and tolerance. He has no choice but to pretend to be a Gandhian because Gandhi is a global icon of non-violence and acts as a goodwill ambassador for India. The Hindu right does not have any ethical commitment to Ambedkar's philosophy or Gandhian ideals, but it tries to appropriate both because of the compulsions of political pragmatism or global diplomatic goodwill, all the while masking its real intentions.

First published in Indian Cultural Forum, April 24, 2018

CONVERSATION: CHANDRASHEKHAR AZAD "RAVAN" ON A BAHUJAN GOVERNMENT

Newsclick

In conversation with Pranjal of Newsclick, Bhim Army Chief Chandrashekhar Azad, alias Ravan, talks about the Bhim Army's agenda ahead of the 2019 general elections. He feels that to defeat the BJP, there is a need to form a strong alliance. The country does not belong to the RSS-driven right wing, he asserts, and these forces will have to relinquish control once the bahujan rise.*

Pranjal (P): Let us start by discussing what happened in June 2017. Yogi Adityanath charged you under the NSA (National Security Act) and kept you imprisoned for a year, in a fabricated case, despite the fact that you were granted bail on one occasion in this period. So let's talk about your experience because there were reports that you were mistreated and not given the facilities that you should have received.

Chandrashekhar Azad 'Ravan' (CA): Jail is no place to expect facilities, but in my case, not even the manual of regulations was followed. Prisoners have certain rights, but in spite of that I was not given proper medical treatment for eight months. I complained many times. I also used to raise these issues with the media, and in retaliation the authorities stopped me from going to court—they would put me on video conference from inside the jail. There were times when I wasn't allowed to meet my family for more than forty days on end. Such things are done

---

*Kanshi Ram, founder of the BSP, contributed the term 'bahujan', or 'multiple peoples', to India's political lexicon. His conception of a bahujan samaj included all castes and communities, apart from the historically privileged ones. The reification of this true majority would bring about social and economic justice, whereas the Constitution had been unable to secure more than political equality to all citizens.

to break a person's spirit. They would give me dry rotis at times, and at times no food at all. They did such things at the direction of the government, to weaken me. But my morale could not be dampened so easily because of the mission, our movement.

P: Coming back to the mission, what are the objectives of the Bhim Army? What was the purpose and intent behind creating the Bhim Army in 2015? And how did you go about its formation? It came up so fast—how did you build it? I remember the rally at Jantar Mantar on May 21, 2017, where you were present and thousands of people had gathered. Already, there was the movement started by Jignesh Mevani in Gujarat; and then in UP, despite Mayawati already being there, you built up such a strong organisation. How did you do that?

CA: Look, there are many political parties. What we are running is a social movement. There are many issues that we take up— every time the rights of people are violated, whenever there is caste-based oppression. So many times, in such cases, the police do not file an FIR against the persecutor, and even if they do, they don't arrest the person, even in matters as grave as rape. People want to be heard, they want their grievances redressed. They want someone to speak on their behalf. Political parties have their limitations; I've been observing this for some thirteen years. We started this movement because social movements do not have those limitations. We do not favour anybody. We will raise our voices against anyone who does wrong. Our movement comprises people from the bahujan samaj—eighty-five per cent of the country. *This* is the big family group. When you look at census figures from 1931, dalits [and adivasis] were over nineteen per cent of the population, and Muslims over fourteen per cent, while the OBCs made up a good fifty-two per cent.* These are people who still haven't come into full enjoyment of their rights.

---

*The census of 1931 was the last one, before that of 2011, to collect data on caste. The 2011 census is known to have yielded 4.6 million castes, sub-castes, surnames, and gotras, but its findings are yet to be made public.

We still do not have representation everywhere. We still do not have anybody in Delhi—in the judiciary. We are lagging behind in most areas. This is why we started this movement—to fight for our rights, to raise the concerns of the bahujan, to make sure the government listens to us. Political parties often reach an understanding among themselves and short-change the public.

P: So when you speak about the bahujan, you are not just talking about the dalits. You are also talking about OBCs, adivasis and Muslims, and we can draw a parallel between your movement and Kanshi Ram's BAMCEF.* Many people are saying that Mayawati sees this as a threat, because the BAMCEF used to work with Mayawati. The Bhim Army has, since its launch in 2015, worked on the same issues as they have, but in a more radical way, and it is growing rapidly. Do you agree with this assessment?

CA: Such interpretations are misleading. Look, the BAMCEF had government employees as its members, after which Kanshi Ram started the DS-4—the Dalit Shoshit Samaj Sangharsh Samiti.† It was a very strong movement. He brought together the entire bahujan community. That the Bhim Army is a threat to Mayawati is just propaganda. Why should anyone feel threatened by a social movement? All political parties have their own social organisations. We're trying to bring about a social revolution. Kanshi Ram gave a slogan: "Rajneeti chale na chale, sarkaar bane na bane, lekin samajik kranti nahi rukni chahiye" (It doesn't matter if we don't succeed in politics, or if we cannot form government, nothing should come in the way of social revolution). We are merely trying to do that.

P: Let us talk about the Modi government and what they did with the SC/ST Prevention of Atrocities Act (POA, 1989), and the

---

*The Backward and Minority Communities Employees Federation, officially launched from Delhi on December 6, 1978, the anniversary of Ambedkar's death.

†Launched on December 6, 1981, and absorbed into the Bahujan Samaj Party with its founding on April 14, 1984—Ambedkar's birth anniversary.

protests that followed. On April 2, 2018, there was an India-wide strike and many people died because of 'upper' caste violence. It has been four-and-a-half years since the Modi government came to power and now elections are imminent. How has this government affected the status of dalits? The increasing number of lynching cases usually targets dalits or Muslims. Dalits are not getting their rights. How do you view this politically?

CA: This government that you are talking about: though Modi is at its helm, it is controlled by the RSS and they have always had an agenda of their own. Their agenda is to subdue various sections of our society—be it dalits, Muslims, OBCs, or other religious groups like Buddhists and Sikhs. This is because they believe in the varna system. The biggest problem of this country is the caste system. Till we can achieve a casteless society, our country will never make progress. The Sangh's agenda is to implement their legal code, the *Manusmriti*, to benefit the social constituency of their membership. They have been fooling the dalits for ages, just as a hunter deceives his prey. They talk big and say they are always working in the interest of the dalits, but they work for their agenda and their people. On the one hand, the government claims to be bringing in an ordinance to protect the rights of dalits; and on the other, its own representative deposes before the Supreme Court that fake charges are being filed under the POA.* Where are all these false cases? Speaking as an advocate, I've known cases of rape where an FIR wasn't filed for forty days. If and when it does get filed, the case disappears under paperwork, the complainant is threatened and browbeaten, and counter-charges are slapped against the victim. As things stand, where do you go to get justice? The administration is the government's domain. The government has penetrated all institutions. It is because of the interference of the government that four Supreme Court judges held a press conference [on January 12, 2018]—a black day for democracy—to complain about this state of affairs.

---

*The SC/ST Prevention of Atrocities Act, 1989.

This government is entirely against the bahujan. They are attempting to fool the OBCs by making an OBC aayog, because they need their support for the upcoming elections. They are back to their politics based on religion, to their agenda of making the Ram Mandir in Ayodhya.

P: Most of the policies of the BJP are seen as anti-dalit, anti-Muslim, anti-adivasi, but the Sangh has been trying to appropriate Babasaheb Ambedkar. They put up his picture in their offices, and they celebrate Ambedkar Jayanti, even though the Sangh and Ambedkar are on diametrically opposite sides. How do you view this ideological war? One would have thought that Babasaheb was the most potent counter to the Sangh.

CA: The Sangh keeps changing its strategy over time. This is the same Sangh that took out a mock funeral procession of Babasaheb. It is the same Sangh that does not believe in the Constitution to this day, the same one that does not want the tricolour atop its buildings.

P: They want the *Manusmriti* in place of our Constitution.

CA: They want to use the picture of Babasaheb because they find it profitable to do so. Just as their talk of samajik samrasta is for their own gain.* The Sangh never speaks up when a savarna Hindu attacks a dalit. If there is even a small incident involving dalits and Muslims, they try to blow it out of proportion. People from the OBC and dalit sections of society have now started to understand who is with them and who works against their

---

*The Samajik Samarasta Manch (platform for social harmony/cohesion) was launched at Pune in 1983, during the tenure of Madhukar Dattatraya Deoras as sarsanghchalak of the RSS. It was, and remains, part of a concerted outreach by the Sangh, to expand the constituency of Hindus and thereby increase its own influence. Another innovation of Deoras was to include Ambedkar among the pratahsmaraniya (great figures remembered at dawn by the RSS), quite disregarding Ambedkar's frequently expressed contempt for Hinduism.

interests. The Sanghis only work with the intention of breaking up the country, which is their agenda. We regularly hear about the people who have run away with money, and then we get to hear that they had met the Finance Minister or the Prime Minister.* These people are running away because the bahujan of the country are becoming aware. Their social movement is becoming strong.

P: Talking about the Bhim Army in the light of the movement in Gujarat, is this another step towards left-dalit-bahujan-Muslim unity? What is your take on this?

CA: My only concern is the rights of people. One hundred and seventy-five million hectares of land is under the control of a handful of people. If that land is distributed among the landless, they will start working on it. The country will develop only if all the sections of society develop. Currently ten per cent of the population controls ninety per cent of the resources and wealth of the country.

P: And the top one per cent has half of all resources.

CA: How is the ninety per cent supposed to survive? The people of the country are very patient and trusting. They believe anyone who talks about honesty. Modi talked about honesty and fooled the people. When demonetisation happened, so many people died. But people did not protest as they felt that some good will come of it all. The same was the case with GST. The rate of unemployment in this country is very high. They made the promise of creating two crore jobs, but that remained a promise. Whenever someone starts talking about the rights of people, they impose NSA on that person and implicate him or her in false cases. They start an

---

*Jeweller Mehul Choksi and business baron Vijay Mallya, accused of defrauding Indian banks of several thousand crores of rupees, left the country days before they would have been arrested. Later, photographs appeared of Choksi in a select gathering with Prime Minister Modi in Davos, and Mallya revealed he had met the finance minister, Arun Jaitley, just days vefore he fled the country.

inquiry into any judge who speaks up against them. They raid any media house that dares to speak out against them. Place anyone who speaks for the weak under house arrest. This is an undeclared emergency. And they will have to pay the price for it—it will be like what happened in 1977.

P: What will be the role of the Bhim Army in the upcoming elections in 2019?

CA: The Bhim Army wants a government of the bahujan. We want the rights and development of the bahujan. And we will fight for it. We are not a political party, but given the atmosphere in the country, we need a strong coalition to get rid of the BJP. This cannot be achieved by a single party or individual. Everyone will have to come together. We have to protect our nation. We have to protect our Constitution. The Bhim Army will help campaign against the BJP in 2019, and we will organise rallies. Kanshi Ram told the bahujan of the country to be united, because otherwise they can easily be misled by rumours, lies, organised riots. I am trying to bring everyone together. Social unity can be very fragile, and I feel a responsibility towards keeping people united. I don't want to fail at it, as I am answerable. People have put a lot of faith in me, I cannot let them down. People expect that if there is ever any problem, the Bhim Army will always be there to help. The first thing the Bhim Army has to do is to remove the BJP from power. I am neither a supporter nor an opponent of any political party, except for the BJP. If you are against the rights of the dalits and bahujan then you are against the Bhim Army. Kanshi Ram had written a book [*Chamcha Yug*; The Toady Age]. Once the bahujan samaj rises to its feet, the toadies will be out. Our only policy is that the dalits and bahujan should get their rights and justice.

Transcribed, edited and translated from Hindi by Ishita Mehta from a video on Newsclick, November 17, 2018

FROM COMMUNAL DEADLOCK TO A COMMUNAL EMERGENCY: AN AMBEDKARITE ASSESSMENT OF "INDIAN CONDITIONS" TODAY

Soumyabrata Choudhury

In his book Ambedkar and Other Immortals: An Untouchable Research Programme (2018), Soumyabrata Choudhary traced the nucleus of political immortality to the position: What is right must be regarded as true, even where it does not obtain as ground reality. This epistemic principle enabled Ambedkar to treat human equality as self-evidently true, while knowing it to be absent on the ground. As a result, Ambedkar transcends his own time and continues to enliven the struggles of those who stake everything on the perfectibility of the world.

In the following piece, Choudhury considers the opposite of political morality: the powerplay of a communal majority. A communal majority need not reason, persuade or even sincerely believe, in order to defend its claims; it need only display vehemence to get away with anything, and have its own way with everyone else. Hostile to ideas, and cynical, all the communal majority seeks to sustain is its overlordship of an abyss.

For Umar Khalid, scholar and activist with a Muslim name

In a speech he made to the All-India Scheduled Castes Federation (AISCF) in 1945, B.R. Ambedkar distinguished between a "political majority" and a "communal majority". According to him, "a political majority is not a fixed or a permanent majority... it is always made, unmade and remade. A communal majority is a permanent majority, fixed in its attitude. One can destroy it, one cannot transform it." Ambedkar then declares that in "Indian conditions", *only* a communal majority exists.

In these circumstances, no simple electoral majority can be trusted to represent all of the constituency. No elected party or individual can be trusted to represent all the constituent communities or be accepted by them as their true representative. This creates, according to Ambedkar, a "communal deadlock", which cannot be solved either by majoritarian bullying of the minority communities or by the endless "appeasement" of those bullied. The deadlock can only be broken by adopting a new principle to supplement the rule of the electoral majority: the principle of *justice*.

According to the principle of justice, mere electoral majority shouldn't determine participation in the political life of a society. So, for instance, the government shouldn't be only composed of members of the majority party in the legislature. In Ambedkar's view, minorities should find a place of participation in government relative to their position in society. The principle is the following: the weaker the social position, the proportionately compensatory opportunity of political participation for the community and individual. This is the way to break the "communal deadlock" such that the majority community does not enjoy an absolute majority in the political process and the minority doesn't have to tolerate either the bully's harassment or the patron's appeasement.

Ambedkar didn't think the British had done enough in this direction and he didn't trust the "Hindus in Congress" (Ambedkar's phrase) to solve the communal deadlock. On the eve of Independence, Ambedkar did not believe that the future constitution of a democracy could be merely a codification of institutions, such as the institution of elections governed by the rule of majoritarian representation; it had to lay down emancipatory principles that would compensate for structural bottlenecks in realising fundamental principles of freedom and egalitarian fraternity. Otherwise, the formal distinction between political majority and communal majority would be perpetually falsified in the real situation of political power. Elections would be a kind of periodic ritual device to reinforce the majority community's rule over the minorities. This was Ambedkar's diagnosis in 1945.

Let us agree that between then and 2014, till when mostly the

Congress ruled, the communal deadlock was carried on. To that extent, the "Indian conditions" formally retained the gap between a political majority and a communal majority. Elections were a complex, deceptive mask of the real conditions. In the short run, the political majority could be occasionally seen to depart from the communal one but in the long run, the "Hindus in Congress" still ruled. With BJP's victory in 2014 and since then, the mask has substantially come apart and the situation has changed from that of a communal deadlock to one of a *communal emergency*.

By "communal emergency", I mean a phenomenon that Ambedkar himself indicated when he said that the Hindus "insist" on an absolute majority: they will not accept a relative majority and they refuse to politically co-exist and co-work with the minorities. Since 2014, we have seen BJP, their party president, the prime minister, RSS personnel, media ideologues…more and more *insist*. Insist that the 2014 election was not just any other election where at least a ritual distinction between the political and the communal majority was still made. This election was not simply a "result": the 2014 verdict was, indeed, a decision, a command that the course of Indian history, once having changed, must never be reversed. And the essence of this change being claimed, even as I write, is that the 2014 Lok Sabha verdict is that one election by which all future elections must be measured. In this sense, we move from a democracy of elections, which itself was the degraded and—congressist—realisation on the ground of a constitutional democracy of principles, to a democracy of *one* election. This is clearly Amit Shah's dream: to engineer, manage and fight the same election in every election where openly, proudly and immaculately the political majority is fused with the communal majority. The long history of congressist rule, with its oscillation between harassment and appeasement, closes in on itself with a sudden flash—when we see the terrible miracle of the Party and Leader speak the Truth: "We *are* a communal and an absolute majority—we *insist*."

The insistence that 2014 was a miracle, everything is renewed since then and New India has no time to waste on thinking about democratic or constitutional principles, is felt today as excruciating violence in a time of emergency by the minorities. For the minorities, everything is staked on thinking; only when the principle of justice is thought, the dalits, the Muslims, adivasis, and women begin to exist in the Ambedkarite sense—they begin to exist *politically*. Otherwise only the communal majority exists, absolutely, stupidly and without thought. Which *is* the miracle of New India as a brand free of the labour and disturbance of thinking, a brand that the miracle-makers advertise and insist on.

However, the violence of the miracle insisted upon 2014 onwards reaches even deeper. If the minorities aren't allowed a political existence, then their lives are reduced to their physical presence as "populations". It is in this context that the situation of Muslims is particularly distressing. If BJP is, in essence, a Hindu majoritarian party which advertises itself as a "communal miracle", and it doesn't have a congressist manipulative interest in Muslims, then what is its relationship with the Muslim "population"? It is, to begin with, negative and tautological. The BJP has nothing to do with or gain from the Muslims. No candidates and hardly any votes from that quarter...

But we soon see the apparent "non-relation" produce a series of imaginary monsters: The Muslim as essentially belonging to a vaguely and malevolently crafted "Muslim world" which includes India's prime "enemy country", the Muslim as intrinsically "backward", as if backwardness were not a matter of historical discrimination but of something like a social and religious *gene*... And this lurid Islamophobic figuration, this breathless denunciation, not only of those with Muslim names, but of the very name "Muslim" is particularly ironic when we recall that in 1945, when Ambedkar was putting the "communal deadlock" to the labour of thought and principles, he was doing it to offer the Indian Muslim a real alternative between a future democratic India and a future Pakistan whose schema was itself based on a communal majority. This he did while accepting the principle of self-determination on which the demand for Pakistan was based. Today when the ideologues of the nation are revolted and crazed by the sound of "self-determination", they disdain to spend any effort on India's self-determination as a popular democracy, which includes *all* the people.

However, just because BJP wants to impose an irreversible electoral miracle (2014) on India's destiny and its president would like every election then to fall in line and emulate that *one* election—just because they "insist"—doesn't mean things have to inevitably turn out that way. So the BJP has lost several state and local polls as well as Lok Sabha by-elections since 2014. However, the party still insists! Based on its doctrine of the 2014 "miracle" out of which the communal majority is reborn, or rather born for the first time, *in principle*, it considers any subsequent election defeat to be an error. Any election, in which the distinction between the political and the communal majority becomes visible again, is now an anachronism. So, by the logic of destiny, even when history rules otherwise, the party (BJP) is entitled to intervene and rectify the electoral error, however illegitimate the intervention might look (for instance, the cold-blooded use of Governors of states). It is a neo-fascist programme of electoral eugenics, which in the short run doesn't require the classic precondition of fascism and political emergency, i.e., the suspension of the constitution. At the same time, this kind of electoral eugenics is not interested so much in tampering with election results as with ensuring that irrespective of these results, any fluid post-electoral scenario of multiple lobbies, parties and groups vying for power can smoothly pass through a porous electoral verdict and be grafted on the fixed pre-electoral body of a communal majority. The stakes don't ultimately lie in democratic legitimation through a tampered or a genuine election; they lie in exercising *power*, in as much as a certain sovereign and obscene glory attaches to this exercise.

However, to reach that ultimate glory, the logic of electoral representation must first be twisted in the following way: the people must be persuaded into submitting to the brute "fact" and the divine "principle" of the communal majority. If they are sure that it is not possible to "make, unmake and remake" a political majority anymore, only the communal majority exists, then elections become the site of a *blackmail*: if you don't vote for the majoritarian party, you forsake the obscene taste of power and rather feel only its sovereign violence. On the other hand, if you do vote for it, you, by proxy, enjoy that very violence (as the lynch mobs do today). For the minority then the choice is either to hide or to politically resist in the face of communal terror—or to fall in love with the blackmailer (enjoin the RSS...). One can detect a tendency towards the Stockholm Syndrome in a lot of the love for BJP and Modi that is sweeping across the country these days.

This, in my view, is the fundamental nature of an ongoing project that is delusional, violent and, in the current phase, distressingly effective. However, all of this perverse success doesn't allow any melancholic liberal consensus contra the jubilant communal one that political exclusion, cultural derision and physical terror directed against the minorities, particularly the Muslims, are the "new normal" of our national life. What can be melancholically—or jubilantly—accepted by the rest of us as "normal" can only be lived as a time of emergency by the minorities. However insistent, the new "Indian conditions", are not, and must never be, normal.

First published in Indian Cultural Forum, August 21, 2018

GAU RAKSHA AND THE WAR AGAINST INDIA'S POOR

Prabir Purkayastha

The mobilisation of rage against Muslims, under the pretext of cow protection, may appear to be a canny move to unite Hindu public opinion, but, as Prabir Purkayastha explains, cow vigilantism is based on a shallow understanding of the economy of livestock breeding and trade. Not only is this economy more complex than the mental processes of the gau rakshaks, but the Hindu consolidation project may come unstuck if they persist with their current tactics.

The toxic activities of the gau raksha samitis that have sprung up all over the country have led to increased attacks, not only on Muslims but also dalits. This was the pattern in the past, and it is the pattern today. Even as protests against the Una attacks rocked the country, the Bajrang Dal, on July 24, 2016, targeted dalits in Chikmagalur in Karnataka, the eighth such attack in the last two years. This was followed on July 28 by the beating of two dalit men in Lucknow for skinning a dead cow. A few years back, under previous the NDA government, five dalits were killed in Badshapur in Haryana, only 60 kilometres from Delhi, again for skinning a dead cow.

The RSS-Hindutva agenda is to homogenise a Hindu identity using hatred against Muslims. Their notion of formulating an Indian identity involves differentiating Hindus from Muslims. The cow is the symbol of this identity: the cow is sacred to "us"; but more importantly, it is sacred to "us" *and* the Muslims eat it. This differentiates Muslims from Hindus and makes Muslims "our" enemy. This is what led to the lynching of Akhlaq in Dadri, on September 28, 2015, Pehlu Khan in Alwar on April 1, 2017 and the numerous other attacks we have seen on Muslims as well as dalits in the last four years.

According to the Hate Crime database in FactChecker.in, "While 115 Muslims were attacked between 2014 and 2018, 23 dalits were attacked between 2016 and 2017. The worst year for dalits was 2016, as they made up 34 per cent of the victims in cow-related violence that year."

Cow vigilantism has been active for quite some time, but had little traction or support from the people. As long as the state was not complicit in this vigilantism, it could be contained. It is the rise of the BJP and its entry into power—in various states and now at the centre—that has changed this equation. Vigilantism, emerging as a major form of mobilisation in rural areas, tries to forge a Hindu unity and isolate the Muslims. If riots earlier were the instrument used by the Hindutva forces in urban areas, it is the campaign in the guise of protecting the "mother" cow that is becoming a major instrument of Hindu mobilisation and riots in rural areas. The attempt is to isolate and disempower the Muslims politically, similar to what has happened in Gujarat.

Though this vigilantism works as a weapon against the Muslims, it also fractures Hindu society. Hindutva's cow vigilantism has brought into the open the deep fissures that exist within the brahminical order. If the cow is indeed to be venerated, how come all those who work for the larger cattle economy are then polluted by this work? How come, if the cow is indeed their "mother", it isn't the gau rakshaks but dalits who are burying dead cows?

The relationship between human beings in the brahminical order is determined by the labour they do. To feed the upper castes milk and produce the footwear they use, other castes are needed to tend to the cattle and skin and dispose of the cow once it dies. The skin is then worked on by others to produce leather goods. All those who labour in production of any kind—productive labour such as producing milk or leather goods—are "polluted". Those who only consume such products of others' labour—by drinking milk or wearing leather goods—remain "pure". Producers are polluted; the parasites that live off the surplus of others retain their purity! This is the complete hypocrisy of the brahminical order.

While those who support a casteist order would have us believe that the caste society was built on "merit", it was actually built on a division of labour in which the ones doing no labour were at the top, while all others were hierarchically arranged based on the kind of labour they did. Disposing of dead animals and manual scavenging, essential for other castes, became the most polluting, and consigned to the bottom of the pyramid. This arrangement was an instrument of extracting labour from different communities as a part of surplus exploitation.

This did not mean that the extraction of labour was the only form through which the surplus was extracted. There were various other forms of surplus extraction as well. The key difference in the Indian form of caste-feudal society is that while European feudalism tied the serfs to the land or their lords, in India, the working people were hereditarily tied to their occupation. They could go from place to place if they wanted, but they were not allowed to leave their occupation.

Various explanations have been given for why beef eating, which was permitted in Vedic times, and was even a part of sacrificial rituals, was banned later. The most widely accepted explanation is provided by Marvin Harris, the well-known anthropologist.* He has said that it is the importance of the bulls and oxen in the agrarian economy of India that created the beef ban. If milk was the issue, then the buffalo, which is much more important for milk production, would also have been banned from slaughter. It was the clearing of forests and spread of settled agriculture in the Gangetic valley, in the first millennium BCE, that created this need for cow protection. Cows not only gave milk but also gave birth to the prized male calves: "The ox is the Indian peasant's tractor, thresher and family car combined; the cow is the factory that produces the ox." True today, this would have been still truer of earlier periods.

The gau rakshak samitis arose in the late nineteenth century not only as a form of anti-Muslim mobilisation but also as

---

*Harris, Marvin. "India's Sacred Cow." *Human Nature* 1, no. 2 (1978): 28-36.

an instrument of asserting upper-caste, particularly brahmin hegemony. All these bodies were formed as Hindu Sabhas, which later joined together in 1915 to form the Hindu Mahasabha.

The Hindutva forces tried to incorporate the other backward castes—the goalas, the ahirs, the gujjars, etc.—and co-opt them into the ranks of gau rakshaks. The flayers and the leather workers who are considered the most "polluted", as they deal with dead animals and dead animal skins, were not co-opted. So they did not "deserve" to be gau rakshaks; unless they gave up their occupation. Quite often, they are also beef eaters: the dead or sick cow would be eaten by these communities. Therefore, they may be treated as "equivalent" to Muslims.

Bezwada Wilson, the leader of the Safai Karmachari Andolan and a recent Magsaysay Award winner, speaking against the beef ban at the Idea of India Conclave in May 2016, identified it as an attack on the poor, because it deprives them of a major source of cheap protein. Various government bodies admit that beef eating is present among the Hindus, particularly dalits, tribals and some sections of the OBCs.

The attack on Muslims in the name of cow protection has also become an economic war on them. That is why the attack on beef eating has now spilled over to the skinning of dead cows, the transportation of hide and meat, and even cattle trade.

The consequence of attacks on cattle traders is that a large number of cows and bulls past their prime are being simply abandoned, particularly in states that have seen severe drought. The price of cattle has fallen drastically; the transportation of cattle—as we saw in the attack on Pehlu Khan in Behror, Alwar—is much more difficult and has become a high-risk activity. Similarly, the production of leather goods and export of "beef", which in India is largely buffalo meat, has come down quite significantly. According to the Ministry of Commerce, the export of buffalo meat came down by almost 11 per cent between 2014–15 and 2017–18 in terms of quantity and 18 per cent in terms of value. There is a drop of about 13 per cent in India's leather goods exports from 2014–15 to 2016–17 as well. The physical attacks on cattle traders and flayers is also an attack on India's economy.

There are reportedly 2.5 million Muslims and dalits in India's leather industry. So this attack on cattle and skin trade is also an attack on the livelihood of Muslims and dalits, who constitute the bulk of the workers in these trades.

The RSS-BJP's beef agenda may sound like a good instrument to communalise society, particularly in UP. Clearly, these are electoral ploys to marginalise the Muslims in the coming elections. Dalit protests now show the danger of such a path. The BJP has to address the dalit slogan, "If she is your mother, you bury her". BJP has no answer to this.

First published in Newsclick, August 6, 2016 and in Peoples Democracy, August 7, 2016. Brought up to date for this publication.

——◆•◆——

CONVERSATION: BEZWADA WILSON ASKS WHO WILL CLEAN THE 12 CRORE NEW TOILETS

Newsclick

The Swachh Bharat Abhiyan has no meaning while manual scavenging remains a reality. In conversation with Prabir Purkayastha, Bezwada Wilson, leader of the Safai Karmachari Andolan and a Magsaysay Award winner, talks about how the inhuman practice of manual scavenging is forced on the "lower" castes. With the Swachh Bharat Abhiyan's new aims of building toilets, the already burdened scavengers will get an added job of cleaning the new toilets. Wilson remarks on how the government has no plans to tackle this problem. The lack of technology adaptation in this area will result in a perpetual oppression of this particular caste of people.

Under the Prohibition of Employment as Manual Scavengers

*and Their Rehabilitation Act, an amendment to the law in 2003
brought the cleaning of septic and sewage tanks under its purview.
Section 7 of the law prohibits local authorities or agencies from
employing a worker to clean sewers and septic tanks. Despite these
provisions, the situation on the ground remains dire, not helped by
problems with the collation of data about such work, as when the
Delhi government found only 32 manual scavengers in its survey
in August 2016.*

Prabir Purkayastha (PP): Bezwada Wilson, let's talk about this
problem we seem to have made for ourselves—people dying
every year as they clean our sewers and septic tanks. What kind
of figures do we have?

Bezwada Wilson (BW): See, we do have figures, but these are
from a few towns—nothing exhaustive, more like a sample.
After the Supreme Court judgement of March 27, 2014 against
manual scavenging, the government was supposed to enumerate
the fatalities, collate figures and give Rs 10 lakh as compensation.
But when we [the Safai Karmachari Andolan (SKA)] began going
to the government, to its many departments and ministries, we
were surprised that none of them had any data on this, leave alone
a consolidated list. We started to compile the data. According to
our list there have been 1370 deaths, but this is [a provisional
finding] from the two years that we have been working to collect
data. It is the number we have given to the ministry, but it is not
comprehensive.*

---

*During its Bhim Yatra—a 125-day march across twenty-nine states, from
December 2015 to April 2016—the Safai Karmachari Andolan (SKA)
documented 1268 cases of fatality among manual scavengers, of which
only 18 had been followed by payments of compensation. Making these
payments is the least of the government's worries. The real reason behind
the government's costiveness with data is that it is the country's leading
law-breaker in the perpetuation of manual scavenging. In November 2015,
IndiaSpend reported that the Indian Railways are the biggest employer
of manual scavengers, disguised on the payroll as regular sweepers, or
hired through contractors. The degree of denial from the authorities

PP: Yes, the real figure would be much higher. A lot of these workers would not be permanent employees of municipal corporations or municipalities. Many are contract workers and casual workers who go undocumented.

BW: It's with the sewage system of the metros that you get workers who are full-time employees of corporations. There are also septic tank cleaners, the majority of whom are contract labour, or workers privately engaged by homeowners. Already, workers on the payroll of municipalities and corporations are not a small number. In Mumbai, Delhi, Chennai, Ahmedabad and so on, there is a large number of permanent employees.

PP: Why do you think people, since it's not just the government, are so callous about this? Do you think it has to do with the kind of people—the castes and communities—who do this kind of work, and a lack of sensitivity towards them?

BW: The sanitation in our country is caste-based. This is very clear and it is the first thing one must understand. The overwhelming number of these workers are "untouchable". Given this, everybody—the country, the people—all think that if a scavenger is cleaning up after them, what's so wrong about that? This is the work they are meant to do. Even our own people—since I belong to the same community—also think: *What else can we do?* After all, we are born into this caste. We can't do any other work. Also, it's very difficult to change professions. This work seems easier to us in that we simply continue to do what we've been doing, taking the path of least resistance. So, there are two angles at play. But the government does not think about this, about what's going on.

PP: Do you think part of the reason we don't think about it is that this caste viewpoint is built into the people who build the cities—those who develop, plan for cities? After all, sewers and septic

---

can beggar belief. Gujarat, in 2016, admitted to a total population of two manual scavengers. That did not prevent six from dying on a single day—September 19, 2017—in the sewers of Ahmedabad.

tanks in urban areas are a global fact, not peculiar to India, but this problem is uniquely Indian. Is it part of our caste-blindness, that we don't want to see the problem?

BW: We don't want to see it, and we don't care about certain lives in this country. Article 21 says we have the Right to Life, but whose life? Which group, which class, which caste? It is clear that some lives count for more than others. In the public sphere, they always say that all are equal; but some are clearly less equal than others. When such deaths occur, the first impulse is to throw money at the problem and make it go away. So, someone died. What's the big deal? How many children? How much money is it going to take to settle everything? Nobody will ask: *How could this person die?* With all our science and technology, why are we making somebody go down into the sewers like this?

Another reaction is this: these people went and died, so what can I do about it? Never mind that it's my septic tank, my sewer line, and I engaged these workers. Even the concept of workers and management responsibility doesn't apply here. Scavengers are easily available. If they accidentally die while cleaning, that has nothing to do with me. This is why the SKA says, *It's no accident.* You are killing us deliberately in the sewer lines and in septic tanks, because you choose not to mechanise the job. You know that we are dying.

It is important for us to insist on this point, that *you* have created the conditions for these deaths. So, don't come around to show your sympathy when we die, because you are responsible for this, and we want a political solution, now.

PP: It's a matter of justice, not mercy.

BW: I don't believe in mercy here, and I also think it is time the government took a stand, a decision on this. They can't keep throwing it back to society, saying it's a societal problem. No, caste is not a social problem. It may have emerged as such, but the solution must come from the field of politics.

PP: Coming back to the issue of Swachh Bharat. There, the government has announced some ten crore new toilets. They're giving out money and so on, but is there any consideration given to providing proper sewage to the toilets or a water connection? Without this, we are back to manual cleaning. How do you see the Swachh Bharat programme in this context?

BW: On October 2, 2014, the prime minister came to India Gate and announced his Swachh Bharat campaign. Immediately, it produced the impression that from now onward, everybody in India would clean up after themselves. It will not be caste-based, patriarchal, or anything like that. Even the prime minister will clean. We [at the SKA] felt that our movement was being taken back by some thirty-five years. All the work we had done to open the eyes of many across the globe was being nullified. And Modi did this without finding a single solution to the problem.*

Toilet construction is not a big deal in this country, it has been happening for a long time. But they are now making a big production out of it, saying twelve crore new toilets will be in place by 2019. The existing toilets are not functioning well; they don't dispose of excreta efficiently; and there aren't enough sewage treatment plants. These are the reasons for the many deaths among sewage workers. Here we go adding another twelve crore toilets. That means another twelve crore septic tanks, because no underground drainage system is being built in many of the places where the Swachh Bharat campaign is in full swing. They argue that they are putting in twin pits. Too often, where is the space for even a single pit? There's barely enough space for a pot

*Anand Teltumbde's *Republic of Caste* (Navayana, 2018, 338) has this to say of Modi's cleanliness campaign of 2007, 'Nirmal Gujarat', when he was chief minister: "The CAG in its report [...] found that despite the state government's claims of significant progress in managing waste, merely three per cent of Gujarat's municipalities have any segregation systems in place. Further, none of the state's municipalities have working sewage-treatment facilities, and only one has any semblance of a sewer coverage system."

to be fitted, leave alone twin pits. These are empty arguments. They have multiplied the number of tiny septic tanks which will have to be cleaned out manually in the future, and multiplied the risk to the lives of manual scavengers. That is not something they have given any thought to. And what about water? They go on constructing toilets with no thought to how they'll supply the water where there isn't any.

The government is imposing a fixed idea upon the people. People need many things, but you have decided to supply only one, the toilet. There is no food to eat, but toilets must be used. If I speak of only my own people, these toilets are going to increase their problems. Here are more death traps. I feel very strongly that you've been killing us till now, and have made provision to kill us *en masse* in the future.

The name itself disturbs me. Swachh suggests a pure, pollution-free Bharat, but it doesn't offer purity or freedom from pollution to the cleaners. Their contribution never gets recognised. Not even when the scheme is announced. For four thousand years a particular community has been doing the cleaning in this country, and you don't speak a single word of them, or to them. They want to leave this occupation, particularly the women. They came out and protested in public, they've burnt their baskets. Such people are eligible to receive rehabilitation from the government, but the government has nothing to offer them. It's not ready to rehabilitate them. Earlier, in 2012–13, the budgetary allocation for the rehabilitation of manual scavengers was Rs 570 crore. This year [in 2016], it is Rs 10 crore.* The 2016 Budget announced Rs 9000 crore for Swachh Bharat. All this money to build toilets and none to rehabilitate the scavengers, nothing for their liberation.

PP: The government does not want them to leave their occupation because it needs them to take care of the new problems it is creating.

The Hindu (October 29, 2018) reports that in 2017 this amount shrank to Rs 5 crore. The same report mentions that no payments had been disbursed from this fund in the previous four years.

BW: Yes, to trap the next generation. If a mother leaves scavenging, her daughter and daughter-in-law aren't going to continue in the same occupation. One woman burning her basket is no small gesture. It is breaking out of four thousand years of caste, which has gripped people like a chain: linking birth to caste and caste to occupation. She is doing no small thing, and the government must step forward and honour such women, say to them: We are here for you, tell us what you want.

PP: The other community to be badly hit is of those who remove dead animals. And we now see in Una and other places, people are beginning to protest and say we will not carry on with this occupation, because we are being persecuted—accused of killing cows—for doing what is an essential service, something you should consider a necessity. In Gujarat they are saying: You have tied us to this occupation. We need an alternate occupation. Give us land. You can keep your cow, which you consider so pure.* Do you think there is scope for a larger alliance among those who are forced into such occupations? Do you think these are some of the demands we should think about?

BW: It's very simple. In Una, the protesters could have said, We have done this for four thousand years. It's your turn now. You

---

*The slogan went "Gaai nu puchdu tamé rakho, amé amaari jameen aapo" (The cow's tail is all yours; just hand us our land). This particular land struggle grew out of the public humiliation of the family of a dalit, Balubhai Sarvaiya, of Mota Samadhiyala village, outside Una. On July 11, 2016, a group of cow vigilantes burst into the Sarvaiya home, assaulted seven people, forcibly dragged out four males who were then stripped half-naked, flogged, tied to the back of a vehicle, dragged to the town of Una, and flogged once again in front of a police station—with a video recording of the events uploaded on the internet. The mass protest that followed saw the emergence of Jignesh Mevani as a new leader. The protest took novel forms, including the dumping of cattle carcasses into the compounds of two district collectorates. This had a remarkable success in concentrating administrative minds. Three hundred acres of land were released to dalit allottees. Mevani was elected to the state legislature the following year, after contesting from Vadgam as an independent candidate.

can take over for the next forty years. They did not say that. They could have said, We've dealt with your dead animals for four thousand years. It's time you returned the favour and cleaned the carcasses of our dead livestock. They did not say that either. They don't want to reverse the inequality and perpetuate caste. What they're saying is, We've done this job for a long time and don't want to do it any more, we're opting out. That's a fair deal. But the casteist groups aren't willing to accept it. They don't want to give up land, or permit a change of occupation. So, what we say is, there can't be a deal, an exchange, this for that. Our position has to be: Whether you give us something in return or not, we're unwilling to carry on like this and we simply won't do this work anymore.

PP: Do you see a link between the cow as the gaumata, and the caste system?

BW: Very clearly. You produce an irrationalism, foist it on everybody and make everybody accept it. You are also taking away the rational basis [of our lives]. I mean, how many people in this country have the freedom, how many are in a position to think that we are all equal?

PP: It's a way of re-imposing the brahminical system on the people.

BW: Yes, the caste system.

PP: And the cow is an instrument for that.

BW: Otherwise, what is the cow? There's nothing there. They may say "The cow is my mother" and all that. But when your mother dies, why do you throw her corpse at me and ask me to deal with it? If she's your mother, keep her, do the rituals you're supposed to do. I might then believe that you have an emotional tie to the cow, and I would consider that to be your personal business. No problem. But you can't make me believe what you do. This compulsion really disturbs me. It has nothing to do with my being born an untouchable. I just don't want the next generation in this country believing or being made to believe such irrational things.

Edited text from a video on Newsclick published on October 15, 2016.

PART THREE

CITIZENS AGAINST ALL ODDS

Orijit Sen, 2018

SHE WILL SEE A BITTER MOON

Manash Firaq Bhattacharjee

On Eid ul Fitr, for the late fifteen-year-old Hafiz Junaid

They broke your body of fasting.

The smell of iftar had barely left
Your tongue, as you left the city,
Dilli, where you came to gather
Little joys to keep as a souvenir.

They broke your body of fasting
To feed the wolves in their heart,
There is no god left, no prayers,
No wound, to heal or remember.

A shadow in your mother's eyes
Will grow so wide, it will envelop
The house, no one will wake up
To ask for suhoor, kiss the dawn.

This Eid, the moon will not miss
You, only your mother will look
For you, in the streets of her dream
Where people still wait for gods.

Your blood will flow in her tears.

First published in Indian Cultural Forum, June 26, 2017

———◆◆◆———

A TRIAL BY FIRE

Teesta Setalvad

Of the decision to form Citizens for Justice and Peace (CJP), Teesta Setalvad writes that it was taken "during the dark days of March and April 2002, as I scoured Gujarat's cities and districts, stunned and increasingly angry at the scale and meticulousness of the organisation behind the state sponsored violence".

On May 2, 2002, some members of CJP filed the first case in the Supreme Court. They relied on the historic interim report of the National Human Rights Commission (March 2002) under the former chief justice of India, Justice J.S. Verma. The Report had recommended that the major incidents, including the train burning at Godhra, be investigated independently of the Gujarat police. The NHRC and, subsequently, the CJP petition, asked for transfer of the investigations into nine criminal cases, including Godhra, to the CBI. Says Setalvad, "Little did we know then that our maiden foray into legal redressal would become a historic trial by fire."

Seventy-two years after Independence, and sixty-nine years after our remarkable Constitution came into effect, it is still rare that the political battle against majoritarian violence and neo-fascist regimes takes the form of a legal battle. Yet that is how the fight for acknowledgement, accountability and justice in the case of the 2002 Gujarat genocidal carnage* has evolved. Waged inside and outside the courts, and marked by an uncommon alliance between survivors and civil and legal rights activists, this battle has by its seventeenth year resulted in 172 convictions, which include life sentences handed to 137 perpetrators of violence, several of them powerful people. Among the latter, till recently, was Maya Kodnani, then a sitting MLA and a minister in the Gujarat government, who was charged with distributing weapons

---

*Over 300 incidents spread over 19 districts of the state had left over 2,000 dead or missing, 19,000 homes burnt down or demolished, 10,000 plus business establishments destroyed, and 297 dargahs and masjids vandalized.

to ensure that a murderous mob gathered in Naroda Patiya, Ahmedabad killed over 100 people.

The verdict in the Naroda Patiya case delivered by a trial court on the morning of August 2012 was historic—and remains so, even if it was partly overturned six years later, when the Gujarat High Court acquitted Maya Kodnani.* The trial court judge, Jyotsana Yagnik, had meted out exemplary punishment for arguably the worst incident of the post-Godhra killings of 2002, and observed that the police had helped Kodnani—whom the judge described as the 'kingpin' of the violence—to escape justice.

It was almost nineteen years ago, on May 2, 2002, barely two months after the Gujarat killings, that some of us from Citizens for Justice and Peace (CJP) had filed the first case in the Supreme Court, relying on the March 2002 interim report of the National Human Rights Commission (NHRC) under former chief justice of India Justice J.S. Verma, recommending that the major incidents, including the train burning at Godhra, be investigated independent of the Gujarat police. The NHRC, and subsequently our petition, asked for transfer of investigations into nine criminal cases, including Godhra, to the CBI. Little did we know then that our maiden foray into legal redressal would transform into a historic trial by fire.

The decision to form CJP was taken during the dark days of March and April 2002, as I scoured Gujarat's cities and districts, stunned and increasingly angry at the scale and meticulousness of the organisation behind the state sponsored violence. All of us who formed CJP had seen Bombay burn in 1992-93, and had been active as citizens in the movement to get the report of the Justice B.N. Srikrishna Commission on the Bombay riots published (when the Shiv Sena-BJP government disbanded the Commission on coming to power in 1995). We had realised that all political parties were in collusion when it came to ensuring impunity for

---

*The High Court while acquitting Kodnani and her personal assistant upheld the convictions of others.

those in power in cases of mass crimes, and this was the main reason behind recurring incidents of brutal, targeted violence against sections of the Indian people, especially minorities.

It was also clear that within this political consensus, and crucial to it, is police and administrative compromise. Officers of the IAS and the IPS rarely step out of the camaraderie of the service and allow serious indictment of their brethren, even when there is unequivocal evidence of complicity. In that sense, people like Gujarat's former director general of police R.B. Sreekumar, or another IPS officer from Gujarat, Rahul Sharma, and senior retired police officers like Chaman Lal (special rapporteur to the NHRC) are rare exceptions.

While this has been the case for decades, the situation has been even more grim in BJP-ruled Gujarat and, since 2014, BJP-ruled India. In a democracy that sits easily with discriminatory norms symbolised by hate speech and democratic institutions like law enforcement bodies—the police and the paramilitary—and even the courts being filled with persons who espouse an anti-Constitutional dream of Hindu India, equality has become a hollow promise. The failure of India's courts, even the higher judiciary, to retain institutional memory of experiences like Gujarat 2002 continues to cause major and violent cleavages within society, and seriously undermines India's Constitution.*

Between 2002 and July 2003, when the developments in the Best Bakery case† forced a key witness, Zahira Habibullah Sheikh, to seek help from CJP and record her statement before the NHRC

---

*In the Muzaffarnagar bout of targeted violence in 2013, for instance, a similar effort was made to approach the Supreme Court to exercise its writ of continuing mandamus—that ensures some rigour in monitoring of the trials at the local levels so that anomalies and breaches may be corrected; but the judgement delivered by the Supreme Court in these batch of cases in early 2014 was a sorry shadow of the judicial pronouncements vis a vis Gujarat in 2002. The lead judge in question was appointed as a Governor by the new dispensation in Delhi.

† The Best Bakery case involved the burning down of a bakery, owned by the Sheikh family, by a mob in Vadodara on 1st March 2002. Fourteen

in Vadodara, making plain the circumstances under which she was forced to turn hostile in the Sessions Court, the judicial system slumbered. The higher courts simply did not respond to the well-documented cases before them.

Shaken by the allegations made by Zahira Sheikh on 7 July 2003, the NHRC moved a special leave petition in the Supreme Court and after a sensational round of legal proceedings, the Court finally rose to deliver the historic judgement, *Zahira Habibullah Sheikh v State of Gujarat, 2004 AIR SCW 2325*, which not only ordered re-trial in a case of mass targeted violence but also transferred the trial out of the state of Gujarat. This widely cited judicial decision pointed out the statutory responsibilities of the Judge and the Prosecutor—not to remain mute spectators during a criminal trial and ensure that public justice is done. It also flagged, again, the crucial issue of witness protection, critical to substantive justice but an issue that has not found an echo within the Indian political class, not even among parties from the centre or the left who vow by India's Constitutional ethos and secularism.* It was this judgement that resulted in an amendment to the Code of Criminal Procedure (CrPC) that introduced, for the first time, victimology into Indian criminal human rights jurisprudence. Section 24(8)(2) of the CrPC now empowers a complainant/victim to also be, as a matter of statutory right, part of criminal proceedings. This was a significant amendment, because too often the state has conveniently allowed crucial cases to drag on or lapse simply through non-pursuance in the courts.

In the long term, the cumulative result of these individual legal battles, over 126 in all since 2002, has meant restoring the faith of despairing and alienated sections of the Indian population, especially its religious minorities, in Indian democracy and the

---

people were burnt to death. All the 21 accused were acquitted by the court due to shoddy police work. It was the first case to be tried with respect to the post-Godhra killings in Gujarat.

*https://www.sabrangindia.in/article/yet-again-supreme-court-raps-indian-state-witness-protection-anyone-listening justice delivery process. This faith has been severely tested by the politics of hatred and division that has taken hold in the country since the late 1980s. After the political ascendancy of the ideology that drove the people accused of being architects and perpetrators of the Gujarat carnage to the highest offices, the state has been carrying on a vendetta, through malicious, manufactured cases, against organisations and individuals that have led this battle (including the author).

The ultimate test of a successful battle is staying the course. After seventeen years of bitter experience, one lasting lesson for this author and others has been that the system works to tire you out. There is also the bitter realisation that in incidents of mass crime and state-enabled violence, there are discriminatory levels of justice dispensation. No bail was granted until judgement delivery (February 2011) to those accused of the train burning at Godhra. Those accused of rape, mass murder and criminal conspiracy in the post Godhra reprisal killings were out on bail in three to six months. Over 500 such accused were all given bail within months of the violence in 2002.

Safeguarding witnesses and gathering evidence

Eyewitness testimonies form the bedrock of evidence and justice, which is why state governments, police and the defence expend so much energy in turning witnesses hostile in court. Seven years after the Naroda Patiya massacre—between 2009 and 2011, in fact—effective and valid testimonies of eye-witnesses were possible due to the regular and thorough legal assistance provided to victim witnesses by CJP and others availing of the amendment in the CrPC following the April 2004 Supreme Court judgement in the Best Bakery case.*

In the Naroda Patiya case, eye witness testimonies also had firm corroboratory evidence in the sting operation conducted

---

*Citizens for Justice and Peace engaged three lawyers to assist Victim Witnesses through the Naroda Patiya trial.

by Ashish Khetan of *Tehelka*. The sting operation—validated through the scientific testing carried out by CBI pursuant to an NHRC order*—was vital in proving further aspects of the criminal conspiracy: in his deposition before the Court, Khetan, as prosecution witness number 322, confirmed what Babu Bajrangi† had boasted in his taped conversation that he had collected 23 revolvers to further the conspiracy. The revelation that ordinary residences in the Naroda Patiya area experienced gas shortages for weeks before the burning of the Sabarmati S-6 Coach at Godhra station on February 27, also pointed to sinister premeditation.

All of this corroborated the brave eye-witness testimonies of survivors, and it was successfully established that a mob, coming from the direction of Krishnanagar and Nartaj Hotel, had gathered between the Noorani Mosque and the ST workshop, at which point Mayaben Kodnani had come there with her bodyguard Kirpal Singh and incited the crowd to kill Muslims ("Cut the Miyans") and also attack and brutalise women. It was the confidence and protection afforded by a powerful person, in this case, Kodnani, an elected MLA, that emboldened the mob to criminal actions. This also establishes a chain of command responsibility, from those who conspired to those who physically instigated to those who actually implemented the criminal conspiracy.

Gender-driven brutalities and violence rarely sustain judicial scrutiny and the narrative of gender violence usually disappears with the onset of trial. In another first, the Naroda Patiyatria case, monitored by the Supreme Court, with quality legal aid provided to witnesses, ensured that the narrative of gender violence returned during prosecution. Women victim eyewitnesses, emboldened by legal assistance and also physical protection given to them by the CISF under orders of the Supreme Court, testified bravely about

---

*Again it was the author, secretary CJP, who moved the NHRC for this when both the Gujarat HC and SC failed to protect this evidence stating, when approached, that it "could wait until trials commenced."

†A leader of the Gujarat wing of the Bajrang Dal, Bajrangi was a central figure in the massacre in Naroda Patiya. He was sentenced to life by a special court in 2012.

the extent of violence and rape perpetrated against Muslim girls and women.*

Equally historic is the ongoing Zakia Jafri case†. Her criminal complaint about the Gujarat killings was filed on June 8, 2006—with 2,000 pages of evidence, provided by serving police officers and administrators. Thereafter, as proceedings meandered through the courts, CJP's intrepid team of activists and lawyers unearthed a nexus through phone call records between powerful accused and policemen. Finally, as we approached the stage of filing a protest petition‡ in 2013, we obtained as a matter of legal rights 23,000 pages of investigation papers that strengthened the case even further. State Intelligence Bureau records, Police Control Room records and Fire Brigade messages, apart from direct statements from protagonists and witnesses, have allowed us to put together a case strong enough to be put to trial. If institutions worked in favour of genuine democracy, this should have been the job of the Special Investigation Team (SIT), appointed by the Supreme Court itself. The conduct of the SIT, which bent to the interest of the powerful is yet something that the Indian judicial system has to honestly confront.§

---

*In May 2004, on an application by CJP and argued by then Amicus curiae, Harish Salve, 570 witnesses were given cluster protection by the central paramilitary including human rights defender TeestaSetalvad. Once trials began, special witness protection was given to all victim witnesses ensuring that they deposed without fear or favour. In June 2010, the CJP submitted a CJP Survivors Report to the CEDAW Committee of the United Nations.

†Ehsan Jafri, a Congress politician, was killed by a mob armed with machetes in the Gulbarg Society massacre on February 28, 2002 when he pleaded with the mob to spare the lives of the women and children who had taken refuge in his home. His widow Zakia Jafri has maintained that the state of Gujarat and its then chief minister, Narendra Modi, were partly responsible for the violence and for the lack of police intervention in favour of the victims at Gulbarg Society.

‡https://cjp.org.in/wp-content/uploads/2017/05/Protest%20Petition%20PART%20I.pdf

§https://cjp.org.in/gujarat-genocide-mystery-of-the-clean-chit/

Still a long road to Justice

While all over India debates rage about the death penalty, survivors of the 2002 massacre*, aided by CJP, have arrived at a judicious and humane stand. While we've seen the vicious prosecution in the Godhra train burning case—even by the Supreme Court appointed SIT—we have asked for life imprisonment, not the death penalty, for the perpetrators of the post-Godhra killings and rapes. Yet, justice eludes a vast number of the victims.

And any serious effort to do justice cannot refuse to address, in a fair, thorough and legally tenable manner, the now famed *Zakia-Ehsan Jafri and Citizens for Justice and Peace* case against Narendra Modi and 59 others which lies before the Supreme Court, in appeal. This complaint, which has gone from prayers to register an FIR to appeals that charges be framed, alleges criminal conspiracy to commit mass murder in 19 of Gujarat's 25 districts, subvert justice, destroy evidence and intimidate public servants upholding the truth. Already the Supreme Court appointed Amicus Curiae Raju Ramachandran has opined in his report that there is enough evidence to prosecute Narendra Modi on charges of dereliction of duty and hate speech (Sections 166, 153a and 505 of the Indian penal Code). Senior policemen, says Ramachandran, should also be prosecuted, not just for criminal dereliction of duty but subverting of the criminal justice system and destruction of evidence. For the Indian justice system and courts, this remains a test case.

For the first time in our history, a chief minister—now the prime minister—and other most senior figures in authority have been accused of criminal conspiracy in a case of mass murder and the complainants have sought that they be charge sheeted. Seventeen years on, will the evidence that has been presented be matched by the rigour of prosecution? What further costs will have to be paid by the survivors, individuals and groups spearheading this journey?

(February 2019)

*https://cjp.org.in/justice-should-be-reformative-not-retributive-teesta-setalvad/

VIOLENCE AGAINST MINORITIES:
THE NEW NORMAL

Sanjukta Basu

Between September and October 2017, the Karwan-e-Mohabbat travelled across eight states, starting from Assam's Nagaon district, site of the Nellie massacre of 1983, to end at Porbandar, Gujarat on Gandhi Jayanti. Meeting at every halt with the forsaken of India— victims of civil and state-sponsored violence—the Karwan brought with it words of support and legal guidance, but more importantly, a willing ear to those who had ceased to expect humanity of their fellow citizens.

"We believe the Prime Minister should have gone on this journey. He didn't, so we have," said Harsh Mander. The Karwan was besieged all the way, by right-wing organisations and disheartening news. The travellers were to learn of Gauri Lankesh's assassination on the second day of their journey. At this low ebb, with state and society far gone into brutishness, the Karwan's work grew more vital, restoring the character and moral imagination of citizenship.

"Humne sabar kar liya" (We've made our peace with it), said an old and fragile Jafruddin Hassan with tears in his eyes, trembling hands resting between his knees and his head stooped low, as he hopelessly looked at the floor. Jafruddin of Khurgain village, Shamli district, Uttar Pradesh, is the face of the traumatised minority communities who have learnt to normalise the violence in their lives, exactly as envisioned by M.S. Golwalkar, the RSS' guruji, in his book *We, or Our Nationhood Defined* (1939).*

---

*On February 24, 2006, the RSS officially disowned *We, or Our Nationhood Defined* as "neither representing the views of the grown Guruji [Golwalkar] nor of the RSS." Approving the removal of We from the official canon, former spokesperson for the Sangh M.G. Vaidya said that the book central to "us is Golwalkar's *Bunch of Thoughts*, since it consists of his views after he became sarsanghchalak on June 21, 1940." However, on September 19, 2018, RSS chief Mohan Bhagwat declared that even parts of *Bunch*

In his book, Golwalkar called Hindus a race that legitimately belongs to Hindustan, "Mussalman" as outsiders or foreigners, and outlined a future for them in which they must forever live at the mercy of Hindus. To quote Golwalkar:

> There are only two courses open to the foreign elements, either to merge themselves in the national race and adopt its culture, or to live at its mercy so long as the national race may allow them to do so and to quit the country at the sweet will of the national race...the foreign races in Hindusthan must either adopt the Hindu culture and language, must learn to respect and hold in reverence Hindu religion, must entertain no idea but those of the glorification of the Hindu race and culture... must lose their separate existence to merge in the Hindu race, or may stay in the country, wholly subordinated to the Hindu Nation, claiming nothing, deserving no privileges, far less any preferential treatment—not even citizen's rights.[*]

This vision seems to be complete, to judge from the stories that emerged during Harsh Mander's Karwan-e-Mohabbat, a month-long journey that started from Assam and travelled to Jharkhand, Karnataka, Delhi, UP, Haryana, Rajasthan and Gujarat, meeting families of dalit and Muslim victims of lynching by caste and religious supremacists including the state apparatus.

Making peace with violence—Jafruddin's story

It has been four years since 2013, when Jaffruddin's son Salim was killed by a mob of cow vigilantes somewhere on the cattle trade

---

of Thoughts (1966) were no longer valid, as circumstances had changed since this collection of speeches was first issued. Whether these disavowals would be followed by any ideological course correction—on the matter of Hindu primacy in Indian citizenship, for example—was not specified on either occasion. Failing that, the import of these declarations is merely cosmetic. They show as an artful manoeuvre to jettison texts that have become indefensible, while their message pervades the Sangh Parivar's outlook and conduct, its very core.

[*]*Nagpur: Bharat Publications*, 1939, p. 35.

route between Haryana and Uttar Pradesh. Till date, the police have not even handed the post-mortem report to the victim's family, even though they exhumed his body for the purpose, an act proscribed by religion that has scarred the family. In a statement made shortly before his death, Salim had mentioned being attacked by a mob of nine—but only one was arrested, to be released on the same day. After the exhumation of the body and post-mortem, a second FIR was filed but no arrests were made. Four years on, Salim's family has no information about the case, and they do not even dare to pursue justice. Instead, the family lives in fear of further attacks on their other sons. "*Humne sabar kar liya,*" is their response to all the violence they have met. Living at the mercy of self-proclaimed custodians of the majority religion has become the norm. Their hopelessness is so profound that Jafruddin blessed Harsh Mander with, "*Aap ko jannat naseeb ho*" (May heaven be yours) on a mere promise of obtaining a copy of the post-mortem report, the last record of his son.

This is a pattern the Karwan noticed in its entire journey, meeting over fifty families across India. The religious and caste minorities are being systematically attacked by cow vigilantes and Hindu supremacists unleashing terror in their daily lives; several victims have lost life or limb, had their only means of occupation taken away, their access to justice made difficult by the biased approach of the police and administration, while the media constantly vilifies them with all kinds of fake narratives. The result is that their lives are disoriented by their misery, they are so broken, scared and isolated that their own lived realities have come to seem like fiction. They are neither aware that their basic human rights have been brutally taken away, nor are they sure whether they have any basic rights to begin with—exactly as Golwalkar envisioned.

Khurshida's story

Khurshida, a middle-aged widow, abandoned by her in-laws after the death of her husband, lives in Bhango, Mewat, with her four children. Her husband, Ajmal, died mysteriously in a police encounter in 2010. In 2012, she suddenly received a bank draft of rupees five lakh—presumably a compensation, from the National Human Rights Commission (NHRC), but no explanation was given as to what had happened to her husband. This story is most baffling: it is obvious that there had been an inquiry into Ajmal's death and the police must have been held guilty of a human rights violation, otherwise this compensation would not have been paid. But the fact that no details about the investigation have been communicated to the widow is proof the administration wants to hush up the findings.

It is hard even to attempt to understand Khurshida's grief. Ajmal used to drive dumper trucks and had no police case against him. One fine morning he went out to work and the next thing Khurshida knows, he was dead and buried. She didn't even get to see his body, no rituals were performed, "*Kucch pata nahi chala, koi mitti bhi nahi mili,*" (I wasn't given any details, not even earth from his grave) said Khurshida to Karwan travellers.

The psychological impact of such traumas, of lives lost without reason, of grief without closure, of violence without accountability are all part of the dehumanisation of the minority community and normalisation of violence in their lives. Today, Khurshida has bought some land with the money she got and is trying to raise her children by working as a labourer. "I am an uneducated villager, where will I go to ask questions?" is the end of the matter for her.

Threats from right-wing groups—a strategy to cut off the victim from empathy and support system

What the minority communities, disoriented by their sorrow, need most is an assurance that their lives matter, that the violence caused to them should not have happened and that we—the people of this nation—are sorry and extend our condolences. That was the idea with which Harsh Mander started his Karwan. But those trying to dehumanise the minority community are also against anybody who would extend empathy and support to them. They are not only perpetrating violence but also cutting off the victim from all support systems.

On September 14, 2017, a day before the Karwan was supposed to reach Alwar, all six accused named by Pehlu Khan in his dying declaration were given a clean chit by the Rajasthan state police.* The timing of the decision was a suspicious coincidence and soon enough, the Karwan received threats from Hindu extremist groups. Harish Saini from the Hindu Jagran Manch reportedly appealed to the Rajasthan administration to not allow the Karwan to hold any event in Alwar. "Any attempt to pay tribute to deceased Pehlu Khan would not be tolerated," said Keshavchand Sharma of the Vishwa Hindu Parishad.

Even though the Karwan received the Rajasthan administration's assurance that it would not be stopped anywhere, local partners in Behror succumbed to the threats. The venue for the peace meeting—"Ganesh Plaza"—became unavailable and no other venue could be arranged. Local traders threatened to close down Behror in case the Karwan held any event. A defiant Harsh Mander however remained steady in his mission to at least pay tribute to Pehlu Khan by offering flowers at the spot where he was lynched. Even this irked the right-wing groups which tried to prevent it. The state police also tried to put pressure on Mander, "If you place flowers at that spot, this would become a trend," said one of the officers. "Let it be one, what is wrong in it?" replied Mander.

The Karwan had to enter Rajasthan with police protection. The travellers were given instructions on what to do if stones were thrown at the bus; "Duck and don't move," they were told. Despite constant threats and pressure, the Karwan arrived at Behror on

---

*On the principle Nemo moriturus praesumitur mentire (nobody at the point of death is presumed to lie), Indian law upholds the evidentiary value of dying declarations. They may even be the sole evidence leading to the conviction of an accused. In the "Nirbhaya" case (2013), a bench of Justices Dipak Misra, R. Banumathi, and Ashok Bhushan, clarified that a dying declaration in writing, spoken words, or even gestures would be admissible as evidence.

September 15 and was met by a large crowd of Hindu right-wing groups. Harsh Mander briefly sat in dharna near the Behror police station, demanding that he be allowed to offer tribute to Pehlu Khan, and finally placed flowers at a symbolic location amid heavy police security. As the bus moved towards Jaipur with a police escort, right-wing goons from the street chanted "*Bharat Mata Ki Jai*" and "*Joote maaro saalon ko*" and threw stones and shoes at it.

Such extreme hate, threats and intimidation towards a group of ordinary citizens with a simple message of love and empathy is a sign of the times we are living in. The message is clear—anybody trying to build peace and harmony is doing so at their own risk. The Karwan members are not the regular protestors in political rallies who face tear gas and lathi charge, or grassroot activists facing the establishment's ire. It is a group of people who usually do not have direct political participation. This is the category of people through whom Harsh Mander wanted to build a bridge between the victims of and those unaffected by street violence. It is also a category of people who might be easily intimidated, and right-wing groups are trying to do precisely that in order to deter any such attempts at solidarity—at building a united front against hate and violence—for all times to come.

The practice of slapping the "cross case" on victims—a pressure tactic to withdraw cases against attackers

Family after family met by the Karwan revealed another dangerous pattern in the police investigation. In almost all the cases of lynching by cow vigilantes, there are criminal cases filed against the victim, casually referred to as "cross-case". Cross cases are filed by cow vigilantes or registered suo motu by police on various grounds—like flouting traffic laws or animal protection laws, etc.—as a means to put pressure on the victim not to seek prosecution of vigilantes. Often these cross cases keep hanging around the victim's neck, while the perpetrators easily obtain bail, and justice turns elusive. In such situations, the victim or victim's family is tempted to make a compromise—leading to the withdrawal of cases by both sides. Although the legality of this is not so linear or simplistic, the truth is that Muslims having any kind of dealing with cows, be it simple transportation, buying or selling for dairy, are scared even to file an FIR against cow vigilantes for fear of getting roped into a cross case.

Immediately after Pehlu Khan and his son were brutally attacked by cow vigilantes on April 1, 2017, criminal cases were filed against the victims on grounds of cattle slaughter and animal cruelty, which were completely baseless, a fact later confirmed by the court.* In Vadavli, Gujarat, a riot broke out between dalits and thakurs in the closing week of March 2017, and FIRs got registered against both communities, although dalit residents of the village claim that any force used by them was in self-defence. This space is too small to share all such cases but suffice it to say that with cross cases, the cycle of violence is complete—dehumanisation, isolation and victim blaming.

Karwan leader Harsh Mander has given a call to every Indian: "*Chalo Porbandar, hum sab Gandhi.*" How much this initiative will achieve is a question to be answered in the proverbial "long run". But one thing is very clear: the powers-that-be are rattled by the potential impact of the Karwan and attempts to throttle the movement have already begun. On September 14, RSS spokesperson Rakesh Sinha openly threatened Harsh Mander on *NDTV*, that his NGO's funding would be investigated. As soon as Mander reached his office on September 22, his NGO—Centre for Equity Studies—received an income tax notice. "They can cancel our FCRA, shut down the organisation. How does it matter? This would be an infinitely small fraction of the suffering that we bore witness to during the Karwan," Mander wrote on a WhatsApp group, signalling the long fight ahead.

First published in FirstPost as "Karwan-e Mohabbat: Uncovering how violence against minorities has been normalised", October 1, 2017.

---

*Hindustan Times, July 19, 2017

BLAMING THE VICTIMS: THE CASE OF THE ALWAR LYNCHING

Harsh Mander

Pehlu Khan, a dairy farmer and cattle trader from Jaisinghpur Village in Nuh, was lynched on a busy Rajasthan highway in April, 2017. Before he died, Khan named six men as his attackers. A year later, Harsh Mander wrote after visiting Khan's village for the second time with the Kawan-e-mohabbat: "...the villagers believe that the police discarded Pehlu Khan's dying declaration, in its striving to protect influential cow vigilantes affiliated to Sangh organisations. The three men they arrested, instead, are out on bail." The police filed charge-sheets against two young men, Azmat and Rafeeq, who had been attacked with Pehlu Khan, and barely escaped with their lives. The charge was "cow smuggling"—under Section 5 of the Rajasthan Bovine Animal (Prohibition of Slaughter and Regulation of Temporary Migration or Export) Act, 1995. But what this statute prohibits is transport of animals for slaughter. Mander writes, "Since Pehlu Khan and his colleagues were transporting expensive milch cattle with calves, it was obvious that there was no intent to take them to slaughter. By continuing to defame Rakbar Khan—and Pehlu Khan before him—as cow smugglers, the police and ministers justify their murders." The journeys of the Karwan-e-mohabbat to families affected by lynch violence in ten states of the country have found that such criminalising of victims of lynching is now commonplace across India.

I held Rakbar Khan's father Suleiman's hand in mine for a long time. His face was creased with grief, his eyes often welled up. Khan's widow lay close by, stretched out on a string cot, her face fully covered with her red dupatta, unmindful of the claustrophobic heat, surrounded by women of her village who whispered around her in solicitous tones. "She has become crazed with her agony," one of them said. "She just gets up and laughs." Earlier, when she spoke publicly, she had lamented that she was left alone to raise her seven children, the smallest a boy who had only just spoken his first words. The children, most of them with light hazel eyes, gazed at us and the large crowd of village men who had gathered outside their home with puzzlement and nervous unease, unable to comprehend why their father had been killed, and why so many of us had collected there.

Some things are by now clear about the circumstances in which twenty-eight-year-old Rakbar Khan, an impoverished, nearly unlettered dairy farmer, was lynched on the night of July 21 in Rajasthan's Alwar district, a few kilometres from his village Kolgaon in Haryana's Nuh district.* Other facts are still disputed or deliberately obscured. The facts beyond dispute are that as Rakbar Khan and his friend Aslam Khan were returning home on foot, after dark, with the two milch cows Rakbar had bought from Rajasthan, they were attacked by a group of men claiming to be *gau rakshaks* or "cow protectors". Aslam managed to escape, but Rakbar was not so fortunate.

As a teenager, Rakbar Khan had laboured on sand- and stone-mining sites in the surrounding Aravali Hills. After the mining was shut down a decade ago, he fell back on the only other vocation his family knew: dairy farming, supplemented with intermittent farm labour. Two milch cows were tethered outside the family's small home. His father had aged, and Rakbar Khan alone could barely bring in Rs 5,000 a month for his parents and children. He decided that his only chance to improve his family's lot was to buy a couple more dairy cows, which are locally known as biyahi or married cows. His father-in-law had loaned him Rs 50,000 to buy two cows. These, Rakbar Khan had hoped, would change their lives. They did, but not in ways he had hoped. What transpired instead was the worst nightmare of every Muslim dairy farmer in Nuh today.

Each of them knows that buying cows and transporting them have become ultra-high-risk enterprises on the watch of the current political regimes in the country, especially in Haryana and

*Eighty per cent of the population in Mewat, Haryana is Muslim and is ethnically "Mev" or "Meo".

Rajasthan. Since Pehlu Khan was lynched last summer for buying and ferrying biyahi cows and their calves in a pick-up truck, dairy farmers are terrified of the risk of being spotted anywhere with cows, and now even with buffaloes. The law bans the slaughter of cows, not their transport for dairying. But who will explain this to a lynch mob? Or for that matter to a state home minister, or police officials, who continue to defame both Pehlu Khan and Rakbar Khan as cow smugglers, thereby directly rationalising their mob killings. Cow vigilante groups, openly supported by the political establishment and the police, rule the streets. It has become routine for those who transport dairy animals to face violence and extortion at their hands. Aggravating matters, the Haryana Police has established an official Cow Protection Force of men and women in uniform, with the official mandate of saving cows. There are now special cow-protection police chowkis that farmers dread for their coercion and extortion.

Rakbar weighed all of these risks before opting to embrace the hazards of buying a cow. The two cows would have doubled his monthly income from Rs 5,000, allowing his children to drink more milk and to go to school, and his parents to eat better. Too poor to hire a vehicle, he decided to walk the dairy cows home. And he decided to avoid the highways and instead walk through fields in the dark. Nuh is a Muslim-majority district, and we find that most incidents of lynching of Muslim farmers from here occur not within Nuh but in districts like Alwar in neighbouring Rajasthan, where Muslims are in a minority. Rakbar and Aslam were just a few kilometres from the border of their district when some farmers alerted cow vigilante groups, who chased down the two men. A terrified Rakbar left his two cows and desperately tried to escape, but the men caught up with him. Aslam barely managed to escape. He reached his home at dawn, his clothes smudged with wet mud. He had crawled face down through the fields, petrified through his nightmarish journey that the vigilantes would spot him.

We could not meet Aslam Khan in Kolgaon when the Karwan-e-Mohabbat team visited Rakbar Khan's family. We were told that since his escape, he felt dragged down with the shame of abandoning his friend and had left the village for a while.

Who killed Rakbar Khan?

What remains bitterly contested about the events of that night is how severely the attackers, who reportedly bragged that they were backed by the Rajasthan BJP MLA Gyan Dev Ahuja, beat up Rakbar Khan. The men claimed they only slapped Rakbar and beat him "a little" to "show off" to the crowd and teach him a lesson. They produced a number of witnesses who told television reporters that Rakbar was able to sit up after the beating. It was at the police station, where he was taken before he was brought to a hospital, that they claim he was beaten to death. Rajasthan Home Minister Gulab Singh Kataria, too, said that this seemed to him to be a case not of lynching but of custodial killing. He seemed more willing to sacrifice the uniformed men under his charge than his party supporters who were given to lynching Muslim men.

However, during the Karwan team's visit to Rakbar Khan's village, the residents insisted it was the mob that had thrashed him nearly to death, not the police. It was only to save themselves that the mob had shifted the blame to the police, the villagers said. The killers hoped that by doing this, they would be spared the charge of murder, and even in the unlikely chance that they were convicted, they would spend just a few years in jail and emerge heroes. The policemen would, at worst, face administrative action, and ultimately be acquitted when public memory faded.

It was the post-mortem report that confirmed the villagers' version: the mob attack had left Rakbar Khan critically injured. It stated that he had suffered thirteen injuries—including a fractured wrist, a fracture in the left femur, bruises, abrasions and a laceration—in the attack, and concluded that he had died of "shock as a result of ante-mortem [before death] injuries sustained over body". It also said the injuries on his body were twelve hours old, calculated from the time of autopsy. Since the post-mortem was conducted at 12.44 p.m. on July 22, the time of the assault that killed Rakbar Khan was around midnight the night before, when he was still at the mercy of the mob.

Not just an "error in judgement"

Even though Rakbar Khan probably died mainly because of the mob assault, the police were far from blameless. If there was any life left in him when they got to him, he could possibly have been saved had they immediately taken him to hospital, which was just 4 kms away. Instead, as is now well known, they took close to four hours, during which they (or members of the mob) cleaned him up and changed his clothes (a wanton and criminal act of destruction of evidence), delivered his cows to a cow sanctuary, stopped by for cups of tea and only then took him to the hospital, where he was declared dead on arrival.

Senior Rajasthan police officials described the actions of their men in Alwar as only an "error in judgement". What they failed to acknowledge was that this failure may have cost an innocent man his life, and therefore was criminal. They also did not admit that the policemen felt emboldened to act this way because of the unambiguous messages they receive from their seniors, both in uniform and the political establishment. A minister in the Rajasthan government, Jaswant Yadav, rationalised the lynching by alleging that Muslims smuggle cows. And Union minister Arjun Ram Meghwal said the rising graph of lynchings reflected the growing popularity of Prime Minister Narendra Modi. In the Pehlu Khan lynching incident too, the Rajasthan home minister and senior police officials had described the victims as cow smugglers, and the police had registered criminal cases against his son and nephew, even as the men named by Pehlu Khan in his dying declaration were either deemed by the police to be innocent or are out on bail.

Thus, the messages junior rungs of the police receive from their superiors, in uniform or from the elected executive, in Rajasthan as in most parts of the country today, are clear—attacks on Muslims by mobs or men in uniform in the name of protecting the cow (or the "honour" of Hindu women) are understandable acts by provoked Hindus who love their religion, the cow and their country (in deplorable contrast to Indian Muslims). These police personnel belong to the same society that is today widely surcharged with communal hatred against Muslims and caste hatred against dalits. There is little in their training and leadership to encourage them to interrogate and, even less, abandon their communal and casteist instincts. If they are then extensively fuelled by open hate speech and encouragement of hate violence by those who control their careers, how can we blame just junior policepersons for the casual disregard they display for the law and for protecting the lives of Muslim and dalit victims of targeted hate violence?

An unsaid message

I end by examining the frank rationalisation of lynching by representatives of the Rashtriya Swayamsevak Sangh and the BJP that I have encountered in every television debate I have participated in (and watched) in recent weeks. This is that lynching is the outcome of understandable and righteous Hindu anger because Muslims refuse to respect Hindu sentiments and continue to illegally slaughter cows. To take just one recent public articulation of justification for lynching, let us listen more carefully to the words of Rajasthan minister Jayant Yadav. He appealed to Muslims to stop the business of cow smuggling and to understand and respect the sentiments of Hindus. "Smugglers stuff 50-50 cows into a truck to smuggle them and sprinkle acid on them," he told the news channel Aaj Tak. "I request Muslims to not take to cow smuggling as this hurts the sentiments of the Hindus." Lynching occurs, he added, because this "boils the blood of Hindus".

There are, of course, innumerable problems with this kind of reasoning that is widely peddled to validate mob violence. Even if it were true that Muslims generally smuggle cows and Hindus as a whole object to cow slaughter, it does not justify in any way the raising of a single hand against a Muslim (or any other person) who is transporting cows. His guilt or lack of it must be resolved only by the process established by law.

But even apart from this, the alleged Hindu-Muslim divide on the question of cow slaughter is a disingenuous, false and communally mischievous construction. Since incidents of lynching of dairy farmers in Nuh have grown in recent years, I have come to know closely the communities to which Pehlu Khan and Rakbar Khan belong. They love cows no less than any Hindu farmer. Both Pehlu Khan and Rakbar Khan were lynched when they were transporting dairy cows that they had bought for milk, not slaughter. Both had borrowed and spent Rs 25,000 to Rs 30,000 on each cow. The maximum a person can earn from selling a cow for slaughter is Rs 5,000 to Rs 8,000. It is, therefore, indisputable that they were legitimate and lawful dairy farmers, not illicit smugglers of cows for slaughter. Despite this, senior ministers, elected representatives of the BJP and the police persist in slandering them as cow smugglers. On the other hand, many Hindus also eat cow meat. The BJP needs to clarify if they regard dalits to be Hindus, and if they do, how can they generalise that all Hindus oppose cow slaughter? What about Hindus who live in Assam and Kerala? And then, of course, the ordinary farmer, both Hindu and Muslim, who may deeply love the cow, but who does not have the wherewithal to feed and rear the cow when her milk dries and she ages?

Adityanath, the saffron-clad chief minister of India's most populous state, Uttar Pradesh, declared that human beings must be protected, but so must cows. "It is the responsibility of every individual, every community, every religion to respect each other's sentiments," he said, days after Rakbar Khan's lynching. What he implied, but did not say explicitly, was that Muslims must respect the alleged sentiments of Hindus, but Hindus owe Muslims no such obligation.

In other words, the BJP unambiguously places the burden of

ending lynching violence on the principal victims of this violence, the country's Muslims. Muslims in India, after all, are themselves responsible for their own lynching.

First published in Scroll as "Alwar lynching shows the government has put the burden of ending mob killings on victims themselves", July 31, 2018.

◆•◆

MANIPUR NOTES, NOVEMBER 26 TO 28, 2018

Karwan-e-Mohabbat

The Armed Forces (Assam and Manipur) Special Powers Act (AFSPA), 1958, emerged out of a snarl of stopgap executive commands and ordinances, but remains in force today. Its presence through the generations has ensured that democracy in Manipur was brutalised beyond recognition. In this mutant form of democracy, a civil society organisation called the Extra-Judicial Execution Victim Families Association of Manipur (EEVFAM) can exist, and may even see its membership grow over the decades. It is a democracy that can shrug aside Irom Sharmila's sixteen-year protest fast; and which sees no shame in coming to global attention when a group of stark naked Imas (mothers) stand outside a garrison and call out, "Indian Army, rape us!" None of it impels any change of heart or procedures.

On its twenty-third journey of solidarity, the Karwan visited Manipur, where fundamental rights have only ever been a textbook concept, and new forms of violence emerge continually, to little surprise, if lasting grief.

In Manipur, we began our journey in Lilong in Thoubal district, visiting the family of twenty-six-year-old MBA student Farooq Khan, who, on September 13, 2018, was lynched to death by a crowd of people in Tharoijam village, almost 40 kms from his home. In a widely circulated video of the incident, one can see the presence of police personnel as well as children, as Farooq lies in a wide field helpless and wounded.

A large group of his friends arrived to interact with the Karwan team. Each of them spoke, with deep emotion and pain, sharing their memories of Khan as a bright, generous and promising young man.

His parents and siblings are devastated by the loss and distraught in their grief, unable to comprehend the injustice of losing their youngest son in this brutal manner. They are anguished at what they see as a very slow pace of police investigation, with the two men who accompanied Farooq still not having been apprehended for questioning seventy days later.

Although the facts of what happened will come to light only after the police investigation is over, what is particularly troubling about this incident is the way it seems to follow the pattern of other incidents of lynching in many parts of the country. These include rumours of a person from a minority religion or caste being a thief, the gathering of a crowd, lynching by the mob being filmed and circulated, many bystanders watching but not intervening, the police standing by, and slow police action to apprehend the attackers.

Our next visit in Thoubal was to the home of Salima Memcha, a widow who had shown great courage and resilience in pursuing justice after her husband, Fazruddin, had been killed in an extra-judicial manner in 2010. Supported by the Extra-Judicial Execution Victim Families Association (EEVFAM), Salima has pursued the case with great resolve and recently been awarded compensation by the High Court.

Salima shared with the Karwan that it was very important for her to pursue justice instead of remaining silent, because her fight is part of a larger campaign to confront the impunity of security forces and assert the rights and dignity of the people of Manipur. The Karwan members were moved by the brave struggle of this barely lettered single woman, to raise her family, to resist all intimidation and pressure, and to pursue justice in order to ensure—as she told Karwan members—that others don't have to suffer the way she did.

On the second day, the Karwan met with a group of people from the Kuki and Naga communities, all of whom represented families of victims of extra-judicial killings and police firing. There were Kuki women whose family members had died in police firing during anti-dam protests against the construction of the Khuga Dam, and Naga men from Nungleibam whose loved ones had died in shootings by the Jammu and Kashmir Rifles battalion of the Army. The solidarity meeting was also attended by pastors from AMCO, the All-Manipur Christian Organisation, and leaders of the All-Manipur Muslim Organisation Coordination Committee.

The team of Karwan members visited Malom to meet with families of the ten innocents who were killed on November 2, 2000, in the Malom firing by a battalion of the Assam Rifles. It was deeply moving to witness how raw the wounds of the surviving parents, siblings and widows are even after eighteen years. All of them also again reiterated that their pursuit of justice is aimed towards the larger goal of peace-building in Manipuri society.

This journey of solidarity in Manipur was facilitated and made possible through the efforts and long-term work of various human rights defenders, notably Babloo Loitongbam and his team at Human Rights Alert, the women who spearhead the work of EEVFAM, and individual lawyers and civil society activists committed to the pursuit of justice and reconciliation in this land.

The Karwan applauds the relentless work of civil society activists, particularly EEVFAM, in documenting 1528 cases of extra-judicial killings that demonstrate a systemic pattern of shootings over the last three decades.

The decades of insurgency and counter-insurgency operations with literally thousands of extra-judicial killings and disappearances have left enormous unhealed wounds in the collective psyche of the Manipuri people. The members of the Karwan-e-Mohabbat are convinced after their travels through Manipur that this is an important historical moment in which these wounds can possibly be healed, if the state, civil society and the victims come together for this. We believe that justice needs to be ensured at least for the cases that are being considered by the Supreme Court for which evidence is available. But for the larger numbers of killings and encounters, what Manipur needs is a Truth and Reconciliation initiative in which the intense suffering and injustice that the people have undergone is publicly acknowledged, the innocence of the victims affirmed, and a public apology made. Manipur needs a policy of reparations for the victims who continue to suffer penury and loss even decades after their loved ones are taken away from them; this must also include monthly pensions for single women whose male relations have been killed or disappeared.

Karwan-e-Mohabbat India, 2018

——◆◆◆——

"NO, THIS LAND AND COUNTRY IS NOT OURS ANYMORE": AN OPEN LETTER FROM AN INDIAN STUDENT

Aslah K. Vadakara

This letter, written in 2015 by a student of Historical Studies at the Nalanda International University, Bihar, speaks from the heart about the pain of your country—your home—having no place for you any longer.

Much love, everyone.

I am Aslah, twenty-one years old, a post-graduate student in history. I have a few things to tell this world.

During our schooldays, we had to study history. The world's largest country was Russia, the smallest country the Vatican, the most populated country China—all this we learnt by heart.

Also, when we were asked about the largest democracy in the world, we would enthusiastically write *India*.

During our school assemblies, while the national anthem was being sung, we were respectful, still. We even smacked any friend on the head if he made a nuisance of himself. Watching police and army on the cinema screen gave us gooseflesh. In my schooldays, I dreamt, with open eyes, of becoming a collector and serving my India.

But I have something different to tell all of you now. This is someone else's country now. Not ours. Yes. That's what we have experienced.

This is a student, who has lived in India for twenty-one years, telling the world, "This country is not mine." I don't intend to open bundles of history. Just a few incidents that took place within the last week.

A fifty-year-old man was beaten to death by a mob in a place called Dadri, near the country's capital. His son was brutally attacked. Why was Muhammad Akhlaq beaten to death? Because he was a Muslim and a rumour spread that he had consumed beef. Who killed him? Followers of the Hindu powers ruling India. Yes, he stored mutton in his refrigerator. And it was rumoured that what was stored was beef, and he was killed because he was a Muslim and he "ate beef".

Oh, and what did this country's government do? They sent the meat to a forensic laboratory to find out what it was. Even ministers justified the murder. The Prime Minister seemed busy and had nothing to say.

The ruling party's ideological guides continue to let us know that anyone consuming beef will meet the same fate.

The second day after this cruel incident, a ninety-year-old man was burnt to death in Uttar Pradesh. Burnt to death. He was a dalit and had tried entering a temple. If he entered the temple, it would become impure; they burnt him alive at the entrance.

Again, two days after this incident, in the same state, a dalit family was stripped naked on the road by the police. Because, according to the Hindu jati system, they belong to the lowest caste.

The same day, a twelve-year-old dalit student was beaten by a teacher for touching a plate "meant for non-dalits" during the mid-day meal at his school.

All this happened in this country, over six days. Whoever opposes this is killed. They shot and killed M.M. Kalburgi, a prominent writer and Kannada University vice-chancellor, because he would always respond.

They jail people for years without a trial, using horrific laws. Thousands of Muslim and dalit youth are in jails.

Sometimes the government may kill directly. They killed Ishrat Jahan, a Muslim woman, in a fake encounter, and they hanged Afzal Guru.

It is very difficult for a Muslim to own a home, even in a city like Mumbai.

This is the country where a young dalit man was killed because the ringtone on his phone praised Dr B.R. Ambedkar, father of the Indian Constitution.

No, this land and country is not ours anymore. I don't feel safe in this country, a Muslim with an Arabic name. My dalit friend's honour has no value in this country.

Because I am a Muslim, I have no right to choose my food in this country.

The world has to know. India is no longer a democracy. The prime minister himself is the inner energy for this violence against humanity. When he was the chief minister of Gujarat, it was his party that led the genocide of Muslims. He even compared Muslims to helpless puppies caught under motor wheels.

I don't know what I may have to face after writing this. But whatever it is, it doesn't matter to me. This is the truth.

Your brother, 11-10-2015, Bihar

First published in Indian Cultural Forum, October 24, 2015

A SYMBOLIC MORAL GESTURE

K.P. Ramanunni

Malayalam writer K.P. Ramanunni's first novel Sufi Paranja Katha (What the Sufi Said) *dealt with an inter-faith marriage and the subsequent dialogue between a convert's past and present, amid the tug of divergent loyalties. In 1995, it was awarded the Kerala Sahitya Akademi Award. His fourth novel,* Daivathinte Pusthakam (God's Own Book) *won the Kendra Sahitya Akademi Award in 2017. Ramanunni, who once fasted in solidarity with Irom Sharmila, now used his award to reawaken the public conscience after the murder of the teenager Junaid Khan. What follows is his statement after receiving the Sahitya Akademi Award on February 16, 2018.*

Dear Friends,

After accepting the Sahitya Akademi Award I now come in your midst in order to make a symbolic, moral gesture. Let me explain briefly. The book that earned me this award is *God's Own Book* which is, so to speak, my extra grief at the present plight of the world and humanity, and a writer's imaginative struggle to renovate them.

But beyond this, in the present Indian situation, *God's Own Book (Daivathinte Pustakam)* carries out an enormous political mission as well, And that is to uphold the love of other religions cherished by true Hinduism, to build a conceptual foundation for religious amity, to put up a bulwark against the country's catastrophic slide into communal ruin, *Daivathinte Pusthakam* is a book where the Prophet Muhammad Nabi, calls Krishnan "ikka" (elder brother) and Krishnan affectionately calls the Prophet "muthe" (precious dear). They are presented as if they are brothers. Both Krishnan and Nabi, who share a number of personality traits, who go through life's predicaments that are similar, do not ask their followers to engage in conflicts but to live in love and harmony.

Since this is the message that the novel presents, I have the obligation to disseminate it on the occasion of the Award function too, that is why I shall now take only three rupees from the award amount, and leave the rest to Junaid's mother (Ammi). Junaid is one who was killed by Hindu communalists just for being a Muslim. Let me place this award amount as an offering at the feet of Junaid's mother, thus doing penance for that wicked sin, for penance is a special observance in the true Hindu tradition. Yes, I am a true Hindu, l am a true Hindu.

I hope our great India's literary world endorse this humble gesture.

What was the incident?

On June 22, 2017, Junaid Khan, a fifteen-year-old boy, and his brothers and cousin, were returning to their village in Haryana after a day-trip to Delhi to shop for Eid, when a murderous mob turned on them. The crowd shouted communal abuses at the Muslim men, also yelling they were "anti-nationals". Junaid's brother Haseeb's cap was pulled off his head and his beard was grabbed and pulled because they looked "different". Finally, Junaid was stabbed to death, and his body was later thrown off the train at a railway station just 30 kms from New Delhi. Junaid, who was killed just because he happened to be Muslim, had new clothes for Eid celebration with him.

◆•◆

NO CLOSURE FOR KASHMIR'S HALF WIDOWS

Gulzar Bhat

Over the last three decades, thousands of men have been "disappeared" in Kashmir—taken away by men in uniform and never seen or heard from again. Governments have changed at the Centre, but the fate of the "half-widows", the wives of many of these men, of the parents, siblings, children of these men, has not changed. As Gulzar Bhat writes, "Although a 2011 investigation by the State Human Rights Commission found nearly 2730 corpses interred in a plethora of unmarked graves across four districts of the Valley, the government is yet to come up with a rehabilitation policy for the families of victims of enforced disappearance."

Whenever she passes by a motor garage, she halts for a while and looks carefully at the men—mechanics, welders, painters—working there. Heaving a deep sigh, she walks past with heavy steps. Among these workers, she tries to look for her disappeared husband who used to paint vehicles in a local garage. Once every month, despite her multiple ailments, fifty-five-year-old Dilshada shows up in Srinagar's Pratap Park to join a peaceful protest alongside scores of family members of victims of enforced disappearances.

In the nineties when the insurgency in Kashmir was at its peak and a constant rat-a-tat of machine guns was heard everywhere, one afternoon, on June 12, 1992, Dilshada's young husband Bashir Ahmad (27), an automobile painter by profession, left home for work and never returned.

A neighbour had seen Ahmad, a resident of Zukura, Srinagar, being bundled into a vehicle by some gun-toting men in uniform. After searching for him a few days, on June 16 Dilshada registered an FIR with a nearby police station.

"I failed to get any trace of him. I looked for him in all the BSF and army camps in Srinagar but I am sure he vanished into some military facility," said Dilshada.

As Ahmad was the sole bread earner of his family, Dilshada, a mother of three—all in the age group of two to nine years at the time—had to confront new challenges on many fronts. To make ends meet, Dilshada took up a number of jobs. She worked in a boutique, washed clothes in her neighbourhood and also did some menial jobs at different construction sites in the city. She worked beyond normal hours and that took a toll on her health.

"I would stitch till late night. That not only affected my eyes but also become a reason for many orthopedic conditions," she said.

After a couple of years, her elder son Imtiyaz Ahmad quit his studies to help his mother. He worked as a bus conductor.

Dilshada's tribulations did not end here. In 2001, her middle son Riyaz Ahmad, fifteen, vanished mysteriously after he had left for school. After many days of useless search, Dilshada visited the office of a prominent local newspaper and got a missing report along with the picture of her son published. The next day, she received a phone call from a resident of Baramulla who said that he, along with fellow villagers, had recently interred the dead body of a youth who resembled the picture carried by the newspaper. A devastated Dilshada did not lose a minute to get there, and found her son interred under an oblong mound of earth.

"The locals told me that he had died after he was hit by a speeding vehicle and when his body was not claimed by anyone for a few days they buried him in a local graveyard," Dilshada recounts with misty eyes.

In 2000, Dilshada joined the Association of Parents of Disappeared Persons (APDP), an NGO fighting for justice for the victims of enforced disappearances. She takes part in its peaceful demonstrations, organised monthly, to seek the whereabouts of those who vanished from the custody of the forces.*

Leading the life of a half widow for more than two decades, all but broken by two consecutive tragedies, Dilshada has received no help from the state or central government.

"Government never ever helped me. My family is still reeling under the worst financial constraints. It is only the APDP that provides me some small financial support," said Dilshada who still searches for her husband.

---

*These gatherings of the APDP take place on the tenth of every month, as December 10 is International Human Rights Day. The number of enforced disappearances is hard to ascertain. The APDP's figure puts it in the range of eight to ten thousand people, since 1989. The uncertainty about the exact number indicates the loss of both trust and control that comes with a military occupation. The state and the people use different yardsticks of measurement and no independent sources exist to verify facts against rumour and propaganda.

Although a 2011 investigation by the State Human Rights Commission found nearly 2730 corpses interred in a plethora of unmarked graves across four districts of the Valley, the government is yet to come up with a rehabilitation policy for the families of victims of enforced disappearance.

Indian Cultural Forum, October 6, 2017. First published in The Citizen, *October 6, 2017, as 'There Has Never Been Any Closure for Kashmir's Half Widows'*

———— •••• ————

THE KASHMIR YOU WILL NEVER UNDERSTAND

Faakirah Irfan

"What nationalism makes you agree with, and defend, genocide, rape, and murder?" This question sums up the estrangement, sorrow and raw anger of many in Kashmir, like the author, a young law student.

As I write this, the Internet connections of various service providers have been shut down. The social media services have been banned, and the only thing working in the state of Kashmir is the ongoing conflict.

The government stands prepared against the wrath of Kashmiris, ready to silence their voices, whether online or with bullets to the chest.

A lot has been written about the ongoing conflict in Kashmir. There is nothing much to add to it. However, as a storyteller, it is my job to let society know the truth that is being suppressed. This is to help those not living in conflict zones realise what it feels like to have virtually any say over your life taken away from you.

Without going into a comparison about the authenticity of narratives, I would like to narrate the reality I know.

I am Sakeena, Raffia, Ayushee. I am a woman living in the strife-torn state of Kashmir. A state that you see often being debated on your news channels, where the anchors, sitting miles away from us, ask us to meet them at a place of understanding. They do not, however, realise the worlds we'd have to cross to reach their smug certitude. Nor will they ever know how it feels to look into the face of your blind daughter, who would never be able to see the marvellous beauty of her hometown. Her eyes and the eyes of the future of Kashmir are bound tight by a big tricolor and marked as "collateral damage".

Nor will the social media warriors zealously defending the integrity of their nation-state by waging an online war ever understand the plight of the mother who lost her only son to a bullet. She will never understand your nationalism or the patriarchal state because there is something called motherhood, which has been snatched away from her.

You will see her rise in a rage against your soldiers; you will see her anger melt into tears. But you will never understand her.

Nor will the people sitting in their drawing rooms, sipping rose-flavoured green tea, understand that the media are selling Kashmiris as terrorists to them. They can paint our demand for freedom as terrorism because you let them do it. Nor will you ever know what happens in the alleys of Kashmir, except what they want you to know. They have maimed a generation back here, while you watched them feed you nationalism.

What country are you trying to build on the bodies of young boys from Kashmir?

What nationalism makes you agree with, and defend, genocide, rape and murder?

You will never understand what a Kashmiri goes through when he hears the sound of a blast. We have had grenades and bullets come at us, and have lost our taste for the fire-crackers of celebrations.

Nor will the ministers residing in posh localities in Kashmir understand how it feels to be stuck outside government offices trying to locate where your husband, child, father went missing fifteen years ago.

Nor will they ever understand the tears that flow from a child's face when he sees burials and death.

Playgrounds in villages turn into graveyards, but you will never understand the wrath in the soul of that child.

Nor will you understand that we try to exist even as the occupation erases us as far as it can. So when you talk about Kashmir and try to see us through your nationalism and occupation-tinted glasses, know that your nationalism consumes the blood of innocents. Ask yourself if it is okay for you to defend your countrymen who loot, kill and plunder on my soil.

While you wave your nationalism at me, I try and wave my humanity before you. Will you ever see that?

By the time you try and begin to reach out in understanding, my Internet connection might be shut down in the name of your national security.

Indian Cultural Forum, August 17, 2017. Published first in Cafe Dissensus, July 27, 2017.

CONVERSATION: NANDINI SUNDAR ON A STATE WITHOUT A CONSTITUTION

Indian Cultural Forum

"We must state that we were aghast at the blindness to constitutional limitations of the state of Chattisgarh, and some of its advocates, in claiming that anyone who questions the conditions of inhumanity that are rampant in many parts of that state ought to necessarily be treated as Maoists, or their sympathisers, and yet in the same breath also claim that it needs the constitutional sanction, under our Constitution, to perpetrate its policies of ruthless violence against the people of Chattisgarh to establish a

Constitutional order." Justices B. Sudershan Reddy and Surinder Singh Nijjar, Supreme Court of India, issued this order on July 5, 2011 declaring the Salwa Judum and other vigilante groups in the State of Chhattisgarh "unconstitutional".

This order was pronounced on the writ petition filed by Nandini Sundar and others following the burning of hundreds of homes, rape and murder of adivasis by the police and security forces in the villages of Tadmetla, Morapalli and Timmapuram between March 11 and 16, in 2011. The Supreme Court ordered the CBI to inquire into the incident and provide a "status report" within six weeks. It took repeated efforts to push the CBI to conduct the inquiry and then release the report, made public in October 2016; a full five years after the Supreme Court passed its order. It indicted the Chhattisgarh state police, the erstwhile Special Police Officers (SPOs) or Koya Commandos (now renamed Auxiliary Armed Forces), and CRPF/COBRA paramilitary force for burning over 200 homes of adivasis in the name of fighting Maoists.

Teaching social anthropology at the University of Delhi, Professor Nandini Sundar deals with some of the oldest inhabited forests of central India, an area far removed from the corridors of power in Delhi, corridors which dictate state policy. This conversation for the Indian Cultural Forum between Vidhya and Nandini Sundar reveals the nature of the case in Tadmetla, Dantewada district.

Vidhya (V): Over the last two decades, what has been the impact of state policy in Chhattisgarh? Could you explain this in the context of Tadmetla?

Nandini Sundar (NS): Tadmetla has been targeted since 2006. The whole area was under attack from 2006 to 2007, homes were burnt, and people were killed over a sustained period of time. Then, in 2010, there was an ambush by the Maoists where seventy-six CRPF personnel were killed. In its wake, the people of Tadmetla were expecting some retaliation by the police. In a way it has always been a very tense area. It has always been cut off and there are no schools functioning there after the Salwa Judum started operating in the area. There is a local sarpanch, Podiyam Panda. When the security forces and police attacked in 2011, he persuaded people to remain in the village. Usually, the people of the area run away when their homes are attacked. This time, he asked them not to flee. He called the press, urged them to take up the case, and got everything going. The people in Tadmetla have been very keen to get some kind of justice. They've been testifying and talking about what happened to them. Three people were killed and three women raped besides the hundreds of homes burnt and looted. The people of Tadmetla have been coming to Jagdalpur whenever they've been asked. But with the recent spate of mass surrenders and arrests, which are clearly false surrenders orchestrated by the police, they are being targeted again. So, for the people of Tadmetla, it is a continuous history of being targeted and harassed.

V: Why did the people of Tadmetla decide to file a petition for a CBI inquiry in the Supreme Court? What about the three people killed and three raped?

NS: Sarpanch Panda gave them the courage to talk about it and take up the case. Initially, people weren't keen on filing it. Rather than running away, the sarpanch appealed to the people to fight it. There were times when many of them couldn't come for hearings in the court of Jagdalpur due to the security forces' ongoing "combing operations" in the village. And, there were times when the people of Tadmetla felt disillusioned, wondered what the point of it all is, especially when nothing appeared to be coming out of all this effort. There was some resistance at times. But, on the whole, the people of Tadmetla have been coming and deposing before the court in Jagdalpur.

The CBI inquiry did take up the question of the three people killed and three women raped during the police operation. The fundamental mistake that the CBI has made, and continues to make, is that they took the police FIR as the primary FIR. The FIR filed by the villagers should be the primary FIR as it is based on the complaint initially filed by the villagers. This is something we have been saying again and again, that the CBI were not directed to take up the police FIR. They were directed to investigate what happened in Morpalli, Tadmetla and Timmapuram in March 2011. So the CBI has all along been helping the government and, despite that, if they found the police guilty, then it counts for something. Even now, they are not indicting anyone for the rapes and murders.

So, by taking up the police FIR, they committed two serious mistakes; one is treating the police officer who filed the FIR (the person who led the operation) as the complainant in the case. So now, even when they file the charge sheet, he is officially listed as the complainant, though he should actually be listed as an accused. Secondly, the police FIR only mentions arson by the Maoists, and does not say anything about the rapes, the killings and the looting. The CBI wrote this strange initial report. Then we wasted a whole year reminding them of the rapes, killings and looting. The way they mentioned it in the status report was that in the course of investigations they discovered that rapes and murders had also happened. So, in December 2015, the court asked them if these rapes and murders happened at the same time as the burning of homes, or are they things the CBI found subsequently. The CBI was supposed to file an affidavit clarifying this. They did not do so for a long time. They did it in August 2016 because we pressed for it in the court.

The CBI was investigating the rapes and murders right from the beginning. But the way they wrote their status reports was really mealy-mouthed and problematic. Fighting that has taken a whole lot of time. Even now they are claiming that the rape cases could not be substantiated as the women could not identify who raped them. This, they argue, is because there was no other evidence available, i.e. forensic evidence. In one case, where a woman was raped, they took her saree. The first time the CBI visited the village was in January 2012, almost a year after the incident. The events happened in 2011. Ten months later they take her saree. This adivasi woman has only two sarees and she has washed them many times since the event. We told the CBI officials that they are not going to get any biological evidence. We told them not to use the saree to say that there is no evidence when it was clearly not worth collecting in the first place. But they've said in the report that the saree revealed no forensic evidence. And that she could not identify who raped her. Therefore, they've argued, the CBI cannot say she was raped. This is simply ridiculous. They've done this with all the women who've filed cases of rape by saying that these women cannot identify who raped them and there is no other evidence to prove otherwise. Now, we are contesting it in the court.

V: After this CBI status report, five years after the incident, what does the future hold for the people of Tadmetla?

NS: The villagers will have to travel to Raipur to depose because the case is now in the CBI special court. So it is actually a crazy system. First, they have taken five years to establish that somebody has done something, i.e. burned hundreds of homes, and they have established this in a half-hearted way. Second, they expect the villagers to come and fight their case in Raipur while they keep putting up bureaucratic hurdles. This procedure appears to be going nowhere. I don't know if the people themselves are disillusioned. I haven't been to the area to talk to anybody in a while.

The people of Tadmetla have had to come and depose repeatedly and, after all this time, all they have heard is that the rape victims could not identify the rapist and there is no evidence on their saree. Which rape victim is going to come all the way to Raipur again to say the same thing? The CBI can't even visit the area without being attacked. With Kalluri, how is the CBI going to investigate any further? There has to be something conducive to normal rule of law, investigation, and, if everybody who takes up this issue is going to have their effigy burnt, attacked and threatened, this will not go anywhere.*

---

*On October 25, 2016, TheWire.in reported a WhatsApp message announcing that security personnel in Kondagaon district would be

V: How do you think this ruling will affect other cases in Chhattisgarh? Will this CBI report set a precedent?

NS: Well, it doesn't seem like the state government is listening to the Supreme Court. They talk about peace talks on the one hand, and burn effigies of the petitioners on the other. I mean, Manish Kunjam's press conference was attacked by twenty-five or so men. One is forced to ask if they believe there is a Constitution at all. They don't seem to think that the word exists anymore. There is a complete culture of impunity.

Postscript

IGP S.R.P. Kalluri has never taken kindly to interference from "outsiders" in his ham-fisted efforts to bring "law and order" to Chhattisgarh. Attacking journalists, lawyers, activists, teachers, doctors and adivasis who speak out against police violence, the Chhattisgarh State police is infamous for its human rights violations and harassment of those who dissent. In the wake of the CBI's report and subsequent charge sheet against seven officials, the temerity of the Chhattisgarh police was evident when it burned effigies of several human rights activists and journalists, including Professor Sundar, threatened the petitioners in press conferences, and, most outrageously, on November 8, 2016, filed a case of criminal conspiracy, murder, rioting under

---

burning the effigies of Nandini Sundar, CPI leader Manish Kunjam, social activists Himanshu Kumar and Bela Bhatia, Aam Aadmi Party leader Soni Sori (herself previously a victim of police atrocity), and journalist Malini Subramaniam—who, while working from Jagdalpur as a correspondent for Scroll.in, had been forced to leave Bastar under mob pressure. This extraordinary political demonstration by men in uniform came on the heels of an October 23 press conference by the IG, Bastar Range, S.R.P. Kalluri, where he claimed that the houses of adivasis had spontaneously ignited on account of the great heat in Chhattisgarh. The effigy-burning was duly carried out by police and armed auxiliary forces, and was followed by personnel in uniform marching through several towns, in a show of strength.

Sections 120-B, 302, 147, 148 and 149 of the Indian Penal Code (IPC) against Nandini Sundar, Archana Prasad (Professor, JNU), Vineet Tiwari (Joshi Adhikari Institute and Communist Party of India), Sanjay Parate (Chhattisgarh state secretary, Communist Party of India [Marxist]) and others at the Tongpal Police Station. They were charged with killing an adivasi, Shamnath Baghel—a charge contested by Baghel's wife. The inspector general went on to declare that, "strongest possible action" would be taken and announced to the media that Professor Sundar faces immediate arrest. The threat of arrest was subsequently rescinded after an uproar from members of civil society all over the country and a damning order by the NHRC summoning the chief secretary of the Government of Chhattisgarh and the IGP of Bastar for abuse of power.

The immediate consequence of speaking up for the people of Chhattisgarh appears to be criminal charges, threats, and sustained harassment. Kalluri, along with other senior officers of the Chhattisgarh State police, met Home Minister Rajnath Singh, held press conferences to defend their actions, filed cases against activists, and proclaimed that activists are enemies who incite the people of India. Declaring a "Mission 2016—to eliminate Maoism" and propping up vigilante groups like Samajik Ekta Manch and AGNI (Action Group for National Integrity), the Chhattisgarh police has attacked lawyers, journalists and civil rights groups attempting to conduct fact-findings in the area. In December 2016, Advocate Shalini Gera of Jagdalpur Legal Aid Group (JagLAG) along with others who were part of the legal team for Kumma Pottam (father of a thirteen-year-old boy allegedly killed during a fake encounter) were investigating his son's case. While in Jagdalpur on the orders of the High Court, they were harassed by the police and accused of laundering money for the Maoists.* Gera and the team managed to avoid being arrested.

---

*The fact that the minor's body had been exhumed for an autopsy, following an order of the Chhattisgarh High Court, may explain the desperation of the police to frame Gera anyhow.

Just days before Gera faced these charges, on December 26, 2016, a seven-member team from the Telangana Democratic Forum (TDF) was picked up from Telangana, declared as arrested in Sukma, Chhattisgarh, and charged under the same sections. They continue to languish in jail.*

On January 7, 2017, the National Human Rights Commission (NHRC) issued an interim report that held the Chhattisgarh State Police guilty of raping sixteen tribal women and asserted that "prima-facie, human rights of the victims have been grossly violated by the security personnel of the Government of Chhattisgarh for which the State Government is vicariously liable." The NHRC came to this conclusion after hearing fourteen of the thirty-four women and is yet to bring out a complete report on the matter. On January 19 and 20, Bela Bhatia had accompanied the team investigating the cases of women who had registered complaints of rape, sexual assault and loot by the security forces in 2015. In a move that is intended to terrorise such social activists, on January 22, Bhatia's home was gheraoed by members of AGNI, she was threatened with physical violence and hounded out of her residence. On January 25, Bela Bhatia met the chief minister of Chhattisgarh, Raman Singh, and appealed to him to ensure the "observation of the rule of law by all state institutions including the police".

When human rights organisations appealed to IG S.R.P. Kalluri to ensure the safety of Bela Bhatia, he responded with abuses and said, "Maoists and their dogs like you will be stoned out of Bastar. Beware."

Indian Cultural Forum, January 26, 2017

———◆◆◆———

*The team remained in jail for the next seven months and were not granted bail till July 2017.

WRITE DOWN "I AM A MIYAH"

Hafiz Ahmed

On April 29, 2016 Assamese poet Hafiz Ahmed posted the poem "Write Down 'I Am a Miyah'" on his Facebook page. Shalim M. Hussain wrote a response to it the same day in English, and, the following day, in one of the Char-Chapori dialects. Soon, a movement had begun: Miyah Poetry. Fifteen poets from all over Assam claimed the term "Miyah"—a derogatory term for Muslims—and spoke powerfully, defiantly of their experience, the hostility and prejudice they face, and their refusal to be cowed down and bullied into surrendering their rights as citizens.

Write
Write down
I am a Miyah
My serial number in the NRC* is 200543
I have two children
Another is coming
Next summer.
Will you hate him
As you hate me?

Write
I am a Miyah
I turn waste, marshy lands
To green paddy fields
To feed you.
I carry bricks
To build your buildings
Drive your car
For your comfort
Clean your drain
To keep you healthy.

---

*National Register of Citizens

I have always been
In your service
And yet
you are dissatisfied!
Write down
I am a Miyah,
A citizen of a democratic, secular Republic,
Without any rights,
My mother a D voter
Though her parents are Indian.

If you wish, kill me, drive me from my village,
Snatch my green fields
Hire bulldozers
To roll over me.
Your bullets
Can shatter my breast
For no crime.

Write
I am a Miyah
Of the Brahamaputra
Your torture
Has burnt my body black
Reddened my eyes with fire.
Beware!
I have nothing but anger in stock.
Keep away!
Or
Turn to ashes.

Translated by Shalim M. Hussain. First published on the Sunflower Collective Blogspot, September 12, 2016.

A RETURN TO THE BAD OLD DAYS
IN ASSAM?

Vivan Eyben

The National Register of Citizens (NRC) came into being after the census of 1951. In 2013, following decades of ethno-linguistic and communal agitations in Assam, the register for that state began to be updated under the monitoring of the Supreme Court, and the complete draft NRC list for Assam was released in July 2018. The initial criterion for recognition as a bona fide citizen was the appearance of a candidate's name in any official Indian document prior to March 25, 1971—with the young obliged to prove the identity of an ancestor, "legacy person" being the term in parlance. In a move seen as favouring Hindu immigrants (primarily from Bangladesh, formerly East Pakistan), to whom the BJP had promised recognition and citizenship during its 2014 election campaign, the central government introduced its Citizenship (Amendment) Bill, 2016. The Bill introduces a new date, December 31, 2014, as the cut-off date for immigrants coming into Assam to apply for citizenship—but specifies that this will apply only to non-muslim immigrants. As Vivan Eyben points out, the Citizenship (Amendment) Bill 2016 has further muddied the waters in Assam, where there is already uproar over the exclusion of over four million applicants in the final draft of the NRC, and no clarity on what is to be done with the excluded. Meanwhile, India is at risk of violating international covenants of human rights to which it is a signatory.

Assam appears to be on the cusp of returning to the bad old days. On November 1, 2018, five Bengali-speaking people were shot dead by gunmen dressed in battle fatigues in Bisonimukh village in Tinsukia district. Targeted killing of non-Assamese people has been a calling card of the United Liberation Front of Assam (ULFA) in the past. Initial reports had pinned the blame on the Paresh Baruah-led ULFA (Independent) [ULFA (I)] faction. However, ULFA (I) has denied any role in the Bisonimukh killings.

ULFA's denial of involvement should be believed, as they

have a history of admitting when they are behind an attack, be it a blast or otherwise. On October 12, a low-intensity blast was detonated in Panbazar, near the migrant majority area of Fancy Bazar in Guwahati. ULFA (I) had claimed responsibility for the blast and stated that it was a warning to all those opposed to the National Register of Citizens (NRC) as well as those favouring the settlement of Hindu Bangladeshis in Assam.

Despite what most media reports would lead one to believe, the issue in Assam is not so much the NRC exercise which aims to update the citizenship register in the state (and is now being monitored by the Supreme Court), but rather the Citizenship (Amendment) Bill, 2016.

Why is the BJP promoting the Citizenship Bill?

The Citizenship Bill, as distinct from the NRC, is an attempt by the BJP to amend the existing citizenship law in India to enable non-Muslims (and—curious specification this—"non-atheists") from Afghanistan, Bangladesh and Pakistan to be treated as persecuted minorities and easily acquire Indian citizenship.* The Bill has faced backlash on many fronts. The mainstream political parties such as the Trinamool Congress (TMC) among others have highlighted that the Bill is discriminatory against persecuted Muslim communities. However, the loudest opposition to the Bill has come from civil society organisations and student groups from across the Northeast. These organisations fear that the Northeastern states would be overwhelmed by Hindu immigrants from Bangladesh.

In Assam specifically, the issue with the Bill is that many believe Hindu undocumented migrants from Bangladesh far outnumber their Muslim counterparts. They also believe the NRC—once completed—will expose this fact.† However, the BJP is worried

---

*In other words, atheists with a Muslim background need not apply.

†Out of 3.29 crore applicants, 2.89 crore were included in the final draft of the NRC, published on July 30, 2018. To enable the excluded to file

that revealing these facts will erode its voter base, particularly in the Bengali-speaking areas of the Barak Valley. Thus, the Citizenship Bill has been thought up in order to ensure that the party's electoral assets are not compromised.

This view appears to be corroborated to some extent by certain events that have taken place in Assam in the past few weeks. Following the Panbazar blast, the founder and president of All Cachar Karimganj Hailakandi Students' Association (ACKHSA), Pradip Dutta Roy, told the press that the blast would not affect the will of the people. He then went on to declare his support for the Citizenship Bill—which would, naturally, be advantageous to the Chachar community, who are Hindu migrants—while alleging that the names of illegal migrants had been included in the NRC. To support this statement, Roy referred to the high acceptance rates in the districts of Dhubri, Karimganj, Goalpara and Barpeta, all of which have significant Muslim populations.

The Citizens' Rights Protection Coordination Committee and the North East Linguistic and Ethnic Coordination Committee have also voiced their contempt for Paresh Baruah's ULFA(I) while expressing their support for the Bill. However, perhaps what is most telling is the role of Shiladitya Dev, the BJP member of the legislative assembly from Hojai. He questioned Baruah's motives for the blast and told *The Telegraph* that if Baruah was genuinely in support of the Assamese people, he should question the inclusion rates in Dhubri.

Shiladitya Dev is also the mastermind behind organising around twenty-six [Hindu] Bengali associations to hold a rally in support of the Citizenship Bill. The rally was initially to be organised on November 17 at Khanapara ground in Guwahati. However, due to opposition from various groups, including Akhil

---

their claims and objections, the Supreme Court extended the deadline till December 31. Among the excluded were former chief minister Anwara Taimur, and the family of former president Fakhruddin Ali Ahmed. Out of 40,70,707 applicants for reconsideration, 37,59,630 names had been rejected by December 12, and 2,48,077 been put on hold.

Gogoi's Krishak Mukti Sangram Samiti (KMSS), the venue was shifted. Interestingly, Dev made a u-turn on the Bill on October 28. But, the u-turn also reveals the BJP's agenda—Dev had told reporters that the Bill would be unnecessary if the names of all Hindu Bengalis are included in the NRC.

The BJP is probably well aware of the polarising nature of this agenda. The party is also probably aware that the Citizenship Bill issue has widened the rift between the Brahmaputra and Barak Valleys. Yet, despite this knowledge, it appears to be hell-bent on ensuring citizenship for undocumented Hindu migrants. The fallout of such an agenda is likely to result in communal violence, this time based on language. The killings in Tinsukia were not carried out by ULFA(I). However, the tragedy may be the start of a trend.

Indefinite detention for those without documents

The report by Amnesty International on Assam's detention centres has once again highlighted the procedural lapses and lack of policy or law on the matter.

On November 23, Amnesty International released a report on foreigner detention centres in Assam.* The report highlights the procedural lapses in determining a person's citizenship status through the proceedings in the Foreigners Tribunals under the Foreigners Act, 1946. Further, the report also pays attention to the absence of policy, let alone regulation—whether statutory or otherwise—on how to deal with those declared foreigners. Though the report did note that the NRC process has contributed to anxiety among the Bengali-speaking population of Assam, the focus remained on the detention centres.

---

*Amnesty International had begun to voice its concerns about the NRC the day after the final draft of the citizen's list was published. Like other human rights and citizens' organisations, Amnesty flagged the issues of possible error and bias creeping into the list, and the unrealistic expectation of official documents from people living at subsistence level in remote areas barely connected to electricity, people who were also frequent victims of displacement by natural disasters.

Towards the end of its report, Amnesty International listed some "recommendations" to the Government of India and to the Government of Assam. To the Government of India, it recommended that detention should only be used as a last resort and that a statutory time limit on detaining "irregular foreigners" should be introduced. Regarding the Government of Assam, Amnesty recommended that the detained persons should be separated from ordinary convicts and undertrials, and housed in a separate facility. It also recommended drafting an operation manual as well as making provisions for healthcare, inclusive of mental health. With regard to children living in detention centres—which violates the Convention on the Rights of the Child—Amnesty recommended that the Assam government take steps to fulfil its legal duties in the children's best interests. Lastly, Amnesty International recommended that the Assam government allow independent audits of its detention facilities, and ensure that the principles of natural justice are followed in the Foreigners Tribunals.

The concerns that Amnesty International highlighted were also raised by Harsh Mander in his interlocutory application in *Re: Inhuman Conditions in 1382 Prisons.* On September 12, 2018, the Supreme Court passed an order issuing directions regarding the condition of the detention centres in Assam. The Union government was directed to prepare the manual of detention centres promptly, indicating that till now these centres had been operating in the absence of any guidelines.

The Government of Assam was directed to expedite the construction of a proper detention centre as an amount for the same had already been sanctioned by the Union government. The Court also directed the Assam government to look into the matter of families being separated after being declared foreigners. Since there is only one detention centre for women in Kokrajhar, children up to the age of six years stay with their mothers. After male children attained the age of six, they would be transferred to stay with their fathers. The Court also directed that the detained people be provided with cooking gas as all cooking was being done with wood.

Amnesty International's report also took into account that the friction between Assamese and Bengali speakers in Assam, including over the issue of migration—whether pre- or post-Partition—had been raised in the discussions of the Constituent Assembly, when the Constitutional provisions for citizenship were being debated.* It was argued that migration had to be curtailed with special reference to the inner line areas. At the time, Assam comprised present-day Assam, Meghalaya, Mizoram and Nagaland. The Governor of Assam—along with the Ministry of External Affairs—also exercised powers over Manipur and the North East Frontier Agency, now Arunachal Pradesh. The inner line is still in use by Arunachal Pradesh, Mizoram and Nagaland.

It is quite clear that the demand was not quite heeded by the esteemed members of the Constituent Assembly, which perhaps contributed to a sense of marginalisation and victimhood in the Assamese middle-class. The movements in Assam began within the first decade of the Constitution coming into force. The language movements in the Brahmaputra and Barak valleys were perhaps the first manifestations of this. Then came the infamous anti-foreigner agitation which culminated in the Assam Accord of August 15, 1985.†

---

*The provisions for citizenship occur in Part II of the Constitution (Articles 5–11), which were debated from August 10 to 12, 1949. The Citizenship Act, 1955, sets out the terms for acquiring, renouncing and terminating Indian citizenship.

† The Accord was signed after a six-year agitation (1979–85) led by the All Assam Students Union (AASU) and the All Assam Gana Sangram Parishad (AAGSP). The massacres at Nellie and Khoirabari (1983, both) occurred during the agitation, which asserted the rights of "indigenous" Assamese people against immigrants, demanding that "illegals" be identified and deported. Following the Accord, the leaders of the AASU and AAGSP formed a new political party, the Asom Gana Parishad (AGP), which contested and won state elections in 1985.

Repatriation: What are the possibilities?

The Amnesty International report has quoted Akhil Gogoi of the Krishak Mukti Sangram Samiti (KMSS) as making statements to the effect that the detention centres are inhuman, and that all the foreigners must be returned to their countries of origin in a dignified manner. However, it is clear that the country of origin is usually presumed to be Bangladesh, but the people accused themselves may not be so sure considering how porous and unmarked the border is. This ambiguity is perhaps what makes it difficult for India to have a repatriation treaty with Bangladesh. The only existing mechanism for repatriation is a long and arduous process involving the Government of Assam, the Union Ministry of Home Affairs, the Ministry of External Affairs, and the Government of Bangladesh, along with probably as many levels of bureaucracy. Only when the Government of Bangladesh is able to verify that the person in question is actually a citizen of that country, will the person be repatriated.

The next issue then is what happens in cases where the Government of Bangladesh is unable to verify whether the person is their citizen or not. In such a circumstance, there are few options for the Union Government or the Government of Assam. One option is to let the person go. This option may not be palatable to many in Assam. The other option is to free the person while conferring basic constitutional rights that are available to non-citizens of India, or strip them of citizenship rights. The third option, which seems to be the prevailing practice, is to detain them indefinitely.* Between freedom with limited rights and indefinite detention, perhaps the former is the optimal solution, though many outside Assam would be inclined to argue for a complete amnesty, as the first option entails.

November 2 and 24, 2018, Newsclick

---

*Short of establishing a process of absorption or a repatriation treaty, no other option augurs well for long-term peace. A legal limbo in which people designated as "outsiders" are held in segregation with no definite resolution in view is a recipe for eventual violence against them, as happened with the Rohingyas of Myanmar.

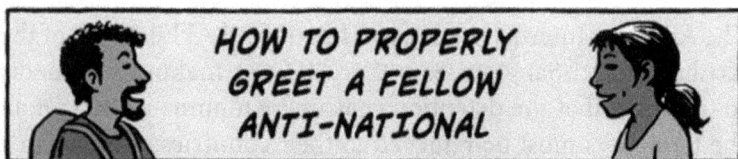

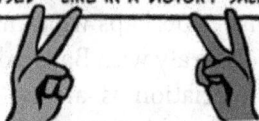

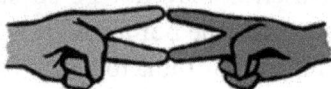

Orijit Sen

PART FOUR

THE BULLET TRAIN TO NOWHERE

Newsclick, 2016

DEMONETISATION—A POEM

Abhishek Anicca

Cycle rickshaw-walas support demonetisation.
Their earnings have halved.
Some days they don't have any work.
They think it will be over, soon.
In a month or two, hopefully, they say.
They are doing it for the country, right?
Maybe they are.

Mandi-walas support demonetisation.
Their supplies are short.
And what they have, is rotting.
They are rotting too, slowly.
They are waiting for things to change.
For many the effects will last,
Some weeks of earning nothing at all
Turning into the big nothings of tomorrow.
But they are doing it for the country, right?
Maybe they are.

Farmers support demonetisation.
They do, they do, they do.
How many times do they have to say that?
The harvest is delayed.
The next season is delayed.
Loan payments are delayed.
Marriages are also delayed.
The last rites, no, they took another loan for that.
They are doing it for the nation.
Jai jawan, Jai kisan.
Hopefully, their compensation is matched
To that of the soldiers
When they commit suicide next year.

Maybe, they won't,
But then, maybe, they will,
For the nation, of course.

Indian Cultural Forum, January 25, 2017

———◆•◆———

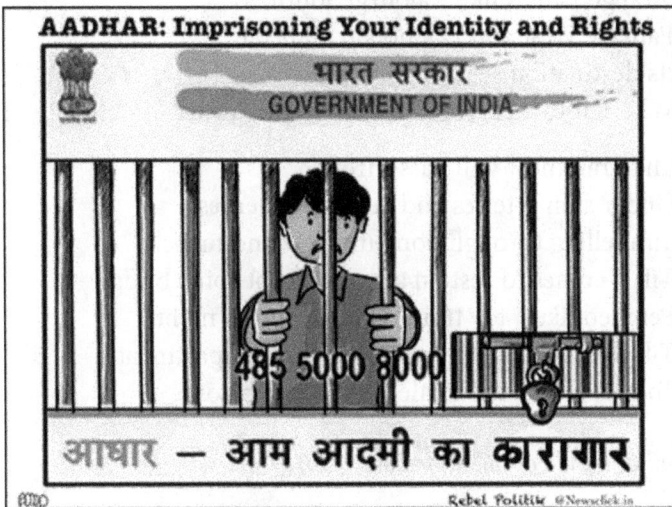

AADHAR: Imprisoning Your Identity and Rights

THE BULLET TRAIN

(The first Aadhaar-linked poem in the world)
Ra Sh (Aadhar No: 9876 5432 1001)

The Shinkansen Model accelerates to
217 miles an hour, cutting journey time
To 3 hours from Ahmedabad to Mumbai.
Mukesh sings "Meri gaadi hai japaani"
On a soulful studio radio.
Born post-war, Shinzo Abe smiles
And waves and hugs like Hirohito.

This Bullet Train is the Brahmaasthra of the epics.
Or, the Narayanasthra or the Rambaan.
Sometimes, it is a Mohanasthra that drugs
Billions of people, putting them in a daze.

There is another Bullet Train.
A 7.65 calibre *Make in India* model
That passes through stations with
Strange names like Kalburgi South
Pansare West and Dabholkar Central,
Its destination set in Bangalore
Where it rockets through a pulsating heart.

This train now will pass through,
Under skin arteries and veins and nerves,
Tunnelling through bone marrow and muscle
Till it comes to rest on a magnificent spine bridge,
Perched like a toy train on a full moon night
Till the slightest breeze causes the compartments
To topple into a depthless soul, one by one.

Indian Cultural Forum, September 7, 2018

Orijit Sen, 2018

STATUES RISE AND FALL,
ONLY THE PEOPLE REMAIN

Prabir Purkayastha

The 182-metre "Statue of Unity" near the Sardar Sarovar Dam in Narmada district was built at a cost of 2,989 crore rupees. It was inaugurated by the Prime Minister in 2018, with a great deal of publicity—about paying tribute to freedom fighter Sardar Vallabhbhai Patel; about "the world's tallest statue"; about a new tourist attraction; about an "icon of unity". Other than outrage about what could have been done for real people with the money spent on the statue, there were protests from adivasis and farmers in the region whose land was acquired by the government for the project. The following piece looks more closely at the multi-crore "monument for the elite", which has extracted a heavy price from people whose homes and land have been submerged.

Prime Minister Narendra Modi's unveiling of the "tallest statue in the world" has been accompanied by a high-voltage campaign on Sardar Patel's contribution to nation-building. Of course, we know—and Modi has made it repeatedly clear—that this recognition of Patel is a part of the campaign to dismantle the legacy of Jawaharlal Nehru, the first Prime Minister of the country. In the game of opposing pairs of icons, sometimes it is Netaji Subhas Chandra Bose versus Nehru; sometimes, Babasaheb Ambedkar versus Nehru; and often, Patel versus Nehru. Nehru remains the constant enemy for Modi and the RSS-BJP.

Why is Nehru the constant enemy? As Prime Minister, Nehru embodied the vision of the national movement: a secular state as the instrument of development and lifting Indian people out of poverty. This was the central impulse of the independence movement against the British. These two elements—secularism and development—distinguish all the leaders of the national movement, whether Patel, Bose, Ambedkar, Nehru or others, from the Rashtriya Swayamsevak Sangh. For the RSS, the British were not the enemies; the nationalists, secularists and the Muslims were.

The RSS is the only political formation that wanted an India based on religious identity; it had nothing to say about development either. For the RSS, Indian and foreign capital should develop the Indian economy, with the state only playing the role of a facilitator. This is similar to what Modi has managed in the Rafale deal. It was such a vision of the state which kept the RSS and its allied movements out of the independence struggle. And this is why the secular institutions of the state and the public sector are seen as key enemies by the RSS-BJP today. These are the institutions that need to be dismantled, along with Jawaharlal Nehru.

The "Unity" Statue of Patel has been built at a cost of Rs 2,989 crore. As Dhirubhai Patel, the 91-year-old grandnephew of Sardar Patel has said, Patel would not have approved of this statue. He knew the value of money. Sardar Patel has been often quoted on his priorities for India: "I have one wish: that India becomes a productive nation; no one should cry for food and remain hungry." Patel would certainly not have approved of wasting Rs 2,989 crore on a statue which will produce nothing but dubious vainglory for Prime Minister Modi.

A number of people have made calculations to list more productive uses of this amount of money. Or with the money our most-travelled PM has spent on his frequent foreign tours. Prime ministers are "allowed" their vanity expenditures. We pay a much higher price when we procure Rafale aircraft at eight billion euros, and that too without any technology transfers or indigenous development. And we might have to "compensate" the US now—because we dared to buy Russian S-400 missile defence systems—by procuring US-made, outmoded F16s at an even higher price. So, perhaps we should overlook the "small" price tag of about $400 million for the 182-metre world's tallest statue!

Consider, instead, who this magnificent monument has been built for, and who has paid the price for it. If we look at the website of the Statue of Unity, it is clear that it is meant for the Indian elite, who can stay in an opulent hotel (part of the statue complex) and look at the Sardar Sarovar Lake. The website describes the venue:

"[Two] guest-room levels above a public floor containing meal services, a ballroom, and other meeting and event spaces. King rooms and suites are located on the river side of the building, where they have access to balconies overlooking generous gardens."

Further, "A heavy-load open lift with a panoramic view will be built alongside the Statue of Unity. Visitors will be able to rise up within [the] statue, walk into a viewing gallery and enjoy a panoramic view of the Sardar Sarovar project and the surrounding region from an astounding height of close to 400 ft." In other words, this statue is a monument to the Indian elite, who can come, look at a beautiful lake, rise without any effort to 400 feet and have a nice view. It is about the elite "consumption" of nature.

You know what you don't see from 400 feet? People. Nor do you see them when you look at the lake that has submerged 377 square kilometres of their land.

What is missing in this picture of development? The people who have paid for the statue, their homes and lands. The people Patel talked about when he envisioned a productive nation.

It is always true that the poorest pay the most in development projects involving dams and mines. Their lands are taken away, the compensation is either not given, or meagre; they have no alternative livelihood. The gains are for capital, who make money out of the projects, and then enjoy the continued benefits. The landed peasantry and big landowners benefit from the irrigation provided downstream. Even the electricity from the power houses of hydro-electric projects does not reach the villages nearby, only towns and industries far away. This is how capital views development and that is how it operates under capitalism.

The Narmada Dams—Sardar Sarovar and Indira Sagar—are no different. The tribal villages that have been displaced for the dams are yet to receive water or electricity, or the affected people their full compensation. The villagers near Sardar Sarovar say that twenty-eight villages near the dam are yet to receive water.

Seventy-two tribal villages kept a day's fast on October 31, the day Modi inaugurated the world's tallest statue. There have been widespread protests by the tribals in the area. Posters of Modi and Rupani have been blackened. The posters now require police protection.

The "Unity" Statue has fared no better. The heads of twenty-two villages wrote an open letter to the PM, saying that they would not welcome him for the inauguration. They wrote, "These forests, rivers, waterfalls, land and agriculture supported us for generations. We survived on them. But everything is being destroyed now and celebrations are also planned. Don't you think it's akin to celebrating someone's death? We feel so."

So much for Modi's unity.

It also appears that there were other issues with the statue project. The relevant environmental clearances were not taken, nor were the villagers consulted, as the law requires for such projects.

Modi's statue project brings to mind the relationship between monumental architecture and the fascist imagination. From ancient rulers to modern "strongmen", they all seem to be fascinated by size. And let us also understand Patel's attraction for Modi: if Patel was the Iron Man of twentieth-century India, Modi wants to be his twenty-first-century version. This is as much a statue of himself as it is of Patel's.

History knows how to deal with such vainglory. Shelley, the English romantic revolutionary poet, wrote about the remains of a mighty statue:

> And on the pedestal these words appear:
> "My name is Ozymandias, king of kings:
> Look on my works, ye Mighty, and despair!"
> Nothing beside remains: round the decay
> Of that colossal wreck, boundless and bare,
> The lone and level sands stretch far away
> Statues rise and fall, Mr Modi, only the people remain.

Newsclick, November 1, 2018.

Newsclick, 2018

THE ECONOMY UNDER MODI

Prabhat Patnaik

Now in its second year, the Oxfam report on The Commitment to Reducing Inequality, released in October 2018, ranks India a dismal 147 on a total of 157 countries, and sixth among the eight countries in South Asia. Looking at government initiatives such as social spending, taxation policies, wages and labour rights, the report mentions India and Nigeria as particularly worrying cases of a want of commitment to redressing economic inequality.

In this essay, first written in 2017 and updated in January 2019, Prabhat Patnaik explains the gap between a much-touted growth rate and the ground realities. When the government applies neoliberal nostrums with an almost superstitious fervour, accompanied by a questionable fidelity to facts, widespread immiseration is to be expected. All the more so when "The country's economy has scarcely ever been in the hands of more unthinking persons."

The Modi government's record in tacitly supporting the actions of a bunch of vigilante thugs who have been terrorizing the country, especially the Muslims and the dalits, in the guise of gaurakshaks or opponents of "love jihad" or "nationalists", has been so outrageous that it has grabbed all the critical attention. In the process, the government's abysmal failures in other spheres have gone virtually unnoticed. One such sphere is the economy, whose dismal state is sought to be camouflaged by hyped-up figures of growth of the Gross Domestic Product (GDP).

In fact, GDP figures these days engage one like an Edmund Crispin detective novel. In Crispin's novels one is forever occupied trying to identify the murderer from the clues the author gives; likewise, with GDP data today one gets primarily occupied trying to discover how truth has been done away with through the estimates. It is the "post-truth" character rather than the data itself which proves absorbing.

But even official data cannot hide certain things about the Modi years, and in what follows I rely exclusively on official data. The gross domestic product at factor cost originating in agriculture is the source of the incomes of all those engaged in this sector: agricultural labourers; peasants of different categories; capitalist farmers; and landlords, both feudal and capitalist. True, some of them, notably the landlords and capitalist farmers, may have incomes from other, non-agricultural sources, such as trade, cinema halls, or the transport business; but with their numbers being relatively small, as long as their share in the GDP originating in agriculture does not fall, we can safely infer that an observed fall in per capita GDP originating from agriculture implies a fall in the per capita income of the agriculture-dependent population.

Income of course should mean net income, i.e. gross income minus a deduction for the depreciation of those one-time investments (land, machinery, etc.) called fixed capital, but the ratio between gross and net incomes does not change much over short periods; so, taking per capita GDP at factor cost for examining trends in per capita income of the agriculture-dependent population seems legitimate.

Now, to see what has been happening, let me go back to an

article I wrote in June 2017, looking at the first three Modi years, and make a point-to-point comparison of the pre-Modi base year 2013–14 with the last of these three years, 2016–17. This way we also avoid the two middle years, 2014–15 and 2015–16, which were poor harvest years because of successive droughts, and whose inclusion would have exposed us to the charge that we are unfairly blaming the Modi government for a natural phenomenon like drought.

Since over such a short period of three years, there is unlikely to have been much shift in the sectoral composition of the workforce, and hence of the population dependent upon it, we can quite legitimately take the rate of growth of the agriculture-dependent population as being equal to the rate of growth of the overall population of the country.

Let us now come to the calculations. From official data it can be seen on this basis that the per capita GDP at factor cost in current prices increased by 16 per cent between 2013–14 and 2016–17— which everybody acknowledges to have been a very good crop year (so that none can accuse us of unfairness). But exactly over the same period the Consumer Price Index for rural India increased by 16.8 per cent. In other words, the per capita nominal income of the agriculture-dependent population increased less than the price index, which means that there was a marginal decline in the per capita real income of the agriculture-dependent population over these three years.

Agriculture accounts for roughly half of the total workforce of the country. Assuming identical workforce to population ratio in agriculture (as elsewhere), what this means is that roughly half of the country's population witnessed no increase whatsoever—on the contrary it saw a marginal decline in its real per capita income over the first three Modi years. This is a fact of great significance.

The agrarian crisis of course pre-dates Modi, and has to do with the withdrawal of state support from peasant agriculture and the exposure of this sector to the operations of agri-business and domestic and foreign monopolists, as part of neoliberal economic policy. The point, however, is that the Modi government has been fully complicit in this squeeze on the agriculture-dependent population by neoliberalism. Indeed, as I suggest below, it has been unthinkingly neoliberal, and for that reason ultra-neoliberal, to a degree far surpassing anything we have seen earlier.

In the non-agricultural sector in general, output and employment (employment here must exclude "disguised unemployment"), are demand-determined. Now, a part of the demand, what one may call the "endogenous" component of demand, comes from the output of this sector itself: larger output means more incomes generated in this sector and hence a larger demand out of these incomes for the sector's own products. To see why the output of this sector is what it is, we have to focus, therefore, on the "exogenous" or the "autonomous" element of the demand for this sector's product—the element not dependent upon its own income.

One important exogenous element of the demand for non-agricultural goods and services comes, obviously, from agricultural incomes. But these, we have seen, were stagnant in per capita terms from May 2014 to May 2017, which means that this source of demand did not grow over this period. Since investment tends to respond to the change in the size of the market and hence to the size of output, it cannot be taken as an exogenous element at all. This leaves us with only two other elements which can be taken as exogenous; one of these is net exports and the other is government expenditure. (Boost to autonomous consumption through asset-price bubbles, which leave asset-holders feeling wealthy, and hence consuming more, play a relatively small role in the Indian economy.)

The demand arising from net exports (i.e. exports minus imports) was fairly sluggish over the first three years of the Modi regime, because of the crisis in the world economy and also the protectionism increasingly adopted by the US. Such protectionism, by discouraging US firms from "outsourcing" service sector activities, hurts the exports of services from countries like India.

True, the lower oil prices in the world economy should have had the effect of boosting domestic demand, if these lower prices had been passed on to the consumers. But this did not happen; on the contrary the government just took advantage of the lower world oil prices to garner larger revenues through excise duty.

With such larger revenues, or even without them, if government expenditure had increased significantly, then we could have had a genuine exogenous boost to demand, and hence an increase in the output and employment in the non-agricultural sector. But here, we come to the real crux of the matter. The total nominal expenditure by the central government increased by 6.7 per cent in 2014–15, by 7.6 per cent in 2015–16, and by 12.5 per cent in 2016–17 (RE), when the Pay Commission's recommendations had to be implemented. The increase in total expenditure proposed in the 2017–18 budget was again only about 6 per cent. Since in each one of these years, the nominal GDP growth exceeded 11 per cent, what this suggests is that central government expenditure as a proportion of nominal GDP kept falling; even the Pay Commission-driven increase in 2016–17 scarcely contributed to an increase in this proportion.

In a situation where per capita agricultural income has not been increasing and the stimulus from net exports has been waning, the need of the hour was an increase in the stimulus from government expenditure. But we find instead that government expenditure as a proportion of GDP kept declining over this period. The government, in other words, was keener to keep finance capital happy by restraining expenditure, than to sustain output and employment growth in the economy. And while this fact may not be manifest in the GDP estimates (because of the flawed methodology adopted by the Modi regime for estimating GDP), it is certainly manifest in the employment figures. The number of new jobs created in the organised sector of the economy, which used to be about 8 to 9 lakhs per year in 2010 and 2011 and which was nonetheless lower than the number of new persons seeking work, had fallen to less than two lakhs per year in 2016-17, which expresses the seriousness of the crisis.

The government's fiscal conservatism arises from an unthinking adherence to the neoliberal prescription of "fiscal responsibility". The effects of such unthinking adherence have been compounded by its unthinking "macho" measures like the demonetisation of currency notes. All these measures reflect the government's generally unthinking character. The country's economy has scarcely ever been in the hands of more unthinking persons.

The Indian economy in a tailspin

Looking at where we are at the start of 2019, it is clear that the Indian economy is in a tailspin. This cannot be attributed only to innocence in economic matters of the command-centre of the NDA government. While that is indubitably a contributing factor, the current travails of the economy point to something deeper, namely the dead-end to which neoliberalism has brought the economy. Without moving away from the neoliberal trajectory, the economy cannot come out of its current difficulties.

India's success in raising the GDP growth rate, the main selling point for the neoliberal regime, was, unlike China's, built upon the quicksand of a persistent trade and current account deficit on the external front. This was covered all this time by financial inflows, which were large enough even to add to the foreign exchange reserves. A major factor contributing to such inflows in recent years were the much lower interest rates, compared to India, that prevailed in metropolitan economies, especially in the US where they were virtually pushed down to zero to revive the economy after 2008.

But now the US itself has started raising interest rates; and uncertainty over the future of neoliberalism in the wake of Trump's protectionist measures is making globalised finance flow massively to the US as its safe "home base". The dollar, for both these reasons, is rising relative to other currencies, especially the rupee. This state of affairs is not going to be reversed in the foreseeable future, which is why the rupee continues to slide vis-à-vis the dollar, even after Arun Jaitley announced a slew of measures on September 14, 2018, to attract finance into the economy to stem the rupee's slide.

The sliding rupee is raising import costs, especially of crude oil; and the latter get passed on in the form of higher petro-product prices. This fact together with the rise of crude prices in the world market following an agreement within the OPEC itself, has now raised petrol and diesel prices in India to dizzying heights; and the rise continues daily. Here again there is no question of any respite within the neoliberal regime from the relentless impact of this exchange-rate-depreciation-cum-inflation syndrome. The only thing Arun Jaitley can think of doing is to attract sufficient financial inflow to stabilise the rupee, but that, as suggested above, is now more difficult; and even if there is some temporary reprieve through such inflows, it cannot but be temporary.

Manmohan Singh and P. Chidambaram attack the NDA government for its economic incompetence, which is undeniable, but they hardly have any better ideas. At the most they may jack up interest rates a bit more. But that, while its effects on financial inflows would be dubious for reasons already mentioned, would amount at best to merely papering over the cracks (since the basic problem of the current account deficit would still remain unaddressed). Besides, it will worsen unemployment and further damage the economy of the small producers.

One way of providing relief to the people against the skyrocketing petrol and diesel prices, whose effects are felt even by the poorest persons because they increase the transport costs of all goods, is to lower the taxes on these goods which make up the bulk of their prices. Some state governments—of whom Kerala was an early example and Karnataka the latest—have indeed reduced their taxes on petro-products to provide relief to the people. But there are limits to the extent to which such relief would be forthcoming, for two obvious reasons, both related to the neoliberal regime.

One is our overwhelming reliance on indirect taxation and the eschewing of direct taxation, because of the compulsion to retain "investors' confidence", so that finance flows in adequate quantities to keep the balance of payments on an even keel. The second is the disastrous move towards a Goods and Services Tax, again in conformity with the demands of a neoliberal economy, which has affected government tax revenues adversely.

In the face of this already adverse effect, the need to maintain government revenues becomes even more pressing, and puts a limit to the degree to which taxes on petro-products can be lowered (unless greater direct taxation is resorted to). Indeed, the only reason that some states have been able to reduce taxes, for lowering petrol and diesel prices, is because these goods fall outside the GST ambit; but naturally they cannot keep doing so beyond a point without raising revenue in other ways. (And such ways are no longer available to state governments, even to the limited extent that they were earlier).

The way out of the current economic predicament however is obvious, though invisible to eyes blinkered by neoliberalism. Since the inflow of finance will no longer cover the current account deficit, the slide in the rupee would require controlling this deficit; and this can be effected only by directly controlling inessential imports. Even in 2013 when the rupee was sliding, the government had controlled gold imports as a means of stemming this slide. Wealth-holders then were moving from rupees to gold. This had boosted gold imports, and direct controls over such imports played a significant role in reducing the trade deficit and halting the rupee's slide. The ambit of import controls now will of course have to be wider, but there is no escape from such controls. The rupee will have to be stabilised immediately with a combination of import controls and use of foreign exchange reserves.

But this may not be enough to stabilise petro-product prices in view of world market trends. These prices will have to be not just stabilised, but actually lowered to prevent down-the-line cost-push inflationary effects on commodities in general. This can be done by significantly lowering taxes upon them, and making up for the revenue shortfall caused by such lowering through larger direct taxation, in particular wealth taxation.

Wealth taxation in any case is the best way to finance public expenditure as it has no adverse effects upon any investment "incentives": since all forms of wealth are taxed without discrimination, there is no special disincentive for holding wealth in the form of productive assets. In addition, it has the effect of keeping wealth inequality in society in check, which, as is commonly accepted now, is an essential prerequisite for democracy.

It is shocking that in India, where wealth inequalities have been rising so sharply of late, there is hardly any wealth taxation. Using direct taxation on wealth as a substitute for indirect taxation on petro-products will thus kill several birds with one stone: it will prevent the inflationary squeeze on the people that rising petro-product price are imposing, and at the same time bring greater wealth equality in society which is desirable per se.

Lower petro-product prices, it may be argued, would encourage larger consumption of such products, which, in the current context of rising world crude prices, would raise the country's import-bill, bringing pressure on the rupee once again. Alongside controlling, and lowering petro-product prices, therefore, the government has to take steps to control petro-product consumption directly. Since much of this consumption occurs within the government itself, with the defence sector in particular being a major consumer, controlling consumption can be effected through a set of directives within the government. As for consumption outside the government sector, several measures can be taken which effectively ration the use of petro-products.

Many of these measures are advocated and even implemented on environmental grounds. The "odd-even" scheme, for instance, that was implemented in Delhi, was also a means of petro-product rationing. In many countries, to avoid congestion in peak hours, a minimum number of occupants per car is insisted upon; this also acts as a measure of directly controlling petro-product consumption. In other words, measures of petro-product rationing would also kill several birds with one stone: they would reduce road congestion; they would reduce environmental pollution; and they would also reduce the consumption of petro-products with beneficial effects for our balance of payments.

A combination of direct import controls on inessential items, reduction of petro-product prices, measures for reducing the consumption of such products, and direct taxation, especially on wealth, is the obvious way of getting out of the tailspin in which the Indian economy is currently caught. But this combination of measures which is desirable, not just for getting out of the current travails, but for other, more long-term considerations as well, runs contrary to the direction of neoliberalism. There is however no alternative to them if we are to avoid the fate of countries that eventually run to the IMF and get caught in the vice-like grip of "austerity".

The dramatic rise in wealth inequality

Oxfam produced a report in January 2018, in which it highlights the dramatic increase in wealth inequality that has been occurring in India. The basic data used is from Credit Suisse, which regularly brings out a Global Wealth Databook. According to Credit Suisse, the top 1 per cent of the population in India cornered 73 per cent of the additional wealth generated in the year 2017.

This is an incredible figure in itself. What is more, this percentage is higher than the overall figure that had prevailed prior to this year, which was 58 per cent. The percentage at the margin being higher than the average percentage means that the average itself, already extremely high, is in the process of rising still further.

Growing wealth and income inequality is not a phenomenon confined to India alone. It is a world-wide phenomenon which has now started worrying even the top leaders of the capitalist world, who gather every year at Davos for the World Economic Forum. The threat of social instability that such growing economic inequality poses has placed it as a major item on the Davos agenda.

But where India stands out is that the growth of inequality here has been more rapid than elsewhere in the world, so much so that it now ranks among the most unequal societies anywhere. Compared, for instance, to the figure of 58 per cent of total wealth that the top 1 per cent owned in India prior to 2017, the corresponding figure for the world as a whole was 50 per cent. And even though for the world as a whole, the top 1 per cent owned 82 per cent of the addition to wealth in 2017—compared to 73 per cent for India—the level of wealth inequality in the world will continue to remain below that of India in the foreseeable future.

What this suggests is that the underlying reason which is boosting wealth inequality everywhere is operating with even greater intensity in India. And this reason has primarily to do with the pursuit of neoliberal economic policies since the 1990s.

There are at least five obvious ways in which neoliberal capitalism boosts wealth inequality. The first is through the increase in income inequality that it brings about. Since the ratio of income that is saved (and hence added to the stock of assets) is greater for higher income groups, a shift in income distribution in favour of the latter increases both the overall ratio of savings (and asset formation) in total income, and also the share of the top asset-owners in total assets.

An example will make the point clear. Suppose, to start with, that the top 10 per cent of the population owned assets worth 250 and earned an income of 50, while the bottom 90 per cent had an asset of 50 and earned an income of 50; and suppose the former habitually save half of their income while the latter habitually save 10 per cent of their income. Then the top 10 per cent would save 25 and the bottom 90 per cent 5, so that each group's asset grows by 10 per cent, and there is no rise in wealth inequality.

But now if income distribution becomes 60 for the top 10 per cent and 40 for the rest, then with the same savings ratios, the growth in assets is 34 or 11.3 per cent of the pre-existing level; the top group's asset growth is 12 per cent while the bottom group's asset growth is 8 per cent. The top group's share in total assets increases from 83 to 84 per cent. And if the increase in income inequality continues then the share of the top 10 per cent would continue to rise.

The tendency under neoliberalism is to keep worsening income distribution. This is because the number of jobs created under it falls woefully short of the number of job-seekers, which increases the relative size of the reserve army of labour, so that wages remain tied to a subsistence level even as labour productivity increases. The share of surplus accruing to the rich therefore keeps increasing over time under neoliberal capitalism, entailing an increase in income, and hence wealth, inequality.

In the above example, we assumed that the ratio of savings to income of each group remains unchanged when income distribution changes. In fact, however, consumption tends to be relatively sticky when income changes, in which case, in the above example the savings of the top 10 per cent would increase to 35 when their income rises to 60 (since consumption remains fixed at 25), and the savings of the bottom 90 per cent would fall to minus 5 since their consumption remains 45 even as income falls to 40. In this new situation then, the share of the top 10 per cent in total wealth increases from 83 to 86 per cent.

This tendency for an increase in the share of wealth of the top percentiles becomes particularly pronounced when there is an absolute decline in the incomes of the bottom percentiles. And one reason among others why this happens in a neoliberal regime is the privatisation of essential services like education and healthcare, which also makes them more expensive, so that the poor have to deplete their meagre stock of assets even to be able to afford a particular level of access to these services. This therefore is the second way in which a neoliberal regime contributes to an increase in wealth inequality.

The third way in which a neoliberal regime accentuates wealth inequality is through an intensive process of primitive accumulation of capital which it unleashes upon the economy. Through a variety of means, ranging from an outright takeover of petty property, including peasant property (or its purchase "for a song"); to encroachment on common property; to appropriation of state property (which is built up through taxes imposed on ordinary people); to the sheer filching of bank credit from the public sector banks (what is commonly referred to as a build-up of their "Non-Performing Assets"), the big capitalists increase their share in the total wealth of the economy.

In fact primitive accumulation increases wealth concentration in two ways: one has just been discussed; it supplements the effect of what Marx had called "centralisation of capital". The other way is that by squeezing peasants and petty producers it forces them out of their traditional occupations to migrate to cities where they join the ranks of the job seekers and hence swell the relative size of the reserve army of labour; this accentuates income inequality for reasons already discussed, and hence wealth inequality.

The fourth way that neoliberalism promotes wealth inequality is by handing over tax concessions and tax breaks to the rich in the name of promoting higher economic growth. Such concessions directly increase wealth inequality. In addition, since they are balanced by reducing government expenditure on education and healthcare, and thereby directly or indirectly privatising these essential services, they contribute to the impoverishment of large segments of the ordinary people, which as we saw earlier, also increases wealth inequality.

The fifth way in which wealth inequality increases under neoliberalism is through the formation of asset price bubbles. Speculative booms on the stock market or in other asset markets give a boost to the value of assets, because of which the top percentiles (which figure prominently among the asset-holders) find the absolute value of their wealth, and hence their share in total wealth, increasing quite sharply within a very short period.

This however raises a moot point. To what extent can an increase in the absolute amount of wealth and its share in the total caused by such a speculative boom be considered genuine? After all, just as a speculative bubble can boost the wealth of the top percentiles, the collapse of the bubble can reduce their wealth overnight; why then should a bubble-based increase in wealth inequality be a cause for concern?

It does become a cause for concern because, under a neoliberal regime, governments try to prevent a collapse of the bubble (which would have seriously adverse repercussions on the economy) by sustaining it through various means. These range from fiscal support (such as what Obama had pledged in the US to stem the effect of the collapse of the housing bubble on the financial system), to the commoditisation of elements of nature like water and air (so that new profitable assets are introduced to keep the boom going), to the privatisation of government assets such as "spectrum" (with the same objective). Hence the view that wealth acquired through an asset market bubble constitutes only fictitious wealth and should not therefore be a cause for concern, does not necessarily hold.

To be sure, wealth estimates, and hence estimates of wealth distribution, are fraught with a host of statistical difficulties. But, notwithstanding such difficulties, there is no gainsaying the fact that something extremely serious for our democracy and freedom is occurring through the extraordinary rise in wealth inequality.

The original version of this article appeared on Newsclick in June 2017 and has been updated and expanded for this collection in January 2019

──────◆◆◆──────

CONVERSATION: SURAJIT MAZUMDAR ON THE PROMISES AND REALITY OF DEMONETISATION

Newsclick

On November 8, 2016, Prime Minister Narendra Modi made a dramatic televised address to the nation, to announce that from midnight the same day, over 86 per cent of the country's currency notes stood cancelled as legal tender. In the years since, it has remained unclear what process of consultation led to this step, or

precisely what aims inspired it. Was demonetisation simply an act
of faith, the emperor showing off his new clothes? The following
exchange between Prabir Purkayastha and the economist Surajit
Mazumdar took place a mere four weeks into the cataclysm, and
is a vivid evocation of those days. The sheer harm demonetisation
did to the lives of India's most vulnerable people was obvious well
before the data confirmed it. All it took to recognise this fact was
some honest observation and questioning. However, opacity and
mystification define the government's pronouncements on the
subject to this day.

Prabir Purkayastha (PP): Surajit, putting it very simply, it seems
the pace at which notes are being printed is slow. We have printed
2000 rupee notes and the next denomination which is widely
available is that of 100 rupee notes. It's difficult to use the 2000
rupee notes for small purchases, and we are not printing 500
rupee notes fast enough. From all accounts it's going to take us
anything between five to six months to be able to get enough 500
rupee notes back in circulation, which means that the shortage of
cash in the economy is with us for now. What's going to happen
to the Indian economy if the shortage persists for the next three
to six months?

Surajit Mazumdar (SM): Well, as far as the shortage of cash is
concerned there's one very simple way in which one can look at
it. Suppose you were to say that all the vehicles on the road today
have to be replaced with new ones. Would the production capacity
of the country be able to replace them in a short period of time?
No, because the existing stock of vehicles has been produced over
a long period of time. It is essentially the same with currency. The
currency in use today is something that has been produced over
time, and every year you add a bit to it. So, basically you have
a capacity to print what you need to add every year. And now
suddenly you are having to replace practically the entire currency.
From the figures that have been put out by the RBI (Reserve Bank
of India) it is quite clear that more than 55 per cent of the value
of new currency being put into circulation exists in 2000 rupee

notes. That's the minimum. It's probably even higher than that, and it is not going to be an effective substitute. You really have to now add currency of smaller denominations in the coming year, which means more units, and so the fact that it is going to take a long period of time is absolutely clear. I think the government has also accepted that they would not be able to reach more than 50 per cent replacement of the currency by December 30 [2016].

PP: That's why I said it doesn't appear that they will be able to print the 500 rupee notes. They require fifteen billion of them and that would take time, given the fact that all four presses put together can only print 3.3 billion notes per month.

SM: The shortage of cash is going to be felt for a period of time. The downside is also that the extent of the requirement of cash also comes down because economic activity itself has shrunk. The consequence of this shortage is that at least one important mode with which people make payments is not available with them in the requisite quantity. And beyond a point, it is not possible to shift to alternative modes of making payment.

PP: Surajit, we have looked at the non-cash transactions in the last month, November [2016], and even that has come down. It is not as if payments in kind and promissory compacts have increased to compensate for the lack of cash transactions.

SM: If you have a situation where economic activity contracts because of the shortage of cash, it is going to affect all transactions. That means the total volume of transactions, the value of transactions themselves, both have come down. Even non-cash transactions may shrink as a result of the shortage of cash. Essentially the problem is this: the amount of money available with people with which they can make payments is less. If the total value of payments that people can make is reduced, then the total value of payments that people can receive is also correspondingly reduced. Ultimately, you only receive what someone else pays. Which means that the total of economic activities, which involves

THE BULLET TRAIN TO NOWHERE 215

all the buying and selling that can be sustained at this particular level of income, has to shrink.

PP: Are we looking at an economy in recession? Right now do you expect that in November–December, the two months of this demonetisation experience, the economy may have actually shrunk?

SM: Definitely. I think we will find the economy has shrunk, and may have shrunk very significantly. I am not so certain that our statistics on the economy will fully capture this. Let me give you an example. Suppose there is a rickshaw puller who used to transport people from one point to another, and because of the shortage of cash, some people decide to just walk that distance and don't use his rickshaw any more. Now that particular service, the total production of that service, and the income that would have accrued to the rickshaw puller as a result of that activity, virtually disappears for a period of time. Which statistical measure or system is going to capture this? A lot of our data comes from highly organised units, and we assume that normally there is some relationship between a set of transactions which we can record, and transactions that we are not recording. But those ratios may not be valid for this particular context.

PP: So the services part will be difficult to capture, services like this one in the informal sector. But if we look at industrial production, and we [in Newsclick] have looked now at Firozabad bangles; in Aligarh, at the lock industry; we looked in Moradabad at the brassware industry; and at Agra's footwear industry. There are precipitate drops in production. Aligarh has 4,000 crores of annual income, but 90 per cent of the factories seem to be shut down. So already we see powerhouse production areas of the semi-formal sector, which *are* visible as data, being shut down. Are we also looking at the organised units which do get reflected in some statistical form or the other? Are they showing much lower production and indicating that we have entered into recession?

SM: Let me put it this way. The organised units are also taking a hit. It is not that organised units don't take a hit. As far as the industrial sector is concerned, the index of industrial production figures that came out for October, which is before demonetisation, showed that compared to the previous year, production was down by two-and-a-half per cent. And this has been going on for some length of time. So these sectors are also going to take a hit. What I am saying is, in addition to all that, even in the industrial sector there are unorganised units, and the distribution of the extent of the downturn between organised and unorganised sector units may not be in the same ratio in which production is normally distributed. Since we tend to estimate what's going to happen in the unorganised sector from the existing conditions in the organised sector, our data may not fully capture the extent of the decline that will take place in the GDP [Gross Domestic Product].

PP: But you are sure that GDP will decline in this quarter?

SM: Absolutely. Compared to what would happen in a normal year, this has to show. There is no way in which you can withdraw such a large part of the currency from circulation and not see the effects of that in terms of contraction of GDP. After all, the production of GDP depends on the use of money.

PP: The black money coming back into the banks is going to be a long process. The initial expectation was that such money would not come back into the banks. That hasn't happened, so the black money side of the ledger looks rather bleak for Mr Modi. But if on top of that we have stagnation in the economy—and the contracts are treating it as recession, it appears—demonetisation seems to be, economically, a very stupid move.

SM: Yes. The opinion among economists is pretty unanimous, and exceptionally so—it is never normally so unanimous on any matter, but this time it is. Everyone can understand that on the one hand, there are serious consequences that will derail the process of economic activity through which people generate their income, through which they find employment. You are going to have that derailing effect, on that there is no dispute. You can quibble about the degree to which it will happen, but you can't dispute this particular effect. On the other hand, everyone realises that the possible hit that the black economy could take from such a move was always minimal. That was a given before the demonetisation exercise. You did not need the exercise to know the result, for the simple reason that the amount of cash that is held by people is a very small fraction of the total income that is generated in a year. It is a very small fraction of the total wealth that is held by people. So, even if you did something to disrupt the flow of cash, the effect on the black economy was not going to be severe. That was a given, right at the beginning. All you could achieve is the disruption of a particular process. Now, black incomes are not generated from a process which is completely delinked from the process by which other incomes are generated. They are not two distinct parts of the economy. They are interlinked. So, those who earn black incomes may not be, or their black income may not be, as severely affected as white income. It is a distinct likelihood that white income is going to be affected more severely, especially the income of those who are most vulnerable financially.

PP: You have already seen that the rich are not standing in queues or spending sleepless nights, while other people are. So that is already there. A lot of daily wage workers have returned from the towns to their villages. This has been going on. But what kind of economic sense was there in the government's decision? Who would have planned it? Do you think they are singularly bereft of economic understanding, basic economics, or do they know a different kind of economics that the world doesn't know about?

SM: Well, if that's what they have then, of course, we don't know about it yet. A more realistic way of looking at it is this: you always knew the effects on the black economy were not going to be significant. That was no error, but a certainty when you took this course. You knew it was not going to affect the black economy significantly, and that was not your intention in any case. You knew that the effects on the majority of the population in India would be pretty drastic and adverse. Despite knowing these two things, if you undertook such an action then perhaps it reflects an attitude towards the Indian people, the belief that you can hit these people at the level of their basic requirements, put them into conditions of adversity, and you can still fool them into thinking that you are doing it for the benefit of the nation. What we need to understand is the contempt for the people of this country that enables them to undertake such an action.

Based on the edited transcript of a video on Newsclick, December 6, 2016.

————◆◆◆————

HOW DEMONETISATION RAVAGED THE RURAL ECONOMY

P. Sainath

While P. Sainath cites many examples of banks going the extra mile to help the poor and downtrodden during the hard times of demonetisation, the general story in rural India was of despair, devastation and starvation.

Just a few days before the first anniversary of demonetisation, actually around the time of the anniversary, I was in a small place called Chitradurga in Karnataka. Chitradurga is famous for three things—one, its proliferation of religious matths, second, its famous sixteenth-century fortress, and the third, the best dosa joint in that part of the country called Lalitha Bhawan Tiffin Home. It is on the tourist map. It is a small place with notices put up on the wall. I asked for a translation since they were written in Kannada. The notice read, and mind you, this is one year after demonetisation: "Please don't bring two thousand-rupee notes here. We do not have change. We cannot give you change." And it said, "Either you tender exact change or do your transaction in small denominations." I asked the owner, "Why? It's been one year, man?" He said, "Sir, the impact was terrible! We lost fifty per cent of our revenue for three–four months. People would come to the hotel and be turned away. So we had to put this up." I asked him, "But you said three–four months. So, after that there must have been a recovery?" He said, "Yes, there was a recovery. After five–six months, we came back to what we were getting earlier, more or less, as the currency had come in." So, I asked, "Why do you still have the notice up?" Essentially, what he said amounted to, who knows what they will come up with next? He added, "I think I'll keep the notices on."

While thinking of that, and the GST, and the political scenario, I'm reminded again of the stand-up comic George Carlin's famous line: "Never underestimate the power of stupid people in large groups." We at the People's Archive of Rural India (PARI) looked at demonetisation not in terms of ATMs in the cities—which was all the footage you got on television—or even in the villages. (By the way, rural ATMs account for a fraction of the total ATMs and their running-time is less than twenty per cent of the urban ATMs.) We at PARI were looking at a number of things across India, from the villages of Uttarakhand in the Himalayas to villages around megacity Mumbai. Try imagining this picture from Maharashtra, it beats everything: on the border of Maharashtra and Karnataka are very poor dalits and banjaras, who earn something once a year and have to live on it for several months. They are sugarcane cutters. These sugarcane cutters come in for the season and work like slaves. They can earn up to five hundred rupees a day, but it depends on the tonnage and how much you cut and all that; tough conditions. They come with their families, and they really slog. Now imagine that demonetisation is announced in the middle of this process. Imagine that the farmers are given these old notes; the old five-hundred-rupee notes used to be commonplace. So, after they are given the old notes, they are told that either you bank this note, or it has no value. Please understand that these people have never set foot in a bank before. Also remember that twenty or twenty-five of them could be earning ten thousand rupees in a day at five hundred rupees apiece, and they do it for sixty days or ninety days, depending upon the season. Imagine the picture of this poor man in his dirty banian and torn dhoti slapping four lakh rupees on the teller's counter. The teller is in a panic. The teller informs the manager, who informs the police, who informs the IT Department, because they all assume that the poor sugarcane cutter is a conduit for some big guy's money. Sure, the big guys actually did a lot of that, but in other ways—they opened accounts for their migrant labourers. Not only did they deposit salaries there, but even controlled the ATM cards of the labourers.

Some of the unseen effects of demonetisation, in health terms, may be irreversible. All over, in most parts of the country, certainly in Telangana and Maharashtra where we looked at it, millions of children went hungry for months because the midday-meal scheme had collapsed. You see, for the midday meal, rice and wheat procurement are done on contract; everything else—vegetables, eggs, milk—is bought daily or weekly. The lady selling you the greens or vegetables can only give you so much credit. Even the self-help groups who were managing the midday meals at the time could not give you open-ended credit. In Telangana, Osmanabad, Bir, in school after school, children were eating plain rice with extremely watery daal. Even when, five or six months later, there was a recovery, what had happened to their health or nutritional status in the interim could include all sorts of damage—physiological, psychological—in ways we will never be able to count and measure.

The other section that really got wiped out is that of migrant labourers, and god knows how many millions of them there are in the country. There are all sorts of fantastic estimates, but we simply do not know for sure. I want to put something on the record, that at least across Maharashtra where I looked at the banks, the bank employees' unions came forward to help these migrant labourers and poor farmers. And they would keep the banks open till late at night to complete the KYC forms and open accounts for the people, and we must acknowledge that the unions did this as a public service.

At one bank, there was a classic conversation. There were eleven migrants from Assam, Madhya Pradesh, West Bengal, UP, and another state that I can't recall. The bank manager was wonderful, trying to help them, making their KYCs, and keeping the bank open till very late because all the computers had crashed. The biometric database that allegedly exists simply does not work. In many cases, it doesn't even exist. But the conversation was fantastic! These are labourers who earn three hundred and fifty rupees a day, in a public sector company. I want you to know that had they come twenty years ago, they would have been absorbed into the workforce of the company after a while. Instead, the company has now outsourced labour to a labour contractor. The three hundred rupees were now being given to them in a cheque. Since they did not have an account, they were opening a fresh account. They had been in the habit of transferring their money through a postal money order, but the postal money order had collapsed. When that collapsed, they had to deposit their income in the bank. They were asking the bank manager, "How do I get this money to my family in a village in Kanpur?" And another person there was from Jamui, Bihar. Of course, there are no cheques, it's a no-frills account, there are no chequebooks. One guy asked, "*Angootha chhaap chalega ATM card mein?*" (Would my thumb print do for the ATM card?) It was a legitimate question because you've done this elaborate bio-metric exercise. Of course the manager had to tell him, not a chance.

In Kolkata, at the same time, a migrant labourer and cook was telling my friend at the bank there, "This credit card system will only work if I can cut it into six pieces because I have six family members, each one living and working in a different place. How does it work out unless we have six different credit cards or cut one card into several pieces?"

It was horrible that those eleven grown men, I call them the BPL Migrant Eleven, were crying because their families were starving. Their agricultural operations in Bihar or rural Kanpur depended on the money they could send, or their families could not buy the inputs. In Uttarakhand, people solved the problem in a simpler way. In all the border villages—Dharchula is the last village on the Nepal border, just a stone's throw from the Tibet Autonomous Region—everybody switched to Nepali currency. This had happened for the first time. Usually the craze is for Indian rupees. Now, everybody switched to Nepali currency. It used to be 160 in Nepali currency for 100 INR. Suddenly, the rate reversed, and all sorts of other things happened, but for the next six months people were using the Nepali currency. Across the country we saw incredible examples of the things that were happening.

In Marathwada, people from PARI did amazing stories showing the extreme damage done to cotton growers and cane growers, many of whom were selling their produce at the time of demonetisation. To this day they have not received their cash, or have received cheques that have bounced three times or more.

In Osmanabad, the DCC Bank tried to loot the peasantry, using demonetisation as an excuse. The bank sent a printed letter to the entire community of twenty-five thousand peasants who, collectively, owed one hundred and eighty crores. Two sugar cooperatives owed three hundred and sixty crores, but no letters or notices were sent to them. The letter to the peasant borrowers said: "We are going to do three things to you. We are going to set up a tent outside your house and perform *gandhigiri* until you're shamed into paying your dues..." This is the Osmanabad District Cooperative Bank speaking.

One must also look at the fact that all this comes atop twenty years of a particular kind of policies. I agree entirely with what Sridhar said—that never in the history of any nation has everybody got together and celebrated a tax.* There is a whole set

---

*In a simulation of the midnight session of parliament at India's Independence, another such session was convened on July 1, 2017, this

of reasons for why the media celebrated the goods and services tax (GST). But one of the reasons is, yesterday [December 8, 2017] an RTI application brought out the fact that in three years, the Modi government has spent three thousand seven hundred and fifty-five crores on advertisements. To give you an idea of the magnitude, this is about sixty to sixty-five times the amount they spend on pollution control. It was sixty crores they spent on pollution. Three thousand seven hundred and fifty-five crores means that you're spending about one and a half million rupees—fifteen lakhs—per hour on advertisements.*

By the way, the media was itself hurt by demonetisation because a lot of channels and publications are all about off-the-book cash transactions. Paid news is all about cash transactions. So, they were really hurt. They whined a little bit where they could, but they couldn't come right out and say, "You are a moron!" to the nation's leader. There was a reason they couldn't say it. It was because the media owners are the biggest beneficiaries of all the privatisation taking place. The richest man in this country is the biggest media owner in the country. Mukesh Ambani is not only the richest man in India, he is three times as rich as the next richest Indian. Look at how inequality has grown in our country in the last twenty years. As far as I know, in 1991, there was not a single declared dollar-billionaire in this country. In the year

---

time in honour of the rollout of the Goods and Services Tax. On the occasion, finance minister Arun Jaitley spoke of a new India with "one tax, one market, and for one nation"—an eerie echo of Hitler's "Ein Volk, Ein Reich, Ein Führer", translated into Neoliberalese.

*The government has since chalked up a still more impressive figure. An RTI application by Ram Tanwar elicited the information that between mid-2014 and September 2018, the Modi government's spending on advertisements stood at just under Rs 5000 crore, and already equalled ten years of spending by the UPA government. To set this figure in perspective, *The Hindu* (October 29, 2018) reported that the central government's budget allocation for the rehabilitation of manual scavengers had shrunk from Rs 570 crore in 2013-14, to Rs 5 crore in 2017, and *not one rupee* from this scheme had been released in four years.

2000, *Forbes*—my favourite website!—declared that there were nine dollar-billionaires in India. In 2012, the year we began our socio-economic caste census, fifty-three dollar billionaires; in March 2017, one hundred and one dollar-billionaires. We went from nine to a hundred and one in a span of seventeen years. This country with one hundred and one dollar-billionaires ranks fourth in the world, after USA, Russia and China. But I would say second, because though the Russians and the Chinese come out ahead of us in the number of dollar-billionaires, the per-capita worth of their billionaires is much lower than that of ours: the Chinese are at a mere 1.2 billion, ours are at 3.7 billion.

The Credit Suisse global wealth database shows us that the concentration of wealth among the top one per cent of the Indian population is way higher than their counterparts in the United States. It also shows us that the bottom three deciles own virtually nothing in terms of household wealth. This kind of inequality shows in every sector, and of course it is going to be reflected in agriculture. That is the weakest sector.

It shows in the political sector also. In 2004, we started the system of self-declared election affidavits of a candidate's wealth. The Association for Democratic Reform (ADR) found that in 2004, thirty-two per cent of all members of the Lok Sabha were crorepatis. In the 2009 affidavits of the successful candidates, fifty-three per cent of all MPs were crorepatis. By 2014, eighty-two percent MPs were crorepatis. These are the people who are going to represent the poorest majority on earth. And these are all self-declared crorepatis…we all know the extent of modesty when it comes to declaring wealth to the state. The rate of increase in the assets of re-elected MPs ranged, in some cases, from three hundred per cent to six or seven thousand per cent. No stock market in the world will give you such returns on investment.

I mentioned that we had fifty-three dollar-billionaires in 2012. The year is important because we did our socio-economic caste census survey in that year. The data began to come out in 2014, and it revealed that in 2012, during the period of our survey, in seventy-five per cent of rural Indian households the main breadwinner took home less than five thousand rupees a month. If you raised the bar to ten thousand, in ninety per cent of Indian rural households the main breadwinner came home with less than ten thousand rupees a month. What percentage of rural households took home more than ten thousand, you ask? Eight per cent.

But if you break it down further and look at dalit and adivasi households, the level of solvency is about half the national average! And most of the fortunate ones are government employees— schoolteachers, railway employees, PWD workers, maybe a chapraasi at the collectorate, that sort of thing. Just think of the inequality! A country cannot sustain this kind of inequality amid an agrarian crisis, to which the present government, even more than previous ones, is blind. Or it just doesn't care, as demonetisation proved.

Apart from demonetisation and GST, there was also this incredibly stupid extension of the cow slaughter ban. It has led to the near extinction of Kolhapuri chappals. Dalits, again, are the biggest sufferers. People tried making up the shortfall by getting cattle in vans from other parts of the country, like Tamil Nadu, and the vans were burnt on the borders by the VHP, Bajrang Dal and others—"independent, autonomous, fraternal organisations", you know, just like the Hindu Mahasabha and the RSS.

Here I must digress for a bit, because we hear about the rewriting of history. Well, we're rewriting it now. Every day we're rewriting the data on different issues and subjects. I want to share a little tidbit about that wonderful gentleman, Mr Savarkar. There is a biography of Savarkar that appeared in the 1930s. It was authored by someone writing under the obvious pseudonym of Chitragupta. Chitragupta is a significant mythological figure, and an appropriate fit for Savarkar's biographer. He was the scribe of Lord Yama, the god of death. So, Chitragupta is the emissary of the god of death. This hagiography, which tells us what a wonderful, handsome figure Savarkar cut, was republished in the

forties and the seventies, and the eighties, and Savarkar's brother
then revealed that the pseudonym was used by none other than
Savarkar himself. So, we do know for a historical fact now that
Mr Savarkar had a very high opinion of Mr Savarkar. Is this the
sort of person to lionise, the sort of fraud to legitimise?

Anyway, with that digression over, let's get back to the beef
ban and the agrarian crisis. Maharashtra is at the core of it. It is
true that sixty-five thousand farmers have committed suicide in
this one state, according to the National Crime Records Bureau.
I should also tell you that all the figures of farmer suicides from
the last two years are lies. It's a fraud perpetrated by successive
administrations. They have changed categories, and switched
them over and over. They got so sick at the numbers of suicides
growing that they simply gutted the National Crime Records
Bureau and are merging it with the Bureau of Police Research
and Development. The NCRB was terribly flawed. But for all its
flaws, it represented data gathered from every police thaana in the
country. This new lot are going to do little surveys, outsourced to
great think tanks in Delhi. It's like replacing your national election
with an opinion poll.

But having said that, and having said that debts and
bankruptcies are going up, I still want to tell you this: the agrarian
crisis is not simply about the loss of human lives, though that
is terrible. It's not just about the loss of production. It's also a
measure of how much we have lost our humanity. It's a measure
of the shrinking boundaries of our humanness, that we can stand
by for twenty years and watch this incredible misery heaped on
farmers and agricultural labourers. Please understand this. Of
course, we have advanced twenty or thirty places in the ease of
doing business. And yesterday's *Times of India* offered the same
solution for farmers' distress: improve the ease of doing business
for companies in the countryside. With all that said and done,
please understand hunger and malnutrition are a choice we make.
Your children do not have to be hungry. Those children did not
need to go without their midday meals. It's a choice we make, to

remain silent in our complicity with the inhumane policies that have been heaped on the people for twenty-five years.

The beef slaughter and the agrarian crisis have devastated the livestock in this country. There is a stupidity in the belief that you can have perpetual and unending growth. Growth for the sake of growth, as Edward Adams said, is the ideology of the cancer cell. David Attenborough said it so beautifully: "You plan an infinite growth on a planet with rapidly depleting and finite resources; you are either an idiot or an economist or both." So, in the middle of all this, you've had livestock dwindling in census after census. Since 2002, a livestock census takes place every five years, and 2017 is the year of the livestock census. Every eighth rupee that an agricultural household earns, comes from the livestock sector. In that situation, there has been a steep decline in cattle, especially indigenous breeds. Overall, the decline has been of two or three per cent. Crossbreeds and exotic species have seen a gigantic rise. All the animals of livestock that poor people have—goats, sheep, pigs—each of these has seen a dramatic fall, which means that the income support for poor people has declined tremendously.

The crisis is one of a consciously structured, relentless, cynically driven inequality. It's a place where you have given incredible power to the corporate world. Your agrarian crisis in five words is: Corporate Hijack of Indian Agriculture. The process through which it is achieved, in five words: Predatory Commercialisation of the Countryside. And the consequences of that are the largest human displacements in history.

Based on the edited transcript of a talk at the Mumbai Collective, December 2017.

Transcribed, and edited, from a video on Newsclick, December 20, 2017.

BRING IN THE GOATS
Keki Daruwalla

Though she never understood
Goddess Lakshmi stood
In full public view
In the Bank of India queue
That serpent-fashion wound
Its sinuous way around
Khan Market right up to
the Lodhi Garden ground.
Goddess Lakshmi said
Even as she smote her head
(pimpled with beads of sweat)
That mirrored the burning sun
"What have these wise men done?
How do I gift a port
To devotee Adani?
A palace or a fort
(I think I am trillions short)
To my favourite Ambani?"
Her Bank in disrepair,
She spoke with not her usual flair
"Please bring in the goats
To whom I'll feed my notes."

Postscript

Goddess, may I point out
(No scope for any quibbling)
You got the wrong Ambani
among the two great siblings.
Nudged by his spotless Pal
South Block and Rafale
and across-the-table fiddling
They ousted trusted HAL.

Indian Cultural Forum, September 4, 2017

NO ROOM FOR THE POOR IN
SMART-CITY BHOPAL

Shreya Roy Chowdhury

Madhya Pradesh's capital is among the first twenty cities chosen for redevelopment under the Narendra Modi government's Smart Cities Mission. But who is the "smart" city for? Roy Chowdhury describes what is being bulldozed in the name of smartness, and who is being affected—and further marginalised—in the process of alleged development.

The brochures sell a dream: new residences, services accessed through mobile phone apps, outdoor gymnasia, automated monitoring of everything from garbage collection to streetlights, and pavements without hawkers.

This dream will unfold in Bhopal once Madhya Pradesh's capital is reshaped into a smart city. Among the first 20 cities selected for redevelopment under the Narendra Modi government's Smart Cities Mission, Bhopal must provide all basic infrastructure and services, it must use technology in their delivery and find ways to generate revenues.

Currently, the most visible feature of this enterprise are bulldozers. Eleven schools, one hospital, 3,000 quarters for government employees, hundreds of shops and two slum clusters have been razed or await demolition by the Bhopal Smart City Development Corporation, a company established for turning Bhopal smart.

Unlike other cities that are "retrofitting" existing colonies to make them smart, Bhopal is developing a "smart area" from scratch. North and South Tatya Tope Nagar wasn't the first choice, however. The Bhopal Municipal Corporation's original proposal was to redevelop Shivaji Nagar and Tulsi Nagar. But their residents protested. With retired doctors, journalists and bureaucrats in their ranks, their voices were heard. The axe then fell on North and South TT Nagar.

Through 2017 and 2018, those in the government quarters were moved to another place. As a consequence, Indira Market on Bhadbhada Road, which separates North from South TT Nagar, started losing customers. Mohammad Israr, a cosmetics store owner who serves as the market association's secretary, estimates that most of over 500 shops have seen their sales halve.

Not far from Israr's shop, a new road is under construction. It will intersect another road that is almost ready. Their names encapsulate the vision of Bhopal's smart city administrators: Smart Road and Boulevard Street.

Bhopal's new roads will have cycling and walking tracks and "smart poles" with cameras to enable the residents to access the internet, read pollution data and charge electric vehicles. Its Dusshera Maidan, or ground, will have eight basketball courts and an academy. Its smart parks will feature wifi hotspots and food courts, and harvest water.

Most people in North and South TT Nagar, however, struggle to understand where they fit in this gilded vision of a sanitised, gentrified Bhopal. Residents of the slum clusters along the Smart Road were placed in transit housing. They do not know where they will finally end up. Teachers at a government school which juts into Boulevard Street do not know where they or the children will be sent.

That is because information from the administrators is hard to come by. Whatever Israr knows about the redevelopment, he has learned from newspapers. Similarly, one of the first smart projects to be completed was an app-based bicycle sharing system. Of its 50,000 registered users, 5,600 are regular. But ordinary people are convinced these are morning walkers cycling for exercise.

Lack of accountability

The proposal for developing the smart city is submitted by the state government and the municipal corporation but executed by a "special purpose vehicle", a company in which the government has the majority stake but may include private firms as well. The company gets the funds—Rs 500 crore each from the Centre and the state over five years—and is responsible for developing smart areas and maintaining the full range of services.

The Bhopal Smart City Development Corporation has state and municipal officers on its board but no elected representative. It is housed in a new luxurious building next to the dingier offices of the Bhopal Municipal Corporation. It is well-funded and empowered to generate revenues by outsourcing services and initiating partnerships with private players. Its budget is separate from the municipal corporation's. There is an advisory body that includes elected representatives, but its recommendations are not binding.

This arrangement is worrying a section of citizens. For, in effect, powers are being shifted from the elected municipal corporation to a body that performs the same functions, but is controlled by the bureaucracy and potentially private investors, explained Gaurav Dwivedi of the Centre for Financial Accountability.

"An elected body would be answerable to the public," said Dwivedi, who is part of a group of researchers tracking the progress of the smart city mission in Bhopal. Since most members of the company's board are from the state bureaucracy, the activists argue the mission undermines the 74th Constitutional Amendment that decentralises governance and empowers urban local bodies.

Politicians resent being kept out of the loop. "We will ask the chief minister to review the entire project,"* said P.C. Sharma, the Congress MLA who represents the area being redeveloped. "Elected councillors must know how rehabilitation will happen, where shops will be assigned and how slums will be managed."

The company's CEO, Sanjay Kumar, is aware of the "anxiety" the mission has caused but argued that involving "political people"

---

*In December 2018, Kamal Nath of the Congress became chief minister of Madhya Pradesh after the BJP was voted out of power. The smart city project had been initiated during the tenure of the previous chief minister, Shivraj Singh Chauhan, when the BJP was in power both at the centre and in the state.

would slow down implementation of the project. In any case, he said, standard services outside the 342 acres of TT Nagar and the smart roads will remain with the municipal corporation.

Raising the money

Bhopal's smart city project was originally estimated to cost Rs 2,718 crore but the amount was later revised to around Rs 3,500 crore. Rs 1,000 crore will come from government and the company must raise the rest on its own.

How does the company plan to raise the money?

Alongside multi-storey government quarters, TT Nagar will have new commercial and entertainment areas. Boulevard Street will have underground tunnels on either side bearing all utilities. This will leave around 100 acres of land "for monetisation". The land will be converted into small plots and sold to private developers. The company expects to fetch Rs 2,500 crore from the sale.

Much of TT Nagar is little more than rubble and tree stumps now. By late December [2018], trees and buildings on either side of what will be Boulevard Street had been cleared and the land levelled, leaving Shaskiya Madhyamik Shala Deepshika, a government school till Class Eight, standing alone. Though its enrolment has not suffered because of the surrounding destruction, attendance has.

"The roads are closed so some children have to walk longer to get here," explained a teacher who requested not to be named. "Attendance of small children and girls has come down."

In class, they must contend with the noise and dust of construction. Many find it hard to concentrate. "Even children living outside TT Nagar attend the school. They will be affected," Sharma pointed out.

While the major overhaul is restricted to a specific area within the city, the mission also mandates "pan-city solutions", essentially technology-based interventions that make systems such as parking, emergency response, traffic management, water supply and sewage treatment more efficient.

In Bhopal, these projects are also potential sources of revenue. They include three multi-level car parks, a biomethanation plant to manage solid waste and the bicycle sharing service. The cycle service has been outsourced to a private company called Chartered Bikes. Once it starts turning a profit, it will pay royalty to the Smart City Corporation.

Similarly, a new website connects the residents with police-verified workers such as plumbers, carpenters, electricians and beauticians. They charge a minimum of Rs 200 a visit and the Smart City gets a small cut of 3–10 per cent depending on the service.

More substantial revenues are expected from "smart streetlights" and "smart poles" being installed by Bharti Infratel and Ericsson at a combined cost of Rs 640 crore. So far, 18,500 of the 20,500 halogen streetlights have been replaced with LED ones. The rights to advertise on them belong to the private installer that must share its profits with the Smart City. Similarly, revenues generated from the 400 smart poles and the 180 km of optical fibre laid underground will be shared by the private firms and the Smart City.

Keeping track of all the smart poles, streetlights and traffic cameras is the Intelligent Traffic Management System hub in the Smart City's office. From this hub, workers of the private firms setting up these systems will watch seven roads and twenty-two junctions for traffic violations and ensure all lights are running.

The Smart City, with the help of Deloitte, has also set up a start-up incubation centre called B-Nest, in the hope that when the start-ups grow enough to generate revenues, the company can own some stake in them.

Throwing out the poor

Ordinary citizens, however, seem disconnected from this grand scheme.

Both the Smart Road and the TT Nagar development projects have resulted in the eviction of the poor. In March 2017, more than 30 families living in Depot Basti, a slum, were moved into a cluster of tin sheds. "Many of the displaced people were employed as domestic workers or handymen in the government quarters. As the quarters came down, they lost employment as well," said Rinky Patel, one of the displaced women.

Another 200 families from Hasnat Nagar, which is part of the Banganga slums bordering the Smart Road, lost their homes and were placed in transit housing. Gauhar, a mother of three abandoned by her husband several years ago, lost both her home and shop. The colony's residents, most of them Muslim, resisted the demolitions but through the year homes were razed and the families moved out.

Gauhar got a document from the officials who moved her out showing that she has been allotted a transit house. The paper does not carry an official seal, though. She does not have anything to indicate where she might end up.

Shabana, also from Hasnat Nagar, has a certificate from the municipal corporation stating that she was chosen for housing under the Pradhan Mantri Awas Yojana. No one could say why some residents have been selected for housing and not others.

In the confusion created by a multiplication of local authorities—a situation activists had warned about—the dozens of families placed in transit housing appealed to their ward representative and municipal corporation for help, but to no avail.

Kumar claimed they will receive "alternative housing" in the area but the families said they have not been told anything and resented being moved. "Some of us had taken loans to build pucca homes," said Ronak Jahan, referring to a brick-and-mortar house. "We have not been told until when we have to stay here. If you throw the poor out, the city automatically looks smart."

First published as "As Bhopal is recast as a Smart City, its poor have a question: where's the room for us?" in Scroll, January 28, 2019.

PART FIVE

REASON VERSUS UNREASON

THE FIRST BATCH OF DELIGHTED RECIPIENTS OF TRANSPLANTS AT
THE DEPARTMENT OF ANCIENT INDIAN PLASTIC SURGERY

Orijit Sen, 2015

RATIONALISTS UNDER ATTACK:
IF WE SHUT UP, THEY SUCCEED...

Vartika Rastogi

The Sanatan Sanstha was founded in 1999, and its affiliate, the Hindu Janajagruti Samiti (HJS), in 2002. A visit to the websites of the two organisations evokes A.K. Ramanujan's distinction between breast and tooth goddesses; the former benign and the latter fierce, but mutually complementary on the semiotic spectrum. The founder of the Sanatan Sanstha, Jayant Balaji Athavale, styles himself "His Holiness Dr", and the page dedicated to him is careful to mention his seven years' practice of "hypnotherapy" in Britain. With this imprimatur of western-style authority in place, the two websites diverge to their separate-seeming tasks. The HJS on December 15, 2018, was exercised about the BJP's recent rout in five state elections. One feature muttered darkly about the new government of Mizoram and the Christian rituals that attended its swearing-in, another demanded that five Elgar Parishad activists be tried for sedition, while an editorial comment grimly concluded that "devout Hindus have no choice but to unite in the forthcoming period". Meanwhile, the Sanatan Sanstha's website advertised services such as ridding your child of the evil eye, followed by an important reminder about donations.

Vartika Rastogi's conversations with rationalists show how the superstitious and the menacing go hand-in-hand, each composed of the same primal bigotry, fear and malice. This makes rationalists the first roadblock to the ambitions of both organisations, and their prime target.

A number of prominent rationalists have faced attacks at the hands of Hindu extremists in recent years, with many having been gunned down in cold blood: the Maharashtra Andhashraddha Nirmoolan Samiti's President, Narendra Dabholkar, in Pune in August 2013; Leftist politician Govind Pansare and his wife, Uma Pansare, in Kolhapur in February 2015; former Kannada University vice-chancellor and scholar M.M. Kalburgi in August 2015; and noted journalist Gauri Lankesh in Bengaluru in

September 2017. All of them were vocal in their opposition to superstition, to Hindutva and its policies.

Investigations reveal a worryingly similar modus operandi for all these murders, committed by multiple assailants on bikes, who were aiming at the chest and the head. The Karnataka SIT also found 7.65mm country pistols similar to the ones used to kill Dabholkar, Pansare and Kalburgi during the probe into Lankesh's murder. A plot against the life of Kannada writer and critic K.S. Bhagwan was also revealed during this probe, along with a list of thirty-four people—all vocal in the same respects, and likely targets for assassination in the near future.

Persons arrested in all these cases belong chiefly to Hindutva outfits such as the Goa-headquartered Sanatan Sanstha and its affiliate, the Hindu Janajagruti Samiti (HJS). Both, while claiming to be "spiritual" organisations, have proved to be involved in subversive activities like communal rioting and bomb blasts. In spite of this, calls to ban the outfits go unheard.

In Maharashtra, where an Anti-Superstition Act was passed in 2013 with the efforts of Dabholkar and other rationalists, there does not seem to be much of a difference between the actions taken by the previous Congress government and that of the BJP. However, support does seem to be implicit in the latter's silence on such issues. "It is a fact that these outfits are now fearless. The Anti-terrorism Squad should see through the operation to ban these outfits before they start killing not just rationalists but common people, too," says anti-superstition activist and founder of the Akhil Bharatiya Andhashraddha Nirmoolan Samiti (ABANS), Prof. Shyam Manav. According to him, "The change in government may not reveal significant change otherwise, but these outfits do feel capable of openly terrorising intellectuals today because the ideology they endorse is running things." As proponents of Hindutva, the Sanstha and HJS are indeed ideological allies for the BJP.

Elsewhere in the country, the government itself appears to be lending a hand to the hostility. "Many members of my organisation have been put into jail for no reason," says Prabir Ghosh, president of the Kolkata-based Science and Rationalists Association of India (SRAI). "The burden of proof has been put on them by the courts and the government, and they have been asked to prove that they are not terrorists and anti-nationalists. How does one prove that?" he asks. According to Ghosh, all of this comes simply for speaking against religious superstition and quackery, or against government policies regarding such issues, on the SRAI's website and on social media.

For Prof. Narendra Nayak, president of the Federation of Indian Rationalist Associations (FIRA), the present "is a scary situation for those willing to get scared". Nayak, whose name was on the list procured during the Karnataka SIT's probe, and who has narrowly escaped multiple attempts on his own life—the latest being in March 2018—is now living under 24-hour security. "However, I am not one of those who shut up out of fear," he says. Nayak's name appears to have moved up the hit-list due to his sustained campaigns against issues such as the mid-brain activation scam that has tricked thousands of people all over Karnataka and the rest of the country.* His trouble with Hindutva groups also owes to his criticism of people of the likes of Sri Sri Ravi Shankar and Jaggi Vasudev, as well as his fight to get justice for the RTI activist and BJP booth-level worker Vinayaka Baliga, who was allegedly hacked to death by his own party-members.

---

*Mid-brain activation purports to "optimise" brain functioning by enabling subjects to perceive visual data intuitively, without needing to see it—reading in blindfolds, etc. Universally denounced as a snake-oil scam, mid-brain activation centres have mushroomed all over India, unimpeded by the government, charging parents between Rs 10,000 and Rs 25,000 to turn their children into prodigies. As *The Hindu* (April 21, 2015) reports, one Vinoj Surendran, who "runs the Kollam-based Ingenium India offering various 'mind-empowerment' programmes for children", accepted Narendra Nayak's challenge to demonstrate blindfold reading in a neutral setting. However, Surendran backed out after learning that Nayak is a rationalist. He said that the children, whose midbrains had been activated using "nada-yoga" techniques, could only perform in a "meditative mode" and not a "defensive or negative" one.

"Sanatan Sanstha and other Hindutva gangs plot to get rid of us [rationalists] because we are teaching people to question things, which hurts their business," Nayak says, referring to the attempts made on his own life and the lives of others by alleged members of Hindutvawadi organisations. He, like many others, is of the conviction that the government is hand-in-glove with these organisations. "It is the attitude of the people at the top that emboldens these so-called 'fringe groups' to carry out their threats of violence. The government claims to have no control over these groups, but makes attempts to protect them." In such an environment, anyone—rationalist, scientist, journalist or activist—who speaks against the ideals of Hindutva is under threat of attack.

It is not merely the person of freethinkers that is being targeted, but the very roots of their ideals as well. This can be seen in the vandalism of statues of E.V. Ramasamy Periyar—the pioneer of rationalism in the country—that took place in Tamil Nadu earlier this year. These incidents occurred directly after a post advocating destruction of these statues was made by BJP National Secretary H. Raja on Facebook.*

While the Constitution of India urges people to "develop scientific temper, humanism and the spirit of enquiry and reform", in Article 51A, the ruling party at the Centre seeks to find—or to shoehorn where it cannot find—all scientific answers in the Vedas. Ironically, the pseudo-science thus established is considered superior to the "superstition" that plagues other religions, and the quest is to establish Hinduism and Hindutva itself as superior "ways of life". When groups such as the Sanatan Sanstha and

---

*On March 3, 2018, within hours of the BJP's victory in state elections in Tripura, a statue of Lenin in the town of Belonia was bulldozed by right-wing supporters. H. Raja's Facebook post welcomed the news and read: "Today Lenin's statue, tomorrow Tamil Nadu's E.V.R. Ramaswami's [sic] statue." A statue of Periyar at Vellore was duly found vandalised on March 7, another at Pudukottai was beheaded on March 20. In quick succession, statues of Gandhi, B.R. Ambedkar, Nehru, and even one of Syama Prasad Mookerjee, came under attack in different parts of the country.

the HJS are the agents of propagating this pseudo-science, they naturally make an enemy out of any rationalists who seek to debunk the hoaxes of these "alternative" knowledge systems.

Despite the precarious situation, rationalists refuse to back down from their criticism, whether of superstition or the government. "Dissenting voices have already decreased today. If we shut up now, they succeed," says Nayak. "After all, we are not bothered about anything but our aim to make the present a better place to live in—to achieve a more rational, humanistic and questioning society."

Indian Cultural Forum, August 27, 2018. First published in The Citizen, August 24, 2018.

THE CURIOUS CASE OF RSS–BJP SCIENCE

Prabir Purkayastha

The RSS and BJP have a curious relationship with science and reason. Two "curious cases" highlight the right-wing aversion to reason. In 2017, the RSS began to push for "fair, tall babies" with "high intelligence"—violating genetic science while promoting sex selection. In 2018, Satyapal Singh, the Minister of State for Human Resources Development (HRD), and a former police officer, attacked the theory of evolution while speaking at the All India Vaidik Sammelan.

Making super-babies: RSS markets illegal mumbo jumbo as science

The RSS-linked Arogya Bharati has been running programmes for producing "fair, tall babies" with "high intelligence"; even if the parents are dark, short and of low intelligence. All this, according to Arogya Bharati "experts", can be done by following Garbhasanskar, i.e. correct protocols for the womb, claimed to be ancient Indian wisdom. They have even set up Garbhavigyan

Anusandhan Kendra, a so-called research centre in Jamnagar, Gujarat. Garbhavigyan Anusandhan Kendra not only promises "getting the best progeny" to parents, but also their "desired sex of offspring". And all by regulating the "mental and physical status of the partners, time of copulation" and a host of such hocus-pocus measures.

The press has already linked the desire for intelligent, tall and fair babies to Germany's eugenics programme and Nazi Germany. Arogya Bharati's Garbhasanskar brings out the underlying racial beliefs of the RSS, regarding colour and superiority—remember RSS man Tarun Vijay's statement about how "we" have been living in harmony with "them", the dark-skinned South Indians?* It was such a eugenics programme for breeding a true "Aryan race" that not only killed an estimated 6 million Jews and half a million Roma (of Indian descent) in Hitler's gas chambers, but also led to the sterilisation of 400,000 "inferior" Germans.

Neither was the practice of forced sterilisation limited to Germany. The US sterilised about 60,000 women under its eugenic sterilisation laws, upheld by its Supreme Court, and repealed only in 1974. Its immigration policy characterised the Irish, East Europeans Jews, Asians and Africans as the inferior races. Eugenics was far more widespread than the West is willing to admit today.

It is obvious that the seeds of the eugenics ideology of a "superior Aryan race" are shared between Nazism and the RSS. B.S. Moonje (1872–1948), one of the ideologues of the RSS, had travelled to Italy and was deeply influenced by Mussolini's fascism and militarisation of politics via the Black Shirts. M.S. Golwalkar (1906–73) writes approvingly of German

---

*In his capacity as head of the India-Africa Parliamentary Friendship Group, Tarun Vijay participated in a show on Al Jazeera (April 7, 2015), where he responded to an African student's charge of racism in India with the blithe rejoinder: "If we were racist, why would the entire south—you know, the Tamils, you know Kerala, Karnataka and Andhra—why do we live with them? We have blacks, black people around us."

racial pride. The passion with which the Hindutva ideologues identify India with the Aryans cannot be understood without understanding their belief in racial superiority; hence the desire to produce tall and fair babies, very much in the mould of Nazi Germany's desire for blond and tall children.

The eugenic inspiration for Garbhasanskar has appeared widely in the press. What has not yet been examined is Arogya Bharati and its Garbhavigyan Kendra claims, and whether they fall foul of the law. While the Kolkata High Court's interim order restricted Arogya Bharati's proposed Kolkata workshop on May 6 and 7, 2017, to a set of lectures, the court is yet to pronounce on the legality of offering services such as "uttamsantati" (super babies) and "desired sex of the offspring".

There are two sets of laws that Arogya Bharati and Garbhavigyan Kendra violate. One is related to what is the The Drugs and Magic Remedies (Objectionable Advertisements) Act, 1954. It is clear that the claims and practices under Garbhasanskar are in clear violation of the Act. According to Hitesh Jani, the national convenor of Arogya Bharati and an "expert" on Garbhasanskar, genetic engineering can be also done in the womb by following Garbhasanskar. This is in violation of all genetics that we know today, and utter nonsense masquerading as ancient knowledge. Such claims are precisely the ones that the Magic Remedies Act bans.

The "corroborative evidence" the propagators of Garbhasanskar offer is equally ridiculous. Ashok Kumar Varshney, an RSS pracharak and the national organising secretary of Arogya Bharati, said to the *Indian Express* (May 7, 2017), that the project was inspired by what a senior RSS ideologue learned forty years ago in Germany. Varshney said, "He was told that it was due to a woman called 'Mother of Germany'. When he met her...she told him, 'You have come from India, have you not heard of Abhimanyu [the son of Arjuna in the epic *Mahabharata*]?' She told him that the new generation in Germany was born through Garbhsanskar and that is why the country is so developed." Of course, neither the RSS ideologue nor the "Mother of Germany" are identified by Varshney.

It is always interesting to see how the Hindutva ideologues invariably quote Western figures to back their claims. Whether it is the unknown German Mother, or a David Frawley, the proof of the validity of the Hindutva cocktail masquerading as "ancient wisdom" is always a Western figure.* All those who rail against Macaulay invariably bow to the superior wisdom of the West, as long as it supports their half-baked and crazy theories.

The Drugs and Magic Remedies Act is not the only one that the Arogya Bharati and its various affiliates violate. By offering to create babies of the desired sex, they are also violating the Pre-Conception and Pre-Natal Diagnostic Techniques Act, 1994 (PCPNDT Act). The main purpose of the PCPNDT Act is to prevent sex selection, whereas Arogya Bharati promises just that to those who follow its Garbhasanskar programme.

The issue is not simply the violation of law. By claiming to be able to deliver a baby of the desired sex, the RSS is reinforcing the desire for male children in India, a desire that has seen female foeticide and steeply declining sex ratios. In some states such as Haryana, Rajasthan and Gujarat, the sex ratio of the girl child in the age group of 0–6 years is as low as 834, 888 and 890 per thousand respectively. Not only does the RSS's Garbhasanskar reinforce racial stereotypes, it also reinforces patriarchy.

Is Garbhasanskar ancient Indian science? If we look at the material that Arogya Bharati and Garbhavigyan Kendra have provided, there is nothing remotely connected to any serious Ayurvedic text or ancient science. There is an air of authority regarding ancient texts and Ayurveda, neither of which is either referenced or quoted. What is offered instead, is finding out the right time for copulation, the kind of diet that both parents should

---

*Frawley, an American Catholic convert to Hinduism, is in lockstep with the Hindu right, from practising astrology to supporting the indigenous-origins theory for the Aryans. Also known as Vamadeva Shastri, he was awarded the Padma Bhushan in 2015.

have, the efficacy of reciting various mantras and listening to devotional music, all offered as "ancient wisdom".

If we examine Garbhavigyan Kendra's website and claims, not as an ideological exercise but as a purely money-making venture using fake science, we get a completely different picture. There is a page on the site, which is supposed to detail success stories regarding infertility. Two pictures of babies, obviously not Indian (yes, they are fair!), named Kate White, The flu 1, and Kate White, The flu 2, with details in Latin are presented as success stories. A casual visitor might believe that these two babies were the result of Garbhasanskar. The reality is that the web template used to create the website has such gibberish Latin as a simple placeholder for text. These are not success stories.

The Kendra has made no attempt to provide any proof that its so-called cures work, presumably since it might open them to investigation of fraud.

The Kendra also has a video; it's the only video I could find on its site. The video was intriguing as it carries nothing remotely resembling the mumbo-jumbo of Garbhasanskar. The mystery becomes clear when we come to the last part of the video: it gives US-based toll-free numbers, and websites to contact in Wisconsin for would-be parents. It is a video ripped off the Internet, and uploaded on YouTube by a certain Barb Scot, who has nothing to do with Garbhasanskar!

Why science scares the RSS/BJP: The case of Satyapal Singh

Satyapal Singh, the Minister of State for Human Resources Development (HRD), and a former police officer, while speaking at the All India Vaidik Sammelan at Aurangabad, Maharashtra, on January 20, 2018, attacked the theory of evolution—which he foolishly calls Darwinism—asking that it be removed from school and college education. In this, he has been backed by Ram Madhav, the general secretary of the BJP, who has quoted the Christian Right on creationism—now called "intelligent design"—being a credible substitute for the theory of evolution. They join a growing tribe of BJP leaders and ideologues, who argue that myth—or what Y.S. Rao, the Indian Council of Historical Research (ICHR) chairperson, termed as "collective memory"—must supersede any scientific study of history. It is on the basis of unreason and mythology that the BJP wants to build a modern India.

Modi talking about myths as historical facts—flying chariots as aeronautics, and Ganesha's elephant head being cosmetic surgery—could be dismissed as eccentricity or aberration. But Satyapal Singh and Ram Madhav's attacks on evolution are not some isolated myths being paraded as history. Evolution is at the heart of biology, or life sciences, today.

The three premiere science academies, for the first time, have come out openly against the BJP minister and condemned his attack on evolution.* The statement from the three academies states:

> The Honourable Minister of State for Human Resource Development, Shri Satyapal Singh has been quoted as saying that "Nobody, including our ancestors, in writing or orally, have said they saw an ape turning into a man. Darwin's theory (of evolution of humans) is scientifically wrong..."
>
> The three Academies of Science wish to state that there is no scientific basis for the Minister's statements. Evolutionary theory, to which Darwin made seminal contributions, is well established. There is no scientific dispute about the basic facts of evolution. This is a scientific theory and one that has made many predictions that have been repeatedly confirmed by experiments and observation...
>
> It would be a retrograde step to remove the teaching of the theory of evolution from school and college curricula or to dilute this by offering non-scientific explanations or myths...

The late Pushpa Bhargava (1928–2017; founder of the Centre for Cellular and Molecular Biology, Hyderabad) had resigned from the academies for their refusal to stand up for science and the

---

*The Indian Academy of Sciences, Bangalore, the Indian National Science Academy, New Delhi, and the Indian Academy of Science.

scientific temper. He would have been heartened that the scientists have at last raised their voice against this attack on science.

Raghavendra Gadagkar, former president of the Indian National Science Academy and an internationally recognised biologist, correctly identifies that Satyapal Singh and the BJP/RSS project is not about science but about politics. Speaking to NDTV, he said it was "politically polarising science and scientists" which is "the real danger we must guard against".

Raosaheb Kasbe traces this project in his book *Zot*, published in Marathi and translated into English as *Spotlight on the RSS*. He shows that Golwalkar, speaking to the Vishwa Hindu Parishad in Allahabad during the Kumbh Mela in 1966, was asserting the supremacy of religion over science. Golwalkar said, "On several occasions, people say that this age is the age of science. So they often argue that we have to bring about changes in religion in order to adapt to the age of science. I say exactly the opposite thing... If you go on changing religion with every research in science, then the religion will not remain religion... The entire mankind will be then disenchanted. Hence, I think that to bring changes in religion with every research in science is not an appropriate way." Kasbe writes that the language used by Golwalkar is similar to that of the Islamists, who want to *Islamise* modernity; the RSS wants to *saffronise* modernity.

Satyapal Singh now claims that evolution, a core tenet of life sciences, has been "disproved" by scientists today. He even advances his PhD, in chemistry, secured from Delhi University before he became a police officer, as proof that he is still a "man of science". He wants to have a debate over this in a conference, presumably to be organised by the HRD Ministry. Creationism, perhaps, will help shore up the "science" of Garbha Shastra/ Garbhasanskar, which the RSS is propagating with the help of various government agencies. According to their racist and eugenic beliefs, this will help to develop fair and intelligent babies by dint of the mother's listening to religious texts, devotional songs and not eating non-vegetarian food *after conception*!

The interesting issue for me has always been the source and validity of such "truths" which the Sangh lobby propagates. After all, Hinduism never had a revealed text—unlike the Abrahamic religions of Judaism, Christianity and Islam—that had to be taken as the basis of science. It is the Abrahamic myth which is inflexible on the point that God worked for six days to create the universe and all living beings.

It is this creation myth in the Bible that has led to the lobby in the US which argues that creationism should be taught in schools and colleges on a par with evolution. It is this lobby's literature, presumably on the internet, that has deeply influenced Satyapal Singh and Ram Madhav. Ram Madhav, in his tweet, mentions his source, Evolution News, a website of the Discovery Institute that is devoted to the so-called theory of Intelligent Design, the retooled, "modern" version of creationism. Whatever such theories might be, they certainly are not intelligent.

Just as the Christian Right/fundamentalists in the US argue against evolution, so do the Islamists or Islamic fundamentalists. In Saudi Arabia the teaching of evolution is banned and referred to only as a blasphemous theory. Yes, Satyapal Singh and Ram Madhav are indeed in very distinguished company.

Why are the Hindutva proponents continually attracted to such "Western" thoughts, when they attack others for borrowing from the West? Why do they use the "arguments" of an unknown and unsourced German woman, who supported the ancient wisdom of Garbhasanskar, and is allegedly the mother of modern Germany? Why borrow from western creationism and attack science in India? Including labelling the theory of evolution as Darwinism?

It is here we must see how the roots of the BJP/RSS influence their thinking. Golwalkar was clear in his book, *We or Our Nationhood Defined* (1939). He was defining a modern nation, not an ancient one. For him, culture (Hindu), language (Sanskrit), race (Aryan) were the characteristics of a "modern" nation. He was defining—following in the footsteps of Mussolini and Hitler—a sectarian nation, that would identify the nation with one section alone of its people, disenfranchising the rest. He was defining a modern, exclusionary nation, in which Muslims and Christians would be subjugated, second-class citizens. But these views should not be confused with any thoughts from the past. As V.D. Savarkar (1883–1966) had argued, Hinduism needs to be militarised and India needs to be Hinduised; he was clear that this Hindutva had nothing to do with Hinduism as a religion.

What we need to register is that the RSS's views are never original, they have always been derived from Western ideologues. Just as they picked up fascism as an ideology from Italy and Germany, they are now picking up creationism from the racist Christian Right in the US, even while attacking churches and Christians in different parts of the country.

Why are the BJP ideologues so keen to attack not only science but also the methods of science? Why do they argue that myth, or faith, must prevail over reason?

The answer is simple. The RSS/BJP fears critical thinking. Instead, it wants to build an Indian nation on the basis of hatred and fear. Their attempt is to identify only the Hindus with India and exclude minorities as outsiders. Even when they have been here for a thousand years, or two thousand. The problem that they have is not just excluding minorities; using religion for defining exclusions demand that they need to overlook the caste system and the internal exclusions within Hindu society. A critical and a scientific examination of the past would raise all these issues. Therefore the need to jettison science and reason.

Just as it wants to borrow ideology from abroad, the RSS/BJP wants to import advanced technology without the scientific capacity to develop it in India. This is the difference between the self-reliance of Made in India, and the shallowness of Modi's Make in India. In the first, we had to absorb and develop technology. In the other, we expect foreign capital to come to India, manufacture parts or assemble parts manufactured elsewhere without a transfer of technology: a policy for perpetual dependence on the West. Both in mind and body.

First published in Newsclick, May 10, 2017 and January 25, 2018.

HOW PEOPLE IN POWER GET AWAY WITH UNSCIENTIFIC STATEMENTS

Tejal Kanitkar

The mental laziness begins with us, with our unwillingness to take a stand against quotidian instances of irrationality, says Tejal Kanitkar, in this edited transcript of her address to the Mumbai Collective in December 2017. She further asks if this occurs because we are reluctant to disturb the peace or because we have made our peace with great wrongs, with the victimisation of others.

All kinds of ridiculous statements have been made about science of late, and I am not going to focus on them. One that's too good to leave out, though, is how the cow exhales oxygen and how it absorbs radiation as well.* So there are many things cows can do that we didn't know about. But the point is that people holding positions of responsibility make these statements, and the question to ask is why they think they can get away with it. Why do they think it is ok? Why is it that there is no deterrent for them to make such statements? And that brings us to the fact of something I would call "everyday obscurantism". It is there all around us. We see it, we make jokes about some of these extremely ridiculous statements, we make memes and pass them around on social media.

But, very often, we just let it pass, this obscurantism we see around us on a daily basis. Parents insist: "Child, it's the solar eclipse. Don't step outdoors." Everyone must have encountered this line, not infrequently either. If you're building a home, or just taking one on rent, it's the done thing to first examine its vaastu (geomantic alignment). You must have noticed this as well, it happens all around you. Horoscopes are very important nowadays.

---

*Vasudev Devnani, Rajasthan's education minister and an electrical engineer by training, shared these and other findings on the "scientific importance" of cow dung, in a speech at the Hingonia Cow Rehabilitation Centre, Jaipur, on January 14, 2017.

I teach at an institute and often overhear students talking. In the first semester, introducing themselves, they'll go: "Hi, I am so and so, and by the way I am Sagittarian." So horoscopes have become extremely important. This is obscurantism and we don't call it out on a daily basis. There is also something a tad lower-key than this, more personal, it parades around as personal choice: wearing a white thread across your torso. I don't know what it is supposed to achieve. But that is very much a part of what we see around us. You have, for example, all kinds of elaborate weddings brimming with rituals. In cities like Mumbai and Pune, there is this new trend that you have the usual wedding with its full complement of rituals. However, you get the mangalashtak mantras recited by women from the Jnana Prabodhini or some place like that, so obscurantism gets to flaunt its "progressive" strain, too.*

There's all of this happening all around and we don't question it. We let it go. Sometimes the reasoning is: "I don't believe in all this but it'll hurt my parents if I don't do it." So we have to do it then. And this goes on all the time. It creates the grounds for all kinds of ridiculous statements on science and, suddenly one day, when they hit us in the face, we wonder how anyone could say this. But they can because all kinds of other things go unquestioned all the time anyway. Questioning these things on a daily basis would require an uncompromising embrace of modernity and we are scared of doing this because, in our country, we are scared of rejecting the past. There is a strange reverence in us for the past. We are not quite sure... and we don't want to let go of it completely. It can exist in extreme proportions, like with our Prime Minister who has glorified all kinds of things—you

*Founded in 1962, with a declared objective of "dharm-sansthapana" (the installation of dharma) for societal resurgence, the Jnana Prabodhini is most active in its home base of Pune and describes itself on its website as a "multifarious institution working in the fields of education, research, rural development, women power [sic], youth organisation, national integration and health", emphasising "the eastern concept of Stree-Shakti [woman power] rather than imitating the Western view of Stree-Mukti" (women's liberation).

know, pushpakvimaan, etc.—as part of it. Also on climate change, I don't know if you have heard this but he has made a statement saying climate change is not actually happening, it is simply a state of mind. It is not becoming warmer, it is we who have become less tolerant. It turns out that our ancestors also faced climate variability; however, they managed it, because they were much stronger.* This glorification and reverence for the past exists in extreme proportion in the Sangh Parivar, but it exists all around us as well. All of us have met this uncle-figure who would say: "People were more scientific in the time of our ancestors. There was little pollution then, the air's gotten worse now. There was no cancer then, whereas more and more people are getting cancer nowadays. The women were physically stronger. They'd bear tens of children and still cook for twenty people every day, without a fridge, mixer, slicer, or any fuss. I'm sure you've met people who have said this and of course we let it go a lot of the time without pointing out that our ancestors probably died at the age of forty, didn't live long enough to get cancer; and not just that, but the fact that this past, this very past, is full of, is riddled with, caste. It is riddled with patriarchy, with extreme levels of scarcity, deprivation, inhumanity and exploitation. The same past. And we are unwilling to let go of it. This is what provides the grounds for such statements, or the attack that comes from Hindutva.

In the morning Professor Raosaheb Kasbe reminded us of this beautiful word *annihilation,* in the context of the annihilation of caste, and I think it is a very important word to remember in this context. If we want to build a new society that is more equal, in which there is no deprivation, in which everybody has a certain

---

*On September 5, 2014, Teachers Day, Narendra Modi took a master class via video conference with schoolchildren from across the country. In response to a question from a student in Assam, the country's new prime minister explained the psychosomatic dimensions of climate change, adding that old people tend to feel the cold more intensely, not because the climate has turned any colder than before but because they have become enfeebled.

level of well-being, then we have to reject this unseemly past. If we only pause to question, as science requires us to, then we will reject this past as unworthy. And this, I think, is at the root of the RSS attack, the attack by Hindutva. Their final target is not really technology, for they like the bomb very much. They might say, don't teach Newton to our kids at school because Newton was a foreigner. But they love to take the Ahmedabad–Delhi flight. So it's not as if they were rejecting technology. However, attacking the scientific method is necessary to them. What they really mean to attack is the scientific study of society, because the minute you have a scientific study of society you come up with questions that they don't want to face.

Science is much more, has been for many, many years about much more than observation, or the documentation of observation; it is not enough simply to see how things appear but also why they appear as they do. And the minute you ask the question of why things appear the way they do in the context of society, you will have women questioning why it is they should stay at home while the men go out and earn and study. You can no longer tell people they are born poor *kyun ki tumhari qismat kharaab hai*—bad karma has brought you to this pass. You can no longer tell somebody that it is because of the sins of their past life that they are born in a lower caste. You won't get away with it. We should understand that the attack on science is meant to prevent a scientific study of society. In that context, I also want to make another point—that the attack on society doesn't come only from the right. Part of the grounds for this attack have been provided by us. Among a lot of people who would not otherwise associate with the right-wing, say, progressive liberal movements, we see a lot of science scepticism, scepticism about technology. Unfortunately, the fight against globalisation, against global capital has somehow segued into a fight against modernity, a fight against modern science, against technology. Technology is seen as being inherently anti-poor. Science as inherently patriarchal, anti-women. These hostile positions are not necessarily taken only by the Sangh Parivar. They exist even otherwise and these are dangerous positions to take. They provide the grounds for the rise of obscurantism.

Does this come of our inability to fight capitalism? Our inability to fight globalisation? We seem to be saying science and technology are basically proxies for these and are easier to fight than globalisation and capitalism. If we want to fight inequality then I think one of our first steps should be that we take back science. Science is ours. It does not belong to the multi-nationals. The fight is against the multi-nationals, and we have to reclaim science by fighting for access to scientific institutions. Take back the technology that was created in the first place by the labour of the working class. Technology does not innately belong to the élite, so it is not science and technology that we must be fighting. We should remember this distinction because the scepticism towards science and technology, along with our everyday obscurantism has, I think, also cleared the way for the kind of attacks we've seen from the Sangh Parivar.

I want to end with a tribute to, or by remembering, that young man whose death two years ago moved a lot of us. Rohith Vemula's death was not just a loss for the student community or the fight against caste discrimination; his death was a loss to the scientific community as well, because he got the point of science. He was inspired by Dr Ambedkar, that unrelenting, uncompromising, untiring advocate of modernity. He was one of the few who were like that in this country and Rohith was inspired by him; he wanted to be like Carl Sagan. He wanted to take science to the people. To bring light into the darkness that is the everyday life of so many people around us. That is why they don't want Rohiths, and that is why more Rohiths must emerge at this point of time and, to this end, we need to save science.

This is the transcribed text of a talk given on December 9, 2017 at the second edition of the Mumbai Collective held from December 9-10, 2017.

THE DOUBLE CURSE OF SUPERSTITION AND COMMUNALISATION

Rajendra Chenni

The communalisation of Karnataka led to the preservation of a superstitious ritual called madésnana in which non-brahmin devotees roll over banana leaves on which food was earlier served to brahmins.

The protest by activists, intellectuals and writers against the practice of "madémadésnana" at Kukke Subramanya and Udupi Shri Krishna temples in Karnataka, has been at low ebb for some time, thanks to the High Court's verdict, and the Supreme Court's stay on the verdict.* "Madémadésnana", commonly known as "madésnana", is the practice of devotees rolling over banana leaves on which food had been served earlier to brahmins in a segregated part of the temple. In other words, the devotees roll over the leftover food of the brahmins. This takes place during the Shashti festival celebrated at the Subramanya temple. While the educated imagination may conceive images of illiterate tribals and dalits participating in this demeaning ritual with little covering on their bodies, the visuals made available by the media are quite unexpected. The devotees rolling on the leftovers are from the shudra and backward communities, with a small, always unconfirmed, number of brahmins included. Some are middle and upper-middle class, while many are educated. They have been led to believe that the practice cures skin diseases, and also purifies them of any sins they may have committed. For other devotees, it is the fulfilment of a vow taken in times of trouble. While rolling

---

*On November 20, 2014, the Karnataka High Court expressed its inability to stop the practice of madésnana, given the ground-level opposition to judicial intervention. In its winter session the same year, the Karnataka legislature dropped a provision from its Anti-Superstition Bill, which would have outlawed the madésnana. On December 13, the Supreme Court put a stay on the practice.

on the ground (usually around a temple), known as "uruluseve" in Kannada, is common in many religious places, madésnana ("madé" means "leftovers" in the Tulu language commonly spoken in South Canara) is practised only in a few temples. It is claimed that the practice is ancient, or at least five hundred years old.

Though there have been sporadic movements against such superstitious practices in Karnataka, a concerted struggle began in 2012. The CPI (M) (Communist Party of India [Marxist]) led by G.V. Sriram Reddy, K.S. Shivaramu of the Karnataka Backward Class Awareness Forum, Mysore, and members of the Komu Souharda Vedike (Communal Harmony Forum) spearheaded the movement. They were also supported by the progressive pontiff Shri Veerabhadra Chennamalla Swamiji of Nidumamidi Matha.

Many religious heads, leading intellectuals like G. Rajashekhar, well-known rationalist Narendra Nayak and Munir Katipalya, state president of the DYFI (Democratic Youth Federation of India), were the other prominent leaders. Meetings and consultations were held at Bengaluru and other places before the long jathas and protest meets were planned.

Nidumamidi Swamiji had categorically said that the practice was superstitious and disgusting. It was done in ignorance, fanned by conservative forces, and also encouraged by the greedy management of the temples. The majority of devotees at the festival, and the madésnana, are shudras and dalits. The brahminical priest-class supported by the temple management does everything to keep the superstitious practice going, because the Kukke Subramanya temple has an annual income of about eight crores. Sociologists have seen this as an example of a casteist social order, with its ideological capstone of brahmin superiority. Like all regional societies in India, that of Dakshina Kannada has a pyramidal structure with brahmins at the apex. In this case, it is the Shri Krishna Matha at Udupi, headed by the highly controversial pontiff Shri Pejawara Swamiji, which has successfully held the line for centuries, keeping brahminical superiority unaffected. Below the brahmin community are the

Nadavas or Bunts, a powerful land-owning shudra community. Below them are the Konkani communities, traditionally business and trade communities. At the broad base are the Billavas and the Mogaveeras. The Koraga community is the formerly untouchable community. The Male Kudiyas are tribals who have played a baffling and unexpected role in the entire episode of madésnana. As writer and activist Vasudeva Uchil explains, the right-wing ideology, initially supported by the brahmins, Nadavas and the Konkani people, is now passionately embraced by the "lower castes and communities". In Karnataka's activist parlance, members of these communities are the "foot soldiers" of the right-wing.

Dakshina Kannada, the western coastal belt of Karnataka, was the first to be transformed by colonial modernity. The Christian missionaries established strong schooling and healthcare systems, the first vernacular press, brought out the first newspaper in Kannada, and laid down the foundations of modern Kannada scholarship. Social reform movements and the freedom struggle were vibrant here. Long before Gandhi's pro-Harijan movement made its impact, Kudmul Ranga Rao had started educational institutions for dalits, and also led a reform-campaign for them. In the Karnataka social imaginary, Mangalore has always stood for modernity, enterprise and a liberal way of life. But in the last three decades, in the post-Babri Masjid period, there has been an intensive communalisation of the region. The RSS and its parivar have made Dakshina Kannada a violent, turbulent region, where right-wing ideology has infiltrated civil society. Not surprisingly, in the last decade, some radical Muslim fundamentalist organisations have entered the fray, reinforcing the communal divide. The pub attack on women in Mangalore led by the Sriram Sene in January 2009, a spate of killings at Sulya and Bantwal from 2015 through 2017, and attacks by cow-vigilante groups in recent years, have made Dakshina Kannada a platform for communal politics. The Communal Harmony Forum, the CPM, farmers' organisations and activists have been fighting to keep the society from reaching a point of no return.

This background helps one to understand the cultural politics behind the resistance to the struggle for banning the cursed practice of the madésnana. The Pejawara Swamiji of the Udupi Matha is a staunch supporter of the RSS, and has always held a high position in the Vishwa Hindu Parishad. He was present at the demolition of the Babri Masjid, though he has claimed that he did not support the demolition. He has also consistently projected himself as a liberal, reform-minded pontiff, with well-publicised visits to dalit colonies, and an "Iftar" dinner for Muslims hosted at the Udupi Matha on June 25, 2017. He has announced that a VHP meet, or a Dharma Sansad, will soon be held at the Udupi Matha, and the date of construction of the Rama Mandir at Ayodhya declared.* An example of the clout of the Pejawar Swami is that he was among those Hindus who signed a petition to counter the claims of dalit groups that there exists caste-based discrimination in England. This petition from a mostly savarna diaspora was submitted to the British Government and Parliament, to put pressure on the parliamentary committee to exclude caste-based discrimination from the ambit of the Equality Act of 2010, and retain only racial discrimination in its recommendations.† In 2010, the House of Lords had voted to outlaw caste discrimination, calling it an aspect of race, and it had at the time seemed inevitable that the Equality Act, amended once in 2013, would be further expanded to recognise caste exclusion.

---

*On December 3, 2018, the Pejawar Swami joined the VHP in urging Narendra Modi yet again to issue an ordinance and commence work on the construction of a Ram temple at Ayodhya by early 2019.

†On July 27, 2018, the Theresa May-led Tory government reneged on its earlier assurance of introducing a law to ban caste-based discrimination in the UK. A 2009 study commissioned by the Anti-Caste Discrimination Alliance (an umbrella group of British bodies) as well as a 2010 report commissioned by the government from the National Institute of Economic and Social Research, had confirmed the prevalence of caste-based discrimination in Britain. Following this, the British government had even set a timetable for new legislation to be introduced, but caved in under pressure from the National Council for Hindu Temples and the Vishwa Hindu Parishad (UK branch).

To return to the protest against the madésnana, it was triggered off by two incidents relating to the humiliating practice of segregating brahmins and non-brahmins at the communal dinners served at the Udupi Shri Krishna Matha and the Paraja Matha. Activists have called for an end to this pankthibhedha—the discriminatory practice based on notions of purity and superiority. In separate incidents, two educated and well-connected women belonging to the Nadava (Bunt) and Gouda Saraswath communities, who were sitting down for dinner with brahmin friends, were unceremoniously and humiliatingly asked to get up and leave.* Both of them later protested against their eviction, their caste organisations made some noise, and everything was somehow patched up. Various progressive organisations came together to demand an end to both the pankthibhedha practice of segregating brahmin and non-brahmin communities at meals in the Mathas, and the horrendous practice of madésnana. The Pejawara Swamiji and the temple authorities merely talked about old beliefs, ancient practices, and above all, denied any use of force on their part. On December 27, 2012, K.A. Shriramu and the CPI (M) had led a long jatha in a protest at the Udupi Matha itself. To foil the protest, the BJP-led government allowed the police to lathi-charge the activists, and jailed hundreds of activists, while slapping cases against CPM leaders and activists. On the other hand, devotees freely vented their anger at the intellectuals and activists for trying to tamper with their personal beliefs and religious practices. Their major argument was that they were participating in the madésnana voluntarily, and that they had the right to religious faith and practice. The highly partisan and communalised Kannada media played an unethical role by denigrating the progressive organisations and painting the protest as anti-Hindu. However, the public debates clearly pointed to the future in the rationalist struggle against superstitious practices.

*On April 15, 2014, Prof. Vanita N. Shetty had visited the Sri Krishna Temple of Udupi, where she was asked to leave the dining hall after an attendant asked about her caste and learned she was a Bunt. She was directed to a separate facility for non-brahmins.

The most formidable challenge would come from a discourse carefully constructed by the Sangh Parivar, conservative religious institutions, and right-of-centre "intellectuals". The discourse relies heavily on the sanctity of the constitutional right of freedom of faith and worship. What has been added to the discourse is the highly effective notion of "hurt religious feelings". This polemical gambit is used to rally forces against the efforts of any government to enact legislations relating to religious practices. It has reinforced the idea that any group, any political outfit, or any association, has the "right" to push back against an attempt to reform inhuman and humiliating practices. Most importantly, the purpose is not to allow any secular move to monitor or control the power of religious institutions. For example, the Karnataka Prevention of Superstitious Practices Bill (2013) was dead in the water even before it was introduced in the Karnataka legislative assembly. Elected members of the BJP swore to sacrifice their lives, rather than allow any discussion of the Bill. The Kannada media ran 24×7 propaganda campaign on the evil designs afoot to destroy Hinduism. Even the Congress government's cabinet was manifestly relieved that the opposition had stalled the Bill!*

All of this happened along with the struggle to ban the madésnana. The Pejawara Swamiji came out with a compromise solution of replacing the madésnana with a "yedesnana". Yede

---

*At the start of its term in 2013, the Congress government declared its intention to pass an anti-superstition law for Karnataka. Over the next three years, three separate drafts of the proposed law were made—one by the National Law School of India, Bengaluru, targeting thirteen superstitious practices; and two by the state social welfare department— but none of them was tabled before the state legislature, even though the murder of M.M. Kalburgi in 2015 had strengthened the demand for such a law. Finally, more than two months after the killing of Gauri Lankesh, the Karnataka Prevention and Eradication of Inhuman Evil Practices and Black Magic Bill was passed by both houses of legislature on November 16, 2017, outlawing twenty-three practices including the madésnana, the menstrual taboo on temple entry, and animal sacrifice. In its present form, the law applies only to Hindu observances.

refers to the prasada, or food offering to the gods. He suggested that the prasada, or yede, would be made available for the devotees to roll over.

In the midst of all this, a shocker came from the association of the tribal Male Kudiya community. The community is traditionally given the task of decorating the festival chariot along with other tasks. The president of the Male Kudiya Association, Bhaskar Bendodi, denounced the activists and protestors for trying to destroy the traditional belief-system of the tribal community. In an effectively worded statement, later placed before the Karnataka High Court, it was said: "... it is a sort of cathartic communication with the supreme divine for many. The ritual should never be gauged simply in terms of logic because it is a subjective matter governed by [the] sentiments and belief systems of the people performing it."

This statement contains the other dangerous ingredient against any attempt to reform traditional practices. Here was the very community whose members were to be protected from demeaning practices propagated by brahminical hegemony, saying that the ancient practices involving the community were too sacred to be tampered with. It even talked eloquently about the intensity of the religious experience involving the loss of the self in the practice of the madésnana. The arguments bore a curious resemblance to U.R. Ananthamurthy's response to the only successful attempt by the government of Karnataka, prior to 2017, at enacting a law to ban a humiliating practice. In 1986, Prof. B. Krishnappa, founder of the Dalita Sangharsha Samiti, had led a struggle against nude worship at the Renuka temple near Chandragutti in Shimoga district. There was rioting and violence by the devotees; and activists were beaten up and chased away. But the government went on to ban nude worship. It is another story, or a sad codicil to this one, that nude worship is held even today—nearly three decades after being banned.

U.R. Ananthamurthy, who had no knowledge of the movement, wrote "Why Not Worship in the Nude", blaming anglicised, "modern" middle-class intellectuals who did not know the metaphysical, mystical implications of nude worship. Curiously, the petition of the Male Kudiyas uses exactly the same discourse. I am sure that if there is a national intellectual debate on madésnana, there will be a deluge of comments on the limits of reason, instrumental rationality, that evil called the Enlightenment, and the subjugation of indigenous knowledge systems. In fact, activists against the madésnana employ the terms of a regional tradition of reason and rationality, one that they know well. This is the rationality which the Kannada Vachanakaras of the 12th century and the poet saints of the Bhakti tradition used to denounce caste-based inequalities, inhuman superstitious practices and the unethical power of the priest-class.

To return to the narrative, with such arguments and counter-arguments, it was inevitable that the matter should go to court. The madésnana issue was heard by the High Court, and it recommended the modified yedesnana in place of the old tradition. What was disturbing here was that the constitutional freedom accorded to religious faith was once again interpreted to deny the secular state its power and mandate to eradicate humiliating superstitious practices.* The Supreme Court then imposed a stay on the High Court's verdict.

First published in Indian Cultural Forum, August 24, 2017.

---

*News reports of the Champa Shashti celebrations held on December 15, 2018, mention isolated observance of the yedesnana ritual—at the Kukke Subramanya temple of Dakshin Kannada district, and the Sri Muchlukodu Subramanya temple at Udupi, which is managed by the Sree Pejawar Math. However, no new reports of the madésnana have emerged since the passage of the Karnataka Prevention and Eradication of Inhuman Evil Practices and Black Magic Bill (2017).

PART SIX

BATTLING FOR INDIA

Orijit Sen, 2018

OUT OF LITTLE MOUTHS

Ashok Vajpeyi

'What do you do?'
I write poetry—I'm a poet.

'Anyone else consider you a poet?'
Not many know my poetry. Some do–and they think I'm a poet.

'Then why leave poetry and talk politics?'
I haven't left poetry: I do what I can as a poet.
When politics trespasses on poetry, on life,
Why can't the poet trespass a little on politics?

'You know where you will end up?'
Yes—but I also know where dictators end up.

'How will you save yourself?'
I'm not even going to try; only want to protect poetry and conscience.

'You want to become a martyr?'
No, sir. Just want to remain human, come what may.

'Do you pay your taxes?'
Yes, sir, according to my income for the year.

'Have you insured yourself?'
I did earlier, but no longer.
At my age, who would insure me and why?

'Do you drive?'
I know how to drive, but no longer drive.

'You have children? What do they do?'
A son and a daughter. The son is an independent architect,
The daughter an independent social worker.

'When the wave came, you fought it instead of swimming with
   it. What did that achieve?'
I don't know about any wave. If there was one, there were many
   who didn't swim with it.
Some swam another way: I was also one of them. And who said
   anything about achievement?

'You can still get into trouble for what you did!'
I know—but I haven't done anything wrong.

'We decide what's right and wrong, not you.'
I too can use the logic you do—that's my right.

'So you're used to talking big out of a small mouth?'
That's what poetry does. A poem becomes a poem when it speaks
of big things out of a little mouth.

'The days left to you: what will you do with them?'
Live with dignity. Let my poetry talk big; let it hold its head high.
Never let my poetry or my head bend for anybody.

Translated from the original Hindi ("Chhote Muhn Badi Baat") by the poet

◆◆◆

"DALITS ARE NOT GOING TO GO AWAY IF YOU DON'T USE THE WORD!"

Geeta Seshu

*An era of empty concepts such as "urban naxal" and "love jihad" is
unsurprisingly also one in which recognising social realities is not
the strong suit of the government. Witness the recent proscription
of the word "dalit" in official communications. Geeta Seshu goes
down the rabbit hole to examine the motivation and purposes that
govern such an upside-down world.*

After the intensive reporting of the initial weeks following the
arrests of human rights activists, it now transpires that the use

of the word "dalit" to describe some of the activists among the so-called "urban naxals" had been advised against early in August 2018.*

In an inexplicable move, a directive by the Ministry of Social Justice and Empowerment to all central and state government departments to refrain from using the word "dalit" in official transactions crept into an advisory issued on August 7, 2018 by the Ministry of Information and Broadcasting (MIB) to the broadcast media. And remained unnoticed till an NGO drew attention to it.

Besides bypassing the historical and socio-political meaning of the word, the move comes in the wake of dalit mobilisation over various issues that has intensified, following the protests over the suicide of Rohith Vemula in Hyderabad in 2016, the Una floggings in 2016 in Gujarat, the continued incarceration of the leader of the Bhim Army, Chandrashekhar Azad "Ravan", in Uttar Pradesh and more recently, the Bhima-Koregaon commemoration in Maharashtra, the protest by dalit groups, the Bharat Bandh call in April following the dilution of the Scheduled Castes and the Scheduled Tribes (Prevention of Atrocities) Act, and the recent arrests of human rights activists.

The MIB issued the advisory titled 'Compliance with court order' to all private satellite television channels advising that "the media may refrain from using the word 'dalit' while referring to members belonging to the Scheduled Castes". The letter refers to "directions" by the Bombay High Court, following a petition filed by Pankaj Meshram before the Nagpur bench of the court.

The channels either did not get the letter or chose to ignore it. As para no. 4 of this letter says:

---

* On August 28, 2018, the Maharashtra police arrested Sudha Bharadwaj, Gautam Navlakha, Arun Ferreira, Vernon Gonsalves and P. Varavara Rao. Police also raided the homes of Stan Swamy (Ranchi), Susan Abraham (Mumbai), Kranthi Tekula (Hyderabad), Anand Teltumbde (Goa) and the homes of Varavara Rao's two daughters and sons-in-law. This followed the June arrests of Roma Wilson, Shoma Sen, Sudhir Dhawale, Mahesh Raut and Surendra Gadling.

It is accordingly advised that media may refrain from using the nomenclature "'Dalit" while referring to members belonging to Scheduled Caste in compliance of the directions of the Hon'ble Bombay High Court and the Constitutional term "'Scheduled 'Caste" in English, and its appropriate translation in other national languages should alone be used for all official transactions, matters, dealings, certificates etc., for denoting the persons belonging to the Scheduled Castes notified in the Presidential Orders issued under Article 341 of the Constitution of India.

This advisory seems to have been ignored so far. And is addressed only to satellite TV channels, not all media.

Oddly, the Bombay High Court order of June 6, passed by Justices B.P. Dharmadhikari and Z.A. Haq, merely directed the MIB to "consider the question of issuing such directions to the media and to take suitable decision within the next six weeks". But clearly, the MIB decided to go the extra mile and send the letter to television channels as a ""compliance" with the court's order!

According to reports, a directive from the Ministry of Social Justice and Empowerment dated March 15, 2018, quotes from a 1982 circular from the Ministry of Home Affairs and an order passed by the Gwalior bench of the Madhya Pradesh High Court of January 15, 2018, that the "Central government/state government and its functionaries would refrain from using the nomenclature 'dalit' for the members belonging to Scheduled Castes and Scheduled Tribes as the same does not find mention in the Constitution of India or any statute."

The order came with regard to a writ petition filed by a Gwalior-based social worker, Mohanlal Mahor, and is the precursor to the Bombay High Court order as well as the MIB letter to the media. In 2016, Meshram, who described himself as a social worker based in Nagpur and secretary of Vidarbha Pradesh, Maharashtra, filed a petition before the Nagpur bench of the Bombay High Court to seek the removal of the word "dalit" from "all government records, circulars, notifications, and schemes" and demanded that social and print media be restrained from using the word. He contended that the word "dalit" was "unconstitutional, discriminatory, offending, casteist and highly objectionable". He said the word must be replaced with Scheduled Caste and Neo-Buddhist.

"Dalits are not going to go away if you don't use the word!"

It is also perplexing how a directive, originally meant for official transactions and the issuance of certificates and documents, is translated into an advisory to the media. Surely there is a clear distinction between official communication and the coverage of issues relating to dalits? How did the MIB decide to conflate the two? And, even if it did, should media houses comply with such a clearly erroneous reading?

The fact is, there is a fairly long history to the terminology to describe members of the Scheduled Castes and Tribes in official communication as well as in the movements against caste discrimination. While social reformer Mahatma Jotiba Phule is credited with casting the word "'dalit" in its current sense, the differences between Ambedkar and Gandhi over the latter's preferred term 'harijan' are well documented.

Today, the word "dalit", which meant "broken", "scattered" or "downtrodden", has acquired a more emphatic meaning of resistance to untouchability and discrimination.* The Dalit Panther movement of 1972 in Maharashtra consciously used the word "dalit" to denote the fight against casteism, as well as the solidarity of members of the Scheduled Castes, Scheduled Tribes, the working class, the landless and women.

J.V. Pawar, a co-founder of the Dalit Panthers, is clear that it is a word that must be claimed, not just for all members of the SC/ST but for all oppressed and neglected. "I understand it is not found in 'official' documents or the Constitution but it is a big word, it

---

* From the Sanskrit word 'daridra', or 'dalidda' in the Pali usage of the Buddha—where it is contrasted with the gahapati (householder) class [B.R. Ambedkar, *Annihilation of Caste: The annotated and critical edition* (Delhi: Navayana, 2015), 188.].

is a huge circle. The SC/STs may occupy just a small part of this circle and I don't understand this kind of restraint on the media. Dalits are not going to go away if you don't use the word!" he said.

While some believe the term dalit is not in consonance with the Ambedkarite movement. V.T. Rajshekar, editor of *Dalit Voice*, wrote that the word denoted an awareness of their (untouchables') identity and was a big step forward in the dalit liberation struggle. He advocated a change of name for SC/ST employees unions to a Dalit Employees' Association.

While the struggle to claim and assert an identity as "dalits" is important, the obscuring of dalits and their issues by mainstream media is a serious reality. Dalit activists and thinkers have criticised the manner in which caste is pushed under the carpet and thus "invisibilised" by the media. Academic work on caste—which is varied, rich and voluminous—is rarely discussed in the Indian media. As Anand Teltumbde pointed out in his book on Khairlanji, media coverage fails to pay attention to the underlying causes of the violence or the continuing divisions in society every time.*

At least 24 per cent of India's population are dalits and adivasis. Yet, their representation, even within the newsroom, is fractured and scattered. Rendered visible only in the context of violence or discussions on reservations, they are stereotyped and marginalised. In a special report for *The Hoot*, Ajaz Ashraf wrote about the discrimination and marginalisation of dalits in news media, discussing how dalits in the newsroom face discrimination and ultimately prefer to opt out of journalism.†

While top-down attempts to redress discrimination have been negligible, dalit groups have organised to build up an impressive presence in online media. Dalit Camera, a YouTube channel,

---

*Anand Teltumbde, *The Persistence of Caste: The Khairlanji Murders and India's Hidden Apartheid* (Delhi: Navayana, 2010).

†Ajaz Ashraf, "The Untold Story of Dalit Journalists," *The Hoot*, August 12, 2013, http://asu.thehoot.org/media-watch/media-practice/the-untold-story-of-dalit-journalists-6956.

began in 2011 to "document perspectives on/voices of Dalits, Adivasis, Bahujans and Minorities (DABM)". Roundtable India provides both news as well as opinions and debates as a vibrant platform for dalit students and writers. Last year, Dr Ambedkar's newspaper *Prabuddha Bharat*, was revived as a print publication and now has an online presence in English and Marathi.

The MIB advisory to television channels flies in the face of this struggle by dalits for dignity and self-respect. If television channels blindly comply, they will only exacerbate an already discriminatory, unfair and inaccurate system of representation.

Indian Cultural Forum, September 4, 2018.

First published in The Hoot as "Now MIB Says Better Not to Use the Term 'Dalit"'.

———— ◆•◆ ————

"I KNEW I WAS GOING TO JAIL THAT DAY"

Sweta Daga

In 2015, Rajkumari Bhuiya of Dhuma village and Sukalo Gond of Majhouli village were among the women who participated in protests against the Kanhar irrigation project. Activists and local communities feared that the construction of the dam on the Kanhar river in Dudhi block would result in polluting their water source or, eventually, displacement. Rajkumari Bhuiya and Sukalo Gond, Treasurer of the All India Union of Forest Working People, tell us about the adivasi struggle in Sonebhadra, Uttar Pradesh.

"I was in jail because I fought for my land, not because I committed a crime. I wasn't afraid of jail then and I'm not afraid now," says Rajkumari Bhuiya.

Rajkumari, around 55 years old, is from the Bhuiya adivasi community in Dhuma village of Sonbhadra district, Uttar Pradesh. In 2015, she spent over four months in jail after participating in protests against the Kanhar irrigation project. Activists and local communities are against the construction of the dam on the Kanhar river in Dudhi block, fearing displacement and pollution of their source of water.

According to news reports, during the protests in April that year, the police fired into the crowd and began arresting people. Rajkumari was picked up a few days later and taken to the district prison in Mirzapur, around 200 kilometres from Dhuma.

Sukalo Gond, a member of the same union as Rajkumari— the All India Union of Forest Working People (AIUFWP)—was at the Kanhar protest too. "I was born in Kanhar, and I wanted to support the community. I wasn't there when the police fired bullets [on April 14, 2015, around ten am, for about two hours]. I went there after that, but it turned violent, so we all left and went in different directions. Rajkumari went her own way, and I went mine," she says. "I was away for weeks," Sukalo continues. "I walked for five hours to the home of a distant relative, an adivasi family who understands our pains. I stayed there for two nights, and then went onto the next home, where I stayed for another ten days, and then the next home."

Sukalo, around fifty-one years old, is from the Gond adivasi community; she lives in Majhouli village of Dudhi block. She too says she was not afraid. "I know my children were worried, but I tried to stay in touch with them over the phone. I finally went home in June."

Later that month, when Sukalo came to Robertsganj town for a meeting with AIUFWP members, she was arrested. "It was June 30, 2015. Soon the [union] office was surrounded by dozens of cops—it felt like a thousand of them to me! I knew I was going to jail that day...."

Sukalo spent around forty-five days in jail. "What is there to say? Jail is jail. Of course it was hard, our freedom was taken away, it was hard not to see anyone. But I knew I was in jail because of this movement, not because I was a criminal. I didn't eat much, even though my comrades asked me to. My heart wasn't in it. But I survived jail, and that made me stronger."

Sukalo was let out on bail but she still has about fifteen cases pending against her, according to her calculations, including for rioting, dacoity, and carrying a weapon. Rajkumari too has multiple similar cases registered against her at the Dudhi police station. It has involved frequent trips since 2015 to the junior magistrate's court in Dudhi town to get court dates, sign papers and confirm that she has not left town.

She does not remember details of all the cases and leaves that to her lawyer, Rabindar Yadav, who says that many of the cases are false. However, he adds, "They [those associated with the AIUFWP, which also covers her legal fees] must have done something, otherwise why would the police file cases?" Rajkumari does not seem surprised by this. "Justice is not straight," she says.

"They [the police] targeted me because I was working with the union. When they picked me up," she recalls, "I wasn't even allowed to drink water. In jail, we got a plate, a *lota*, a blanket, a bowl, and a mat. We were up at five am. We would make our own food. We would clean the jail. Our drinking water was dirty. Inside, there is room for only thirty women but sometimes there would be almost ninety... A baby too was born in the jail. There was a lot of fighting among the jailed women [over space, food, soap, blankets]. The jailors would make us sleep in the bathroom sometimes because there was no space."

When Rajkumari's husband, Mulchand Bhuiya—also a member of the union—heard his wife was in jail, he was upset. "I didn't know what to do," he says. "My first thought was about my kids—how will we manage? I sold my wheat crop to raise enough money to cover her bail. Otherwise I keep my wheat for our family. My oldest son quit his job to focus on getting her out of jail, another son went to Delhi to work to send money back. We suffered such a loss with her gone."

Like Rajkumari and Sukalo's communities, adivasis in several parts of the country have, for decades, experienced harsh repercussions for protesting against projects and policies. When the protesters or prisoners are women, things get even harder.

"Every instance of a woman in prison is a case of double jeopardy. They suffer the burden of social rejection and an unequal legal battle," says Smita Chakraburtty, an independent researcher working on prison reform in India, and the Honorary Commissioner on Prisons appointed by the Rajasthan State Legal Services Authority to study open prison systems. "When it's a male prisoner, especially if he is a bread earner, his family will try to get him out of prison to the best of their capabilities. But women prisoners are abandoned by their families sooner rather than later. Prison is a taboo. A prisoner suffers the burden of the criminal tag, it doesn't matter if the prisoner is an undertrial, acquitted or convicted. Women are additionally vulnerable to social rejection and it is difficult to rehabilitate them."

"The women are fighting on many fronts"

Sukalo joined the AIUFWP in 2006 after attending a rally in Robertsganj, and eventually became its treasurer. "When I got back home [from the rally], I told my husband I wanted to join, but he was working at the thermal power plant [in Rihand] and said, how can you join, who will look after the children? I said no, I think this will be good for us, so then he said okay." She smiles.

Sukalo and her husband Nanak are farmers too; they have four daughters, and had a son who died. Two daughters are married, and two, Nishakumari, 18, and Phoolvanti, 13, are at home. "I got involved right from when I went for the first meeting. I jumped right in and never missed a meeting. It felt good because we were building a strong community, and for the first time in my life I felt strong. I had never thought about my rights before; I had just got married and had kids and worked [at home and as a farmer]. But after I joined the union, I realised my rights, and now I am not afraid to ask for them."

The AIUFWP (originally the National Forum of Forest People and Forest Workers, formed in 1996) was set up in 2013. It has roughly 150,000 members in around fifteen states, including Uttarakhand, Bihar, Jharkhand and Madhya Pradesh.

In Uttar Pradesh, the union works in eighteen districts with about 10,000 members. Around 60 per cent of its leaders are women and their main demand is the implementation of the Forest Rights Act (FRA) by recognising the authority of gram sabhas (village councils), and giving self-governing options to forest communities. The FRA was enacted in 2006 to address historic economic and social injustices faced by adivasi and other communities for decades.

"These women are fighting on many fronts," says Roma Malik, general secretary of the AIUFWP. "The FRA is supposed to give communities access to land, but it is a struggle. Tribal women have tougher obstacles—they are invisible to most people. The men in power don't want to give people land even though we have the law on our side now. Sonbhadra district is still run like a feudal state, but the women are working together to fight for their land."

Rajkumari joined the union in 2004. She and her husband Mulchand used to grow vegetables and wheat on a small plot of land, and they also worked as farm labourers. But it was not enough to feed their family. In 2005, Rajkumari and Mulchand, along with many other families, reclaimed land in Dhuma—taken by the forest department—as their own original land. A year later, while continuing to cultivate on the old plot, they built a new house on the reclaimed land.

Rajkumari wants to continue her work on land rights through the union. She says she needs help from the other women in her community because of her fear of the forest department. But she does not want to back down and give up her land. "Powerful people play with adivasis," she says with a grimace. "We are toys for them."

On June 8, 2018, Sukalo was arrested along with two others at the Chopan railway station in Sonbhadra, after complaining about anti-adivasi atrocities at a meeting with Uttar Pradesh forest officials. They were taken to the prison in Mirzapur. "Her name was not in the FIR," says Roma Malik. "Yet she was caught to teach her a lesson. Her health has gone bad and she has not eaten food in protest. She is surviving on chana and fruits brought by friends. She has not been granted bail."

A habeas corpus writ petition was filed by lawyers in the Allahabad High Court alleging Sukalo and the others were illegally detained. The petition was dismissed on September 19 [2108]. On October 3 [2018], Sukalo was granted bail.

PARI, October 30, 2018*

———————— ◆◆◆ ————————

SONEBHADRA'S DAUGHTER SUKALO

Citizens for Justice and Peace

Sukalo is a leader, and she also takes care of her family and her cattle. But she can recall a time when there was no awareness among the forest dwellers about their rights and claims on forest land. Violence against them was rampant. The police would often barge into their houses and destroy their hutments or physically abuse them. Then, in 2006, she joined the movement to demand the implementation of forest rights. "We will not beg, we will claim our lands back. It is clear to us that the Government is not supporting us. Our movement will win our rights back, I am sure!" So said Sukalo Gond, marching in a forest rights rally in 2006, her first such experience. She went on to become one of the leading women activists of the forest struggle of adivasis in Sonebhadra, empowering other women through her experience. Though she is the only one from her family to be involved in the movement, that fact does not deter her; she says, "The collective strength of the women—their pains and joys—is what gives me strength too. The struggle is not just for land, but the dignity of existence of an adivasi woman."

*This is a lightly edited version of an article originally published in the People's Archive of Rural India (PARI) on October 30, 2018. The article was written as part of the National Foundation of India Media Awards Programme; the author was a recipient of the fellowship in 2017.

Sukalo was arrested in 2015. She describes the experience of the month-long incarceration in the Mirzapur jail: "It was a life-changing experience. A lot of women and children were fabricated in false cases and imprisoned. Some women had just given birth to children." However, Sukalo continued the struggle even from within the four walls of the jail. She, along with her other inmates sent multiple letters to the higher ups. She sat for multiple hunger strikes within the prison, both for basic facilities within the prison and the rights of land and resources outside. She would hand over the letters to other activists during Mulaqats. Her struggles combined with the resilient efforts of her comrades and their unity within the jails, won all of them minimum wages for the work they did inside. Though she was released later, all the fabricated cases still remain foist on her.

Describing the experience in the jail and how their collective strength turned it around into a struggle for rights within the four walls she often goes back in time. She remembers a time when daily wages that the adivasis would receive were as low as Re. 1 or Rs. 2. Mostly, the wages would be much lesser than minimum wage, a concept they did not quite know at the time. She literally grew with the struggle not just for forest rights but also labor rights of the adivasis residing in the area. When she got involved, most adivasi women were oppressed, both in the family and in the society outside and were not aware of their rights. However today she resolutely speaks, "We have a right to live if we are born on this earth. While there was a time when I could not look any man up in the eyes, today I even negotiate alone, whether it be a minister or police officer."

On June 9, 2018, the CJP team put out an alert: "Adivasi Forest Movement leader Sukalo arrested Even as UP's Forest Minister assures Action on Incidents of Police violence, Police Carry Out Clandestine Arrests".*

An establishment rattled by this flurry of claims, decided to launch a vendetta campaign against strong leaders of the

---

*See https://cjp.org.in/urgent-alert-adivasi-forest-movement-leader-sukalo-arrested/

movement such as Sukalo. She, and another leader Kismatiya Gond were picked up by the police when they were returning from a meeting with state Forest Minister Dara Singh Chouhan and the Forest Secretary in Lucknow. This prompted Citizens for Justice and Peace (CJP) and the All India Union by Forest Working People (AIUFWP) to file a Habeas Corpus Petition in the Allahabad High Court. The court not only demanded an explanation for the detention, but also ordered that the women be produced before it. The women were not produced before the court. The police claim they released the women, but that they remain untraceable.

Sokalo Gond was granted bail on October 4. But technical and procedural issues kept Sokalo behind bars. After four long months in jail, she walked free only on November 1, 2018.

In a video shot by the Citizens for Justice and Peace (CJP), Sukalo spoke about the process of fighting for community rights to the land and the forest: "We have been fighting for almost 15-20 years now. This struggle is against the Forest Department, against companies, against capitalists, against exploitation. It is a struggle for our rights. We have been successful in some ways… It has been a slow process but we have come a long way. Now, it is as if we have reached the bank of the river. We just need to cross it now. We won't stop fighting for our rights… We had initially filed for Individual claims; then we filed claims for the rights of the community over the forest land… over medicinal plants, herbs, *tendu* leaves, fruits…"

She also describes the long resistance to the Kanhar Dam project, and how their numbers have increased since they filed the claims of the community despite the threat of false cases, arrest and even bullets. "We sacrificed a lot for that struggle, we had to face bullets but we survived by the grace of God. But this is the truth of being in a struggle. We had to face bullets and then go underground. We reached Delhi via Chattisgarh and Uttar Pradesh. We stayed in Delhi for a month and then returned to Sonbhadra. We had a programme on June 30 in Sonbhadra and we were arrested on the same day. When they were taking us to jail, the Police Officer present was rough. They were the ones who had stolen from us, but they made us the thieves. He kept moving us from one place as though we were pieces of luggage that could be hidden anywhere. I told him: We are not scared, we have not stolen anything, and we have not killed anyone. We are leading a struggle, we are fighting for our livelihood."

But Sukalo is clear that there is no turning back: "We can't look back. We are moving forward. They can't stop us and we won't be able to stop ourselves either. We have a long way to go; we are fighting for the rights of the generations to come."

Sukalo Gond speaks on being granted bail

In a video shot by the Citizens for Justice and Peace (CJP), Sukalo spoke about the resistance led by the All India Union of Forest Working Persons (AIUFWP).* She describes the process of fighting for community rights to the land and the forest: "We have been fighting for almost 15-20 years now. This struggle is against the Forest Department, against companies, against capitalists, against exploitation. It is a struggle for our rights. We have been successful in some ways… It has been a slow process but we have come a long way. Now, it is as if we have reached the bank of the river. We just need to cross it now. We won't stop fighting for our rights… We had initially filed for Individual claims; then we filed claims for the rights of the community over the forest land… over medicinal plants, herbs, *tendu* leaves, fruits…"

She also describes the long resistance to the Kanhar Dam project, and how their numbers have increased since they filed the claims of the community despite the threat of false cases, arrest and even bullets. "We sacrificed a lot for that struggle, we had to face bullets but we survived by the grace of God. But this is the truth of being in a struggle. We had to face bullets and then

---

* Translated extract from a video by Citizens for Justice and Peace (CJP), 2018.

go underground. We reached Delhi via Chattisgarh and Uttar Pradesh. We stayed in Delhi for a month and then returned to Sonbhadra. We had a programme on June 30 in Sonbhadra and we were arrested on the same day. When they were taking us to jail, the Police Officer present was rough. They were the ones who had stolen from us, but they made us the thieves. He kept moving us from one place as though we were pieces of luggage that could be hidden anywhere. I told him: We are not scared, we have not stolen anything, and we have not killed anyone. We are leading a struggle, we are fighting for our livelihood."

But Sukalo is clear that there is no turning back: "We can't look back. We are moving forward. They can't stop us and we won't be able to stop ourselves either. We have a long way to go; we are fighting for the rights of the generations to come."

This piece combines a piece on CJP.org by Sushmita (see https://cjp.org.in/sonebhadras-daughter-sukalo/), December 7, 2017 and a CJP video shot in 2018.

◆◆◆

CONVERSATION: MOHSIN ALAM BHAT ON RESPONDING TO HATE CRIMES

Newsclick and Indian Cultural Forum

Founded in 2011, IndiaSpend has broadened its scope from being a public 'agency of record' for data on the Indian economy, to tracking hate crimes, and since 2014, fact-checking the claims of public figures. Its database prioritises citizens' concerns in a country where the government does not collect data on cow-related hate crimes.

In conversation with Vivan Eyben and Abhilasha Chattopadhyay, Mohsin Alam Bhat discusses the methodology and issues involved in recognising a hate crime, and also the scope for citizens' participation in the redressal process.

Vivan Eyben (VE): How do you determine what constitutes a hate crime?

Mohsin Alam Bhat (MAB): The nature of hate crimes is actually quite entrenched in transnational legal literature, because there are a lot of countries which have legislations on hate crimes, and also lots of different institutions, organisations and countries have documentation systems in place which use the category of hate crime. The distinction between a hate crime and other categories of crime is the idea of motivation; that is what hate crime as a category really refers to. So, the ordinary definition of a hate crime is "any crime committed by the alleged perpetrator, which is motivated either partly or wholly by hostility towards the identity of the victim". Now, this motivation need not be the dominant motivation. It could be one among many other motivations, but if the motivation of hostility towards the identity of the victim plays any role in the act, it would be classified as a hate crime. What we have been doing, along with India Spend, in what we've called "Hate Crimes Watch" is documenting religion-based hate crimes in India over the last ten years.

Abhilasha Chattopadhyay (AC): Can you tell us a little bit about the methodology adopted for collating the data with respect to the hate-watch initiative?

MAB: There are two things apart from the definition. As you would have guessed, any assessment of motivation is quite tricky, especially when it comes to adjudication. Even in countries where there are categories of hate crime in the law books, courts find it quite difficult to assess if such motivations exist or not, and it's really a question of evidence.

The first thing we decided quite early is, whenever we are deciding whether a particular incident should be included as a religion-based hate crime, we would require some affirmative evidence. There must be evidence and we won't merely infer that the alleged perpetrator held religious hostility. Sometimes this evidence comes in direct form, for example, the alleged perpetrator himself says that he/she attacked this person because of their religious identity. In many other cases, there are circumstantial or contextual factors. We look at the facts, and where the only reason that some people could have been attacked is because of their religious identity—say, because the victim may be a complete stranger to the alleged perpetrator, or, for example, the victim has a religious garb—and there is no other motivational factor in play, one can infer that the only possible motivation could be hatred towards a particular identity. So, there are certain contextual factors. Sometimes the alleged perpetrator claims that he did this against "Love Jihad", so the person may not explicitly say religion, but we know from the context that this must have something to do with religious hostility. There are sometimes more complicated factors involved that are potentially controversial. We have included cow-related violence, ostensibly perpetrated for the protection of the cow, as also falling under the category of religion-based hate crimes.

In international literature these tell-tale signs are called "bias indicators". We are treating the reason of cow protection as a bias indicator. What that actually means is, there is a certain overriding contextual factor: even where there is no direct evidence, we can infer that such violence must have something to do with religion because of data predicting that. For instance, India Spend had done a survey which showed that most cases of cow violence happen against caste and religious minorities, particularly religious minorities. So there is already a strong correlation based on data, between religious hostility and cow-related violence. We presume unless proven wrong, that if there is a cow angle and the violence is perpetrated against a muslim by a non-muslim, this may be an act of religious hostility. It is a presumption based on data and strong correlation, so that's the evidentiary side of it.

Speaking of the sources we're using, ideally, we would want to use ground-level verification but since you start at the moment the news breaks, in the first phase we're only looking at English media sources. Once we have surveyed and audited English media sources, we get to looking at non-English media reports and also start including human rights reports and other organisations' findings. We hope, over a period of time our own ground-level fact-finding volunteers will be in place, but at this stage we are primarily using English media sources as our main source, and hoping to expand in the future.

VE: As far as India goes, what kind of legislation actually exists that specifically mentions or can be placed under the category of hate crime legislation?

MAB: At this stage in India we do not have an anti-religion hate crime law although we do have a caste-related hate crime law. I would argue that the SC/ST Prevention of Atrocities Act (1989) is actually a hate crime legislation. Already, anti-Scheduled Caste violence was covered under the Civil Rights Act (1955). The category and phraseology of the act was, '"any act committed on the grounds of 'untouchability"—again, that goes to motivation, and the phrase tries to capture if the perpetrator was motivated partly or wholly because of untouchability or caste; so the structure was one of a hate crime legislation. Many would argue that gender-related laws are also anti-hate crime legislations. At this stage we do not have an anti-hate crime legislation when it comes to sexual minorities, religious minorities or racial ethnic-linguistic minorities, so that's not covered.

AC: With respect to the recent discussions in the judiciary, I was reading your article in *The Wire*, regarding the Supreme Court's directions of July 17, 2018, given to state governments about the preventive measures that need to be taken against mob violence. How effective do you think that really is when you observe these from three different sites: the legislation angle (comparison with POA Act, and lack of legislation on religion-based hostility), judiciary, and from the end of the civil society groups?

MAB: I think we still have to wait for the implementation of the Supreme Court guidelines. What happened was, this case was filed by variety of different organisations and supported by some really good lawyers of the Supreme Court. The primary frame of the judgement was the notion of lynching. As it turns out, the Supreme Court judgement did not define what lynching was. It wasn't clear if this was a hate crime or mob violence, but it could be understood implicitly from what the court was trying to say when asked to respond to a wide range of problems such as cow vigilantism. Many of the cases that do get documented under Hate Watch are covered by the Supreme Court guidelines. Most of us welcomed the guidelines, but at this stage most of the states have not even filed compliance reports although the Supreme Court had asked for this. It has not happened and there is a huge responsibility on legal academia and civil rights groups to make sure that we continue to survey and audit the implementation of the guidelines. The information we have gathered is not completely clear about how many cases actually received the kind of attention that the guidelines mandated. I think we still have time and to get our act together and make sure that these guidelines are implemented.

AC: Let's talk about civil society. As citizens, what do you think we should do to help with this initiative?

MAB: There are a couple of things; first, any respectable hate crime or documenting–monitoring system must have a component of fact-finding, which is done by volunteers or people who a're part of the documentation work. Our big aim, from the hate watch initiative, is to expand as soon as possible and as far as possible to the depth and breadth of a rigorous documentation. That is definitely one thing that different civil society organisations, students, journalists and others can help in doing while we are in the process of creating models and questionnaires that fit in with our methodologies. We would want people to take up this challenge. Whenever they hear about a certain incident or witness an incident, they may adopt these modules and protocols and conduct fact findings based on our questions. That would contribute to the documentation work we are doing and this has to be a collective activity. It is to be hoped this will also generate some sort of a local groundswell and local-level mobilisation, both for documentation and also for responding to these kinds of incidents because these incidents are not taking place in isolation, but are part of a larger problem of civil rights in this country.

If people do start contributing to local level fact-finding and documentation, they will also be able to get in touch with the families affected by hate crime and provide them rehabilitation support and legal aid support. These are some concrete deliverables from civil society organisations, individuals and students who want to participate, and I do see them working in tandem. But success will really depend on the extent of the outreach to all sorts of stakeholders and asking them to contribute.

First published by Newsclick and Indian Cultural Forum, November 9, 2018

CONVERSATION: NATASHA RATHER ON WOMEN'S CONTINUED FIGHT FOR JUSTICE IN KASHMIR

Newsclick

On February 23, 1991, Indian armed forces entered the twin villages of Kunan and Poshpora in Kupwara district of Kashmir, under the guise of a cordon-and-search operation. The soldiers dragged the men of the villages out of their homes to three ad-hoc interrogation centres set up in houses and barns in the village. The women, now alone in the houses, were then raped. No woman was spared that night—minor girls, teenage girls, married women or older women. The men were brutally tortured all night. The army made no attempts to look for any militants or weapons.

It's been twenty-eight years now, but there has been no action against the perpetrators. While the initial demands for justice by the survivors of that fateful night were ignored by the state, in 2013, a

group of Kashmiri women started the struggle again. Fifty women
filed a Public Interest Litigation (PIL) to re-open investigation into
the Kunan Poshpora case.

   Surangya Kaur of Newsclick spoke to Natasha Rather, one
of the petitioners in the PIL, and one of the authors of Do You
Remember Kunan Poshpora?, a book about the history of the case
and the current developments.

Surangya Kaur (SK): After the rapes and violence first took place
in February 1991, the villagers filed complaints and tried to get
justice for a long time. Can you tell us about what happened in
those years before the PIL? How did the government and the
judiciary treat this case?

Natasha Rather (NR): The mass rape and torture in Kunan
Poshpora took place in the intervening night between February
23 and 24, 1991. The FIR was registered after almost a fortnight,
on March 8, 1991. The case was closed as untraced by the Jammu
and Kashmir (J&K) Police in October that year. The survivors
approached the State Human Rights Commission (SHRC) in 2004.
In 2011, the SHRC ordered fresh investigations into the case, and
compensation for the survivors. There was no action taken on the
SHRC order. Following this, a group of fifty women filed a PIL in
2013 for reopening the case.

   In all these years before the PIL was filed, there have been
denials from the Army and the Indian Government, who refuse to
acknowledge that the rapes happened. B.G. Varghese, in a report
called "Crisis and Credibility", called the mass rape a "militant
hoax" and accused women of "acting at the behest of militants".
The then Divisional Commissioner, Wajahat Habibullah, wrote in
his confidential report that he doubted whether the allegations of
rape were true and recommended investigations. The government
machinery has been complicit in trying to silence the people, to
frustrate them with denials and accusations against the people
of Kunan Poshpora.

SK: What are the developments since the case was reopened after
the PIL you filed in 2013?

NR: The PIL filed in 2013 by the Support Group for Justice for Kunan Poshpora (SGKP) for reopening the case was not admitted by the High Court, which stated that it was premature. The J&K police filed the closure report for the case after the PIL was filed—twenty-two years after it was closed as untraced, in 2013. The survivors approached the Sub-Judge, Judicial Magistrate, Kupwara, who ordered further investigations within three months. There was no action taken by the police. The survivors then filed a fresh petition in the High Court for orders on compensation and reinvestigation following the SHRC recommendation. The army approached the High Court and got the orders for compensation and investigation stayed. The J&K Government challenged these orders in the Supreme Court of India in December 2014, so as to get a ruling to not pay compensation. In 2016, the Union of India filed a fresh petition in the Supreme Court questioning the SHRC's jurisdiction to pass an order in six cases involving the armed forces, referring to AFSPA. The Supreme Court stayed the orders for reinvestigation and compensation in 2016. The case remained in the registry of the Supreme Court for three years, but has not been listed for hearing.

SK: What is the status of the compensation? Why do you think it has not been given yet? Is it another way to protect the army?

NR: The compensation has not been paid to the survivors. Paying the compensation would mean that the Indian army accepts that the mass rape and torture did happen in the village, something that they have been denying all through these years. But where the question of compensation is concerned, it is important to mention that in 2012, the then MLA of Kupwara paid thirty-nine families an amount of rupees one lakh each and an additional Rs 25,000 to a survivor who was disabled. But through an RTI (Right to Information) request that was filed, we came to know that no money had been paid to the survivors as compensation.

SK: You are one of the authors of the book, *Do You Remember Kunan Posphpora?** You write, "People in Kashmir ask us why we have filed the petition, can we expect justice from the oppressors in their own court?" The judicial system of the state and centre has repeatedly failed the Kashmiri people. What made all of you go ahead and file this petition and fight the case?

NR: The PIL was filed after the Nirbhaya gang rape case† shook the entire country and people were out on the streets. People were discussing sexual violence; but no one was taking about the systematic form of sexual violence perpetrated in Kashmir by the Indian Armed Forces. It is true that no case of human rights abuse involving the army has ever been tried in a civilian court and the pursuit of justice is never ending, but to reopen the case and talk about the rape and sexual violence by the Indian army as part of its counter-insurgency operations in Kashmir was important to break the culture of silence, which the state is so comfortable with. This case especially needed to be talked about because the survivors had chosen to speak up in a social and political milieu where these discussions were discouraged. The people of Kunan Poshpora chose to fight, knowing that justice may just be a dream. Their struggle was inspirational. It had to be talked about. Hence fifty women got together to file the PIL aimed at breaking the silence, seeking answers to the crime that the Indian state conspired to pass off as a "blatant lie".

SK: In the chapter you have written in the book, you talk about rape as reprisal, and how rape is also linked to the idea of

*Mushtaq, Samreen, Essar Batool, Natasha Rather, Ifrah Butt and Munaza Rashid. *Do you Remember Kunan Poshpora?: The Story of a Mass Rape.* New Delhi: Zubaan Books, 2016.

†The brutal gang rape of a young woman in Delhi on December 16, 2012 (which subsequently led to the death of the woman) called attention to the violence against women in Indian cities, particularly the capital. There were nationwide protests, and the media named the woman "Nirbhaya", meaning fearless.

nationhood. You also describe the different manners in which rape is used as a weapon by the oppressors, and what kind of effect it has on the people. Can you tell us about that?

NR: In Kashmir, rape/sexual violence has been used widely as part of the counter-insurgency operation by the Indian Armed forces. We talk about Kunan Poshpora here, but it is not the only case of mass rape. There are other incidents but those survivors remained silent while people from Kunan Poshpora fought a legal battle. Sexual violence has also been a part of torture of men. Passing electric current through the penis and inserting objects into the rectum have been widely reported by torture survivors. Many men were rendered impotent through sexualized forms of torture. While torturing the men is an attack on the individual and his idea of manhood, sexual violence against women is aimed at humiliating the entire community, since honour is attached to women in patriarchal societies like ours. Many of the women who were raped were related to militants. The women from Kunan Poshpora were raped because they were believed to be "militant sympathisers".

SK: You also repeatedly talk about the importance of keeping this incident alive in public memory. Why is it important, particularly in a place like Kashmir where human rights violations are regular occurrences?

NR: If violence is the Indian State's weapon to repress the people of Kashmir and crush our struggle for Azadi, memory is our tool to counter it. India has an atmosphere of fear in Kashmir and has been comfortable in the culture of silence. People have been prevented from exercising their civil and political rights, justice has been denied strategically so as to wipe out memories of incidents of human rights violations. But memory is what has kept the struggle alive and memory is our greatest tool. Forgetting would amount to being complicit with the Indian state's tactics of repression. Remembrance is important for resistance. So we keep the memories alive and we continue to resist India's unwarranted rule in Kashmir.

First published in Newsclick, February 23, 2018

◆•◆

CENSORSHIP, SECTION 377 RULING AND THE RISE IN RIGHT-WING ASSAULT

Bindu Doddahatti

The Indian Penal Code (IPC) was drafted in India by the British in 1860. The code was a compilation of the then existing British laws governing punishment for crimes. Section 377 of the IPC was modelled on a sixteenth-century law, called the Buggery Act. It criminalises "unnatural sex"* between two individuals. The offence is punishable with imprisonment up to life. In a landmark judgement on September 6, 2018 (Navtej Singh Johar vs. Union of India), the Supreme Court legalised gay sex by holding that sex between two consenting adults is not a crime.

But now that Section 377 has been read down, the conservative communal elements have been targeting sexual minorities in a variety of ways to reinforce regressive social morality over constitutional morality. They misuse existing laws such as the Beggary Acts of different states; Section 36A of the Karnataka Police Act, 1963, which still has the potential to victimise transpersons; and the Karnataka Dramatic Performances Act, 1964, which gives the power of censorship to state machinery.

On October 13, 2018, the play "Shiva", a performance on sexuality and gender directed by artist Dayasindhu Sakrepatna, had to be

---

*"377. Unnatural offences: Whoever voluntarily has carnal intercourse against the order of nature with any man, woman or animal, shall be punished with imprisonment for life, or with imprisonment of either description for term which may extend to ten years, and shall also be liable to fine. Explanation: Penetration is sufficient to constitute the carnal intercourse necessary to the offense described in this section."

shelved. Right-wing elements from the Bharata Punarutthana Trust, an affiliate of the Vishwa Hindu Parishad (VHP), filed a complaint against the individuals involved in the play, as well as Jagriti Theatre, which was hosting the play. In their letter to the DCP (District Commissioner of Police), Whitefield division, Bangalore, the Trust claimed that Shiva was their devata (God), and that this play hurt their religious sentiments. These right-wing elements arrived at Jagriti Theatre with the police. The police claimed that Jagriti had not informed them about staging the play, and also that they did not have valid permission for sound systems. The police served a notice to the organisers, asking them to appear in the police station. At the station, the police asked the organisers to halt the shows "fearing a law and order situation", and added that they cannot provide adequate protection to the cast and crew of the play.

When the members of the play confronted the complainants, they found out that not one of the complainants had even watched the play. But in their complaint dated October 12, 2018, they have described the play as "communal and targeted to HINDU community, Religion, & GODS" [sic]. On the basis of this frivolous complaint, the Commissioner of Police, T. Suneel Kumar, said the police would review the contents of the play to assess whether it offended religious sentiments; if it did not, they would provide protection. How did the police get such unhindered power to censor artistic expression? What special qualifications do they have to appreciate or dismiss art?

Performances in colonial India depicted the plight of the indigo planters ("Nil Darpan"), the visit of Prince of Wales ("Gajadananda and the Crown Prince") or representing the ill-treatment of the common people by the English police ("The Police of Pig and Sheep"). These, among other performances, enraged the British government, and the Dramatic Performance Bill was introduced in 1876. It was later enacted into a law.

The Karnataka Dramatic Performance Act, 1964, was drafted along the lines of the colonial law. Section 2(1) of the Act defines an "objectionable performance" as performances that are likely to incite violence, deliberately outrage religious feelings of any class or are grossly indecent or obscene. The Madras High Court deemed the definition to be too vague to act as a restriction to the freedom of speech and expression.

The State Government and the Deputy Commissioner have been empowered to prohibit performances that they deem "objectionable". The Deputy Commissioner has the authority to pass such an order without issuing a notice to the concerned performers. An appeal from the said order is dealt with by the same authority. The Act makes no mention of any express procedure to be followed by the authorities to ensure that the principles of natural justice are upheld. Further, Section 13 of the Act protects any acts of the authorities carried out in good faith, paving the way for arbitrary decisions.

The Bombay Police Act, which ordered that a performance must be reviewed and approved by the relevant authority, and the necessary censorship put into effect, was challenged in the Bombay High Court in September, 2016. The case has been pending before the Court; several orders of adjournment have been passed, and the petitioners have not been granted any interim relief.

The theatre group Pareeksha in Tamil Nadu received approval to present a censored version of their play just an hour or two before their performance, leading to its inevitable delay. Subsequently, the Madras High Court was moved to challenge the validity of the Act.*

The Court stated that in the case of a play, time is of the essence, and a defective order cannot be cured by an effective appeal. The mandate of review that requires submission of the script was questioned, as a live play would be improvised to some extent every night. The nature of the discretionary powers given to the evaluating authorities was questioned, along with their

---

*In 2012, playwright and director N.V. Sankaran alias Gnani petitioned the Court, saying that whenever his theatre group Pareeksha wanted to stage a play, they had to get the script cleared by the Police Commissioner in

artistic integrity. The Court cited a case to state that fundamental rights of citizens cannot depend solely on presumed fairness and integrity of officers of the state. This indicates a statutory defect, as the power has not been channelled through the appropriate machinery. The findings of the Court led to the ultimate dismissal of the Act.

Since the decriminalisation of consensual same-sex relationships by the Supreme Court, there has been a sudden upsurge in attacks and cases filed against the LGBTQ+ community by various right-wing elements. In September, right after Section 377 of the IPC was read down in Navtej Singh Johar vs. Union of India, a complaint was filed at the Cubbon Park police station by the Cubbon Park Walkers Association, specifically by a lawyer who is associated with right-wing organisations. The complaint alleged that homosexual individuals were indulging in illegal activities in the park. LGBTQ persons have always had safe access to Cubbon Park; but suddenly, after the judgment, they became a "nuisance". Similarly, in October, trans-women were brutally attacked in Maharashtra, Kerala and Telangana, simply for accessing public spaces. The most recent assault on the play "Shiva"—which navigates the complicated terrain of gender and sexuality by portraying the difficulties faced by LGBTQ+ population—only exacerbates the malaise.

In such a situation, it is important to note that Justice D.Y. Chandrachud in the Navtej judgment observed:

> Confronting the closet would entail ensuring that individuals belonging to sexual minorities have the freedom to fully participate in public life, breaking the invisible barrier that heterosexuality imposes upon them. The choice of sexuality is at the core of privacy. But equally, our constitutional jurisprudence must recognise that the public assertion of identity founded in sexual orientation is crucial to the exercise of freedoms... It must

---

Chennai. In January 2013, the Court termed some provisions of the Tamil Nadu Dramatic Performances Act, 1954, as "unconstitutional", including the requirement for theatre groups to get permission before staging a play.

be acknowledged that members belonging to sexual minorities are often subjected to harassment in public spaces. The right to sexual privacy, founded on the right to autonomy of a free individual, must capture the right of persons of the community to navigate public places on their own terms, free from state interference.

Justice Rohinton Nariman stated that,

"...all government officials, including and in particular police officials, and other officers of the Union of India and the States, be given periodic sensitization and awareness training of the plight of such persons in the light of the observations contained in this judgment."

Now that the Section 377 of the IPC has been read down, the conservative communal elements are targeting sexual minorities by resorting to cunning ways to reinforce regressive social morality over constitutional morality. The Navtej judgment might be a positive and much required step forward. But we continue to have laws such as the Beggary Acts of different states, Section 36A of Karnataka Police Act, 1963, which still has the potential to victimise trans-women, and the Karnataka Dramatic Performances Act, 1964, which gives immense power to state machineries. One way ahead is to challenge the constitutionality of these draconian laws. Simultaneously, police complaints need to be filed; and collective action taken against those who misuse existing laws to humiliate or discriminate against sexual minorities, citing "reasons" such as public nuisance or offending religious sentiments.

This is a lightly edited version of an article which first appeared in The Leaflet, November 20, 2018. Eshani Vaidya, intern at the Alternative Law Forum, assisted in the writing of the original article.

TRANSGENDER BILL:
DENYING CONSTITUTIONAL RIGHTS
TO THE COMMUNITY?

Yogesh S

On December 17, 2018, the Lok Sabha passed the Government of India's Transgender Persons (Protection of Rights) Bill, 2018. Amid heated debate on the Rafale deal in the Lower House, the decision that would affect lives of lakhs of transgender people was taken within the short span of an hour. The Bill that was passed was introduced by the BJP-led central government, watering down the Rights of Transgender Persons Bill, 2014 that was earlier passed in the Rajya Sabha.

On April 15, 2014, the Supreme Court passed a landmark judgment that recognised the third gender, and also discussed, in great detail, the everyday violence faced by the transgender community in India. But till recently, the Indian Penal Code still hosted the draconian Section 377 that criminalised homosexuality. The LGBTQI+ (Lesbian, Gay, Bisexual, Transgender, Queer, Intersex) movement in India, as elsewhere, fought a legal battle. On September 5, 2018, the Supreme Court of India read down Section 377. Just when the transgender community was breathing a sigh of relief, the government passed a Bill that criminalises the community. It is telling that in the case of Section 377, the Narendra Modi government distanced itself, in a sense, from the proceedings, saying that the Court must only talk of decriminalising sexuality, and not about the economic and political rights of the community. So, this transgender Bill does not come as surprise.

Before this Bill, the Rights of Transgender Persons Bill, 2014, piloted by Tiruchi Siva, Member of Parliament, was introduced in the Rajya Sabha on December 10, 2014. This private member's bill was discussed in detail by all the members in the Upper House across party lines, and the Bill was approved. The Bill offered remedies against the abuse and violence faced by transgender persons by equipping them with job skills, and offering employment opportunities, rehabilitation and social security. But the discussion of this Bill in the Lok Sabha was delayed. On December 26, 2015, the Ministry of Social Justice and Empowerment website published a revised bill, calling it the "Transgender Protection Bill". This made the intentions of the government clear: it did not want to reaffirm the constitutional rights of transgenders.

Across the country, the transgender community protested against the bill. Earlier, the community had organised various consultations and submitted amendments to the government's bill. But the bill that was passed does not reflect any of these suggested amendments. Apart from this, the bill also violates the directives of the Supreme Court's judgment in the case of *National Legal Services Authority vs. Union of India,* popularly known as the NALSA judgment.* The transgender community is, once again, out on the streets, protesting against the new discriminatory bill, and quite rightly, calling it the "Transgender Persons (Violation of Rights) Bill, 2018".

In a press conference organised by the community on December 18, 2018 at the Indian Women's Press Club in Delhi, the activists asked if this bill was nothing but contempt of court. Tripti Tandon, a lawyer from the Lawyers' Collective said that while the Supreme Court has passed some progressive judgments such as those on privacy, Section 377 and adultery, the legislature under this government continues to pass regressive bills. The Transgender Bill that has been passed presents transgenders as

---

*Through the NALSA judgement (April 2014), the Supreme Court declared transgender people a 'third gender', and affirmed that the fundamental rights granted under the Constitution will be equally applicable to them. It also gave them the right to self-identification of their gender as male, female or third gender. In addition, the court held that since transgenders are treated as socially and economically backward classes, they will be granted reservations in jobs and in admissions to educational institutions.

aliens; it deprives transgenders the possibility of social justice; it ignores the socio-economic realities of the community; and as in many other cases, the government has not paid heed to the protests of the affected community.

The bill suggests that screening committees be set up to recognise transgender persons. This dehumanising suggestion says: "A transgender person may make an application to the District Magistrate for issuing a certificate of identity as a transgender person... District Magistrate shall refer such application to the District Screening Committee to be constituted by the appropriate Government for the purpose of recognition of transgender persons." This is an outright violation of the NALSA judgment directive: "...any procedure for identification of 'transgender persons' which goes beyond self-identification, and is likely to involve an element of medical, biological or mental assessment, would violate transgender persons' rights under Article 19 and 21 of the Constitution."

Again, those who have not had gone through Sex Reassignment Surgery (SRS) can only identify as transgender, and not as male or female. The identification as transgender depends on scrutiny and certification by a District Screening Committee. Those seeking to identify as male or female need to have had SRS. This misreads transgender identity—not as a gender identity, but a sexual identity.

Due to social stigma and lack of education, the community is forced into begging and sex work. In the case of hijras, however, the *badhai* ritual* is a cultural source of income. A clause in the current Bill criminalises the very source of the community's livelihood—begging. The clause reads, "Whoever compels or entices a transgender person to indulge in the act of begging shall be punishable with imprisonment for a term which shall not be less than six months but which may extend to two years and with

---

*This is a ritual followed mostly in the northern parts of the country during weddings and the birth of a male child. Hijras bless the couple/newborn and collect some money and gifts.

fine." Who can be "enticed" to beg? The community resorts to begging out of necessity and not because it enjoys begging. This clause is likely to be misused against transgenders in the name of protecting them. Besides, most transgender persons are harassed or booked under the begging prohibition laws, even when they are not begging and are merely present at public places.

The bill not only dehumanises and criminalises the community, by deciding where they should live it also violates the constitutional Right to Freedom of Residence under the Article 19 (I)(e).* A clause in the Bill reads: "Where any parent or a member of his immediate family is unable to take care of a transgender, the competent court shall by an order direct such person to be placed in a rehabilitation centre." A clause that compels transgenders to live with parents ignores the fact that the biological families are the primary centres of violence, and that transgenders depend, for their survival, on the families and kin they choose. In the case of sexual violence and abuse against transgenders, the bill dictates punishment of six months to two years with a fine. This is less than the punishment for rape under section 376, which is for seven years.

The transgender community has demanded the complete overhauling of the bill that violates their constitutional rights. The community plans to mobilise across the country to remind the government of the NALSA verdict. It has also demanded that before the bill is presented again, the community's feedback, given via the Parliamentary Standing Committee to the bill, be taken into account.

First published in Newsclick, December 21, 2018

---

*"Everyone lawfully within the territory of a State shall, within that territory, have the right to liberty of movement and freedom to choose his residence. ... No one shall be arbitrarily deprived of the right to enter his own country."

"PRODUCTIVE WORK HAS TO BECOME A PART OF EDUCATION IN ORDER TO CHALLENGE THE CASTE SYSTEM"

Anil Sadgopal

In the second part of a talk titled "End of Legacy of Freedom Struggle: Education for Exclusion and Enslavement" educationist Anil Sadgopal traces the history of education in India from the pre-Independence era to the present, and calls for a major change in the system to address historical inequalities such as caste.

In 1911, when Gopal Krishna Gokhale presented the first bill of free and compulsory education in the imperial legislative assembly, it was not passed. It could not pass because of resistance from two sections of society. One was feudal and the other was the emerging bourgeoisie. From the feudal section, the Maharaja of Darbhanga collected 11,000 signatures from big landlords, rajas and maharajas. Their objection was: If you ensure all children go to school then who farms our lands? At least they were honest enough to say that if all children went to school there would be no one left to do the farming.

Today's government is not honest, nor were the preceding governments either. These governments do not want to acknowledge that more than half of India's children continue to be child labourers. Their names will be enrolled at school; yes, there will be a hundred per cent enrolment. Some people wrongly say that this began to happen after the Right to Education Act of 2009. No, my dear friends, just look at the data. You'll see a hundred per cent enrolment from 1990 onwards. It is so because enrolment is merely a matter of entering names into lists and all headmasters are under orders to record the name of every child in the village. They duly write the names of all the children into their enrolment registers, but at least half of India's children are not in school.

The other resistance to universal education came from the bourgeoisie. The representatives of the bourgeoisie, then in the process of shifting from Calcutta to Bombay, rose in the imperial assembly and said: Don't make haste. India is a poor country, we don't have the resources to fund this, so let us not rush into trouble. Now, if we leap forward by some decades, the same argument was heard in 1946–47, when the Constituent Assembly was discussing what should be regarded as fundamental rights in the Constitution. There was a special committee, the Advisory Committee on Fundamental Rights, to decide whether to accept the proposals coming from the Drafting Committee led by Dr Ambedkar. The Drafting Committee had proposed that education up to fourteen years of age must be made compulsory and free, and must be a fundamental right. So it was placed in Part III of the Constitution. Sardar Vallabhbhai Patel addressed the Advisory Committee on Fundamental Rights and said: Look, this proposal has come before us from the Drafting Committee, and it is going to be very difficult for us to decide whether to accept education as a fundamental right or not. Everything under the sun cannot be accepted. After all, India is a poor country and our resources won't run to it. We must be very careful about accepting proposals on fundamental rights, keeping in mind that we are a poor country. When Patel had spoken to all the Rai Bahadurs and Sardar Bahadurs and Khan Bahadurs of the committee, since that was the social composition of the Constituent Assembly, none of them found the courage to say that we do have the resources to do this. So, education was shifted from Part III to Part IV of the Constitution, and never became a fundamental right until the Unnikrishnan judgement of 1993 declared it as one.*

The intervening period between Gopal Krishna Gokhale's bill and the Constituent Assembly's decision not to make education a fundamental right, is very important. Much happened in this

---

*Part III (Articles 12–35) deals with fundamental rights, while Part IV (Articles 36–51) contains directive principles of state policy which are non-justiciable, or non-enforceable. They cannot be pursued in court.

time, which is of relevance to our story. After Jallianwala Bagh in 1919, Gandhiji gave a call, pained by what had happened there; a call to all young people. He said, quit the British government's schools, colleges and universities, come out and set up national educational institutions. It was a revolt against the very idea of a British education system, because these institutions were enslaving the minds of children and youth. So Gandhi said, rebel against them, come out and set up your own educational institutions. A story to cherish from that time is, when a young person doing his MA in Economics quit at the call from Gandhiji, quit the AMU, he came out and set up a two-room college and started teaching an MA in Economics course. When he caught the attention of the Hamdard Dawakhana people in Karol Bagh in Delhi, they invited this young man to come to the Hamdard campus and set up a college for Economics there. That college grew alongside the freedom struggle and when we got freedom it became the present day Jamia Millia Islamia. That young person was Dr Zakir Hussain.

In 1928, Bhagat Singh wrote a short article, only two-and-a-half pages long, called "*Vidyaarthi aur Rajneeti*" (Students and Politics). In that article, Bhagat Singh refers to the viceroy visiting Lahore and the college authorities forcing students to welcome the viceroy. He writes, when the viceroy comes to Lahore, we are told to attend all his events and be present there, but when Nehru comes to Lahore, or Gandhiji comes to Lahore, or Subhash Chandra Bose, and we go to attend those meetings we are told you are doing politics. Why is attending the viceroy's meeting not politics, why is it politics to attend a Gandhi, Nehru and Subhash Chandra Bose's meeting? This is the question he raises. Then he says, we are told that our task is only to study, not to do any politics. We agree our task is to study in the college, but while we are studying are you going to keep us from trying to understand the economic and social condition of our country, and what is happening in the country? It seems you don't want us to understand. If you don't want us to understand, what kind of education are you imparting to us? He questions the very character of the education that was being imparted. Then he says, such an education is not meant to educate, it is only meant to turn us into clerks of the British Empire and we are not ready to accept such an education. That's a very rich discourse taking place there.

Babasaheb Ambedkar raised the slogan, "Educate, Agitate, Organise", and gave the slogan to the dalits who [along with adivasis] are about 22–23 per cent of our population.* Why does a dalit have to agitate and organise alongside being educated? Dalits are still fighting. To be educated, you have to fight. In order to be educated you have to form student organisations, like the Ambedkar Students' Association. When they form the ASA on campus at Hyderabad Central University then they are called anti-national, casteist and extremist, simply for forming the ASA. What were they asking for? They were saying, please pay our UGC scholarship in time because we come from poor families, we cannot support our families if you do not pay us in time. Because they are asking for the scholarship to be paid on time, they are called anti-nationals and casteist and extremist. Ambedkar's formula, which he gave to the dalits, can be applied to all sections of Indian society. All have to fight to be educated, they have to agitate to organise themselves. Whether they are called anti-nationals or not is besides the point. And when a Kanhaiya Kumar and Rohith Vemula are created by such processes, then the education minister of the BJP government in Rajasthan declares that the education system we are going to establish shall not produce Kanhaiya Kumars and Rohith Vemulas. This is a statement with a lot of deliberation behind it. In the education system now being set up, of course, no world-class institute will ever allow Kanhaiya Kumars and Rohith Vemulas even to be admitted. Forget about creating Kanhaiya Kumars and Rohith

---

*A Socialist League (estd. 1885) slogan from the end of the nineteenth century, "Educate, Agitate, Organise!" came to Ambedkar via the Fabian Society and appealed to his pragmatist outlook. The slogan appeared below the mast of his newspaper *Bahishkrit Bharat* (estd. 1927).

Vemulas, they will not even be admitted under the new rules and regulations that have come out under UGC guidelines.*

In 1937 Gandhi organised an all-India conference on education at Wardha, and addressing the conference, he said: When I spin thread from cotton, while spinning I'm also measuring its length, I am also weighing it, learning how to calculate. I am learning mathematics, I am also learning physics. And as I do it, I am learning about the history of exploitation in the cotton mills of Lancashire, I also think about the exploitation of Indian farmers by these cotton mills and therefore I learn History as well. And he says, I know only spinning, therefore I give you this example. But you can choose your own trade and production activity, whatever you want to choose, but combine a productive task with the curriculum. He proposes a nayi taleem (new education) as a totally new concept which will break the 5,000-year-old dichotomy between labour and knowledge.† When a tribal person called Eklavya had dared to challenge this dichotomy, he had to forego his thumb to Dronacharya. Here was a proposal in 1937, that productive work has to be organically at the centre of the curriculum in the classrooms of independent India. Very few have even tried to understand it, it has not been implemented by any government from the time of Independence till now. And every time someone talked about productive tasks people said: Oh, Gandhi must have meant it for poor people, for villages, urban slums, he never meant it for us, for our children. On the contrary, he meant it exactly for us because he saw that as long

---

*In 2017, the JNU was asked to strictly abide by the UGC guidelines of 2016 for admission to MA, MPhil and PhD programmes, doing away with the innovative scheme of "deprivation points" that had facilitated the entry of students, especially women, from backward areas.

†Developed from Gandhi's experience with his ashram communities in South Africa and India, the nayi taleem was also based on his ideal of small, self-reliant societies based on an economy of handicraft. The nayi taleem expressed Gandhi's view that "Literacy is not the end of education, nor even the beginning." And, "Literacy in itself is no education." (*Harijan*, July 31, 1937)

as the dichotomy between productive work and knowledge is maintained, in the classroom as much as society, the caste system cannot go away. In order to challenge the caste system, productive work has to become a part of the education system. It was a revolutionary proposal from Gandhi. Curriculum, financing of education, the issue of caste, class, language, gender, all becomes a part of the discourse of education. Instead of developing the proposal and taking it forward and finding ways and means of introducing it in the classrooms of India, it was given up forever.

In 1938, the Indian National Congress passed a three-point resolution on education. One, all education up to class eight shall be in the mother tongue. 'Mother tongue' does not mean state approved languages, it means the mother tongue. In MP, where I come from, mother tongue means Malwi, Nimadi, and Bundelkhandi. These are the mother tongues of Madhya Pradesh. So the resolution talked of mother tongues. Second, this education shall be entirely free up to class eight. That was the immediate aim—somehow to take all children up to class eight—which we have failed to do even until today. Third, it will be based upon the nayi taleem conception of curriculum and pedagogy. We have failed in all three respects.

I'll refer to 1985, where the first evidence of the attack of globalisation became apparent. Of course the formal arrival of globalisation was in 1991, we all know that. But there is evidence available to show it goes back even earlier. In 1985, the name of the education ministry was changed to Human Resource Development ministry, without any debate in Parliament, without any discussion; suddenly, one morning we come to know this name had changed. It was not a change of nomenclature alone, it was a change in the very conceptualisation of education.

A year later, the 1986 policy came into being. This policy was passed by Parliament with unanimity, not a single dissenting voice. The '86 policy declared that half of India's children shall not be provided a school. Instead they will be provided an evening non-formal centre. The report on the acts of '86 passed by Parliament said: Why evening centre, why not a day centre? Evening centres, because these are child labourers and when child labourers return home they will be very tired, so they should be given one or two hours to have food and be ready for a non-formal centre under candle-light. The teachers there shall not be regular, properly trained, properly paid teachers; these are poor children, the poorest of the poor sections of Indian society, therefore they will be provided underpaid untrained contract teachers.

After 1991, India faced structural adjustment. This readjustment was non-negotiable, a condition that had to be met if the Indian government wanted to raise more loans from the international market. The International Monetary Fund and World Bank together told the Indian government, we'll give you the loans provided you accept this essential condition, of structural adjustment. You have to make a solemn promise that you shall start reducing public expenditure on education, health, schemes of social welfare, poverty alleviation, and all such subsidised programmes. If you don't—we will stop the loan. India not only accepted the terms, but we capitulated totally. At the end of the decade we even introduced an act in Parliament to ensure that we don't cross the limits set by the IMF and the World Bank. It is called the Fiscal Responsibility and Budget Management (FRBM) Act, introduced in 2000 and passed in 2003. It remains in effect; even Finance Minister Arun Jaitley said we agree with and accept the dictate of the IMF and the World Bank that our deficit will not go beyond 3 per cent as set by the FRBMA—itself a product of orders from IMF and World Bank.

In 1992–93, the World Bank tells us how to renew primary education. Can you imagine this? India with this legacy I've been talking about is being told how to run primary schools. And they give us a programme called the District Primary Education Programme, which within ten years covers half of the districts in eighteen states of India. The programme was designed to destroy public-funded primary and upper-primary schools. The surprising thing was that when this was happening, the teachers' unions kept quiet; all the more surprising because the very first step under this programme was to turn all teachers recruited from then onwards into contract workers—underpaid, untrained contract teachers. As we go further into 1993, the teachers are not just to be of two kinds—contract teachers and regular teachers—but the contract teacher will be further divided into layers, several layers of contractualisation are to take place. Each layer will become weaker than it was before. Earlier, if all contract teachers mobilised themselves, there would be trouble. So, the formula was to divide them into *samvida* (contract) levels 1, 2, 3—with varying terms of employment. This happened in Madhya Pradesh and continues to happen. Now, every section of the contract teachers has to fight its own battles separately. Then came a time when single-teacher schools were promoted under the Sarva Shiksha Abhiyan. You've probably never heard of them. These schools were called education guarantee centres. They guaranteed everything except education. From the year 2000 onwards, the Sarva Shiksha Abhiyan accepted the formulation of education guarantee centres. The first formulation of the Sarva Shiksha Abhiyan, approved in the tenth five-year plan, says very clearly, that henceforth we will provide primary and upper-primary education either through schools or through education guarantee centres or yet other alternative forms of schooling. Schools are no more going to be institutions through which we will provide education. School is increasingly going to be, from the nineties onwards, for the better-off sections of society and not for the poor.

A lot of euphemisms were developed, as I found out. This is a neoliberal policy framework under globalisation, and neoliberalism has a way with words, beautiful new words. At the time they talked of contract teachers as shiksha mitra, bal mitra, and other heart-warming coinages. In different languages they have different names. All kinds of names were thought of for those teachers in the education guarantee centre, those single-teacher schools meant only for dalit and tribal hamlets, not for any other section of the society—only for SC/ST children. The teachers were called guruji, as if the rest of them are not guruji. So, this designation is intended give them more respect. By more respect, you mean more exploitation will take place again. All these formulations were perfected during the nineties, and then the time came to apply these principles to higher education. The global market had learned that we can succeed in destroying an elementary education system of many decades and nobody really will protest. The intellectual class is also silent. The economy is structurally adjusted, the intellectual class is intellectually adjusted and not raising a voice. Otherwise if the higher education academia had raised its voice in the nineties, you would probably not have seen this day we are seeing now, so what I'm saying is meant as a self-criticism of the higher education academia also.

Transcribed and edited from a video,
Indian Cultural Forum, October 26, 2017.

First published in Newsclick, October 25, 2017.

◆◆◆

GROWING ANGER, GROWING RESISTANCE

PARI and Newsclick

The year 2018 witnessed widespread protests from large sections of Indians who could no longer remain silent in the face of government policies that seem to have nothing to do with either the rights of citizens or their well-being. Farmers, women, adivasis, workers, the youth: everyone seemed to be on the streets at some point or the other. The year began with over 2,000 workers from ten trade unions gathered in the National Capital on January 8 and 9, to protest the anti-worker policies of the Modi government. An explosive farming crisis and sustained protests over the past two years converged in the historic march to Mumbai from March 6 to 12 by 50,000 farmers. In another instance of growing anger, on October 30 tens of thousands of adivasis from Maharashtra gathered in Thane, demanding land rights, employment, food security and other long-pending measures. And towards the end of the year, on November 29 and 30, thousands of farmers marched again, this time to the capital, demanding that Parliament respond to their suffering and hold a special session on the agrarian crisis.

We won't leave until all our demands are met!

The sun had set. Darkness was spreading fast. With firewood on their heads and utensils, bricks, uncooked rice, dry fish and spices in hand, many thousands of adivasis—50,000 estimate the organisers—walked towards the old octroi post in Mulund in north-eastern Mumbai. This now-defunct compound became the camping ground for the protesters.

"We will settle here. We have brought along all the things we need. Firewood for the stove, vessels to cook in, rice—we have got it all," said Manubai Gawari as she adjusted the load of firewood on her head. "We will not leave until all our demands are met." Manubai, sixty, is from the Warli community and lives in Dighashi village in Bhiwandi taluka; she came for the morcha along with seventy–eighty others from her village.

Since eleven am on Thursday, October 30, groups of adivasis— from the Warli, Katkari, Mahadev Koli, Ma Thakur and other communities—poured into Thane city from Nashik, Palghar Raigad, Thane and Mumbai districts. They came in groups by hired tempos, by bus, by train. Around noon, the tide of women and men marched towards the collector's office in Thane city from Saket Naka, two kilometres away. Among them were farm labourers, porters, sanitation workers and construction labourers.

"Our adivasi families have been residing in the forests in and around Mumbai for many generations. We don't have any proof of ownership [of land or house]. We don't have caste certificates. My mother gave birth to me at home, that is not registered anywhere. I am fifty-two. My children need a caste certificate for their education. That means proof of fifty years of life. Where will I get that from?" asked a distraught Nalini Bujad at the rally outside the collectorate. She's from the Warli community, and has come here from Amboli in Andheri, a north-western suburb of Mumbai.

"The padas around Mahanand Dairy [hamlets in Goregaon in north-western Mumbai] don't have electricity or water. Give us caste certificates, include our padas in the development plans. Rehabilitate us in the same area," she continued. Close to 2,000 adivasis from ten tribal padas in Mumbai participated in the march, estimates Nalini Bujad, a representative of the Shramajeevi Sanghatana.

The march was organised by the Sanghatana to highlight long-standing issues of adivasis in the state. The organisation is headquartered in Vasai in Maharashtra, and works on adivasi rights. Many times before this, the same communities have taken to the streets in protest. Each time, the government placates the protesters with assurances and sends them back. So this time, the adivasis resolved not to back off.

By five pm, the morcha turned towards Mulund. The protesters walked the five kilometres from Saket Naka to Mulund's Jakat Naka (the old octroi post). It had started to get dark. There was no electricity at the camp ground. "If you don't provide for electricity here, we'll camp on the highway under the lights there." This demand from the people in unison forced the cops there to take some action. In a short while, the light bulbs on the electricity poles lit up.

People from each village chose a spot and brought their firewood, bricks, pots, utensils, grains and provisions there, to set up a makeshift basti. The darkness around them slowly diffused in the light of the cooking fires. There were at least 500 such fires burning at the open ground.

After dinner, the people played drums and sang their songs. Many stayed up all night. Others were exhausted from the day's walk and from carrying the load of firewood and bricks and spread out small sheets of cloth on the ground to rest for the night. Many used their bundles of belongings as pillows and fell asleep under the open sky.

One of the main demands of the protesters was the implementation of the Forest Rights Act of 2006. Even twelve years after the Act was passed, adivasi communities across India have not received rights to the forest land they have cultivated for generations. Another major demand was that before the ambitious Direct Benefit Transfer policy of the central government (introduced in January 2013), to transfer monetary amount in various welfare schemes is set in motion, internet connections must be made available in every village. The protesters also asked for employment opportunities for adivasis; they demanded that the needs of adivasi communities in Mumbai should be included in the development plans; and that solutions should be found to eradicate the increasing levels of hunger among adivasis.

The protesters waited all night in the open ground for Chief Minister Devendra Fadnavis to respond. At midnight—twelve hours after starting out for the collector's office in the relentless heat—ten representatives of the adivasi groups from various districts met the chief minister at his official residence in south Mumbai. They were given a guarantee that what they were demanding would be implemented. The chief minister would also give orders to various department heads, including the forest department, to resolve the issues and would appoint a nodal officer to follow up and steer the process.

At three am, the representatives returned to Jakat Naka. The waiting protesters at the ground expressed happiness at the outcome of the meeting. By five am, they started returning to their villages—with hope.

Mamata Pared, PARI, 2018 (Translated from Marathi by Samyukta Shastri, with inputs from Jyoti Shinoli)

The how and why of the farmers' long march to Mumbai

Over the past six days, India has slowly woken up to farmers' distress—and their resistance. On 6 March, about 20,000 farmers from various parts of the state mobilized by the CPI (M) affiliated

All India Kisan Sabha gathered at Nashik in north-western Maharashtra to begin a 200-km march to Mumbai, the state capital. The plan was to indefinitely gherao the Assembly while the Budget session was on and demand immediate resolution of the life-and-death issues facing farmers. By the time the march entered Mumbai on 12 March morning, it had swelled to over 50,000 people, the government was scrambling to deal with the red tide sweeping in, political parties were falling over each other to show support, and residents of the commercial capital of India were wondering what they had been missing all this while.

Like everywhere else in India, farmers in Maharashtra are reeling under the double whammy of falling incomes and rising indebtedness. In 2017–18, agricultural economy of the state shrank by 8.3 per cent, according to the state's Economic Survey tabled in the Assembly on 9 March [2018]. The Survey predicted that cereal production will dip by four per cent, pulses by 46 per cent, oilseeds by 15 per cent and cotton by a whopping 44 per cent in the current year's kharif season. Cotton is a major crop in the state, but a massive infestation of the standing cotton crop by the pink bollworm has destroyed crop worth Rs 15,000 crore, affecting nearly 20.36 lakh hectares—that's 50 percent of the area under cotton. The Economic Survey also had a dire prediction for the forthcoming rabi crop—acreage is down by 31 per cent, and production is expected to fall by 39 per cent for cereals, six per cent for pulses and 60 per cent for oilseeds.

All this is just the current calamity. Distress of the farmers has been building up over the years because of rising input prices and falling returns as they fail to get remunerative prices. Indebtedness is another dimension of the same problem. Last year, the BJP government had announced a farm debt waiver worth Rs 34,022 crores to supposedly benefit 70 lakh farmers. But the finance minister admitted in his budget speech that just Rs 23,102.19 crores have actually been sanctioned for 46.4 lakh farm households, and further, that only Rs 13,782 crores have actually been disbursed to 35.7 lakh farmers' accounts.

But the core of the farming crisis lies in the fact that farmers' incomes are not at par with what they are spending to raise their crops. A Niti Aayog paper admitted that according to a government committee on agricultural prices, farming output prices have increased by just 6.88 per cent between 2011–12 and 2015–16, while the prices they pay for goods and services have increased by 10.52 per cent.

Another factor is the steady decline in landholding size over the years. In 1971, the average landholding size in Maharashtra was 4.28 hectares owned by 49 lakh landholders. This has slipped to 1.44 hectares owned by 137 lakh landholding farmers. About 78 per cent of these farmers are "small and marginal", that is, they own less than 2 hectares of land.

Despite it being considered an advanced and rich state, Maharashtra has just 25 per cent of its cultivable area under irrigation. Thus, with three-fourths of farmed area dependent on rains, and the increasingly erratic monsoon, farmers are constantly facing a water crisis that destroys their budget. A bizarre feature of this crisis is that sugarcane, which covers just 4 per cent of the state's sown area consumes 71.5 per cent of the water consumed for irrigation.

Another key factor fuelling the farming crisis is the refusal of the state government to speedily implement the Forest Rights Act (FRA) that gives tribal farmers land rights over forest lands that they have cultivated for years. Maharashtra is lagging behind several other states in such distribution of land right deeds (pattas). This has angered tribals in the Thane belt in north-west Maharashtra and the Vidarbha region.

Faced with this immense crisis, Maharashtra has seen a spate of farmers' suicides over the years. Just last year, 2,414 farmers reportedly committed suicide despite the state government's debt waiver. But, that's just one way the hapless farmers found escape from harsh life. All over the state, thousands of farmers found new strength and hope in the collective protests organized mainly by Left organisations, led by the AIKS.

Two years ago, on March 29 and 30, 2016, the AIKS had led an unprecedented one lakh-strong peasant siege for two days and two nights at the central CBS square in the heart of Nashik, which had paralysed the city. Maharashtra's BJP Chief Minister Devendra Fadnavis gave assurances to AIKS, but since these were not fulfilled, the AIKS-led a 10,000-strong 'coffin march' in Thane city in May 2016 to focus on the issue of peasant suicides.

Then, in October 2016, over 50,000 adivasi peasants gheraoed the house of the Adivasi Development Minister at Wada in Palghar district for two days and nights. Written assurances on issues like FRA and malnutrition-related deaths of adivasi children were given. Meanwhile, AIKS held protest actions at Aurangabad in the Marathwada region in May 2016, and at Khamgaon in the Vidarbha region in May 2017 on issues of drought, loan waiver and remunerative prices.

A historic united peasant strike was held from June 1–11, 2017, led by a coordination committee of farmers' organisations. On June 11, the state government was forced to hold talks with the Coordination Committee and agreed to give a complete loan waiver to the peasantry. But the deceptive loan waiver package of Rs 34,000 crores that was announced imposed several onerous conditions that would prevent a great majority of farmers from getting any relief. This betrayal sparked massive joint protests— fifteen large district conventions in July, in which over 40,000 farmers participated, followed by a state-wide chakkajaam (road blockade) on August 14 in which over two lakh farmers blocked national and state highways at over 200 centres in thirty-one districts of the state. Finally, on 16 February 2018, at an extended meeting of the AIKS Maharashtra State Council at Sangli on February 16, attended by over 150 leading activists from twenty-five districts, the decision to hold the Long March on 6–12 March [2018] was taken. A vigorous campaign was carried out throughout the state and it received enthusiastic response all over.

Subodh Varma, Newclick, March 12, 2018

Trade unions announce nationwide strike on January 8–9, 2019

A congregation of over ten central trade unions and independent federations assembled in Delhi on the birth anniversary of Bhagat Singh, to up their ante against the BJP government's pro-corporate and anti-worker attitude, and announced a nationwide strike on January 8-9, 2019. Addressing over 2,000 workers, Amarjeet Kaur, from the All India Trade Union Congress (AITUC) said, "There is an attempt to suppress working class and people's voices in the name of branding them as 'anti-national'. But let it be clear that it was the working class that fought for development and betterment of this country, and not the members of RSS and BJP. We are the real patriots of this country."

The call for organising the congregation was given by ten major central trade unions that included the Centre of Indian Trade Unions (CITU), Indian National Trade Union Congress (INTUC), All India Trade Union Congress (AITUC), Self Employed Women's Association (SEWA), etc.

The unions highlighted the ignorance of the government and asserted that the government is yet to ratify the ILO convention of 1989, and has systematically failed to organise the international labour conference, despite persistent efforts. Additionally, the central government has failed miserably at all fronts as far as the rights of the workers are concerned, failing to pay any attention to the 12-point charter which demands a dignified existence for the workers, including demands of regular minimum wages and universal social security at its base.

Tapan Sen, General Secretary, CITU, said, "The working class is fighting in such a situation where the national and international corporate class are hell bent to destroy our country." He added, "We have to resist this onslaught, and remove the anti-labour and anti-people ruling class."

The event comes at a time when thousands of workers are fighting against attacks on the working class across the country— the Tea Estate Workers' strike, Rajasthan Transport workers's strike, and the Yamaha and Royal Enfield workers' strikes in Tamil Nadu, to mention a few.

The unions also asserted that the Centre has refused to respond to their just and genuine demands. Instead it has been increasing its aggression against the rights of workers, trade unions and its very own employees—the central government employees have been protesting to demand their legitimate salaries in accordance with the 7th Pay Commission.

Expressing concern over the deteriorating conditions of the national economy, they launched an attack on the anti-worker and pro-employer codifications of the government. The unions also critiqued the attempts made by the government to privatise strategic public sector undertakings as well as to sell the Indian Railways to private players. Railway unions, including the AIRF and NFIR, were also present at the venue.

Speaking to Newsclick, Shiv Gopal Mishra of the AIRF said, "It is time to create a new history. If the railway federations hadn't put strong opposition, the government would have sold off the railways. The resistance by the railway unions has halted the attempts to push for full FDI in the railway sector. If the government continues its attempt to privatise railways, we warn that the railway federations will embark on a blockade. Railways had always been the instrument of poor people in this country and now, the government is dismantling it."

As the government pushes its agenda of "ease of doing business", the unions sounded the poll bugle by stating that the January strike is a preparation towards a massive nationwide indefinite strike. Kaur added, "The government in the centre and the states which are engaging in anti-worker policies will be fought by strengthening the workers' movement. We will go to every factory and street to ensure that such attacks on the working class come to an end. We have to prepare and strengthen ourselves before the January 8–9 strike."

Sonia from SEWA also said, "We need to unite and strengthen the unorganised and home-based workers, and put forward a consolidated movement opposing policies that are against the working class."

"Our slogans are clear: 'Modi Hatao, Mazdoor bachao; Modi Hatao, Desh Bachao' (Remove Modi, Save the Worker; Remove Modi, Save the Nation). In four years of this Modi government, we have witnessed that not only attacks on workers have increased but free speech and any kind of voices of dissent are being suppressed. This government has turned into a government of destruction—of employment, of working class, of farmers and of democracy," added a determined Rajiv Dhimri from AICCTU.

The 12-point charter of demands of the trade unions includes urgent measures for containing price-rise through universalisation of the Public Distribution System and banning speculative trade in the commodity market; containing unemployment through concrete measures for employment generation; strict enforcement of all basic labour laws and stringent punitive measures for violation of labour laws; universal social security cover for all workers; minimum wages of not less than Rs 18,000 per month with provisions of indexation; a halt to disinvestment in Central/State PSUs and strategic sale; halting "contractorization" in permanent perennial work; and payment of the same wage and benefits to contract workers as regular workers get for the same or similar work.

First published in Newsclick, 28 September 2018

◆•◆•

CONVERSATION: P. SAINATH ON WHY THE KISAN MUKTI MARCH IS NOT A CULMINATION BUT A BEGINNING

Newsclick

In the lead-up to the November 29–30 farmers' protest, P. Sainath, founder-editor of People's Archive of Rural India (PARI), spoke to Pranjal of Newsclick about the significance of farmers coming

together in Delhi, as well as the importance of building common
ground between the working class and the middle class.

Pranjal (P): Let's start with the background to this march. I
remember your article in People's Archive of Rural India, where
you called for a special parliamentary session to be held to
discuss the agrarian crisis. So, where did this idea of a long march
originate?

P. Sainath (PS): All of us were incredibly inspired by the long
march from Nashik to Mumbai organised by the All India Kisan
Sabha in March 2018. Now, that was a really long march—182
kilometres—where 40,000 adivasi farmers, the poorest of farmers,
really marginal, marched for a week with their demands. And
one of the things we saw there, which was unusual compared
to earlier marches, and I say this having lived thirty-six years in
Mumbai, is that it was the first time the middle classes came out
in large numbers in support of the farmers. They came in their
thousands, in sympathy or empathy with these very poor people
who had touched the conscience of the city. The demands of the
farmers were reasonable, and they also reached out to the middle
classes by marching in the dead of night so as not to disrupt the
board exams of the children of Mumbai. People really appreciated
that and responded with warmth and generosity. They came out
into the streets with water and food, and gave out free pairs of
chappals because there were so many thousands that had no
footwear. These middle-class people had not been mobilised by
any organisation. When we saw that, we thought this should be
happening in Delhi—that's where the power lies.

The call for a march on November 29 and 30 [2018] has been
given by the All India Kisan Coordination Committee (AIKSCC).

P: It is a group of around 180 farmers' organisations.

PS: Almost 200 farmers' organisations, big and small. Our role
as middle-class professionals was to decide how to reconnect the
middle classes with the primary classes and workers. In September

you had a march of the All India Kisan Sabha where you had farmers and agricultural workers…

P: And just one day before that [on September 4] was the women's march in Delhi.*

PS: So the idea was, why can't we bring all these together and bring the middle classes in? I think there is some sensitivity growing around the country. A middle-class platform, Nation for Farmers, sprang up in solidarity. Within this there are doctors, teachers, students and techies for farmers—there have been groups forming in Hyderabad, Bengaluru, Chennai. They might wear their separate armbands or headbands or T-shirts, but they will come with "Nation for Farmers" as their main banner in front. That's the idea. On my visits to college campuses and elsewhere there has been a very good response to it.

Of course, there are problems…with elections [for five state legislatures] coinciding with the dates for the march, especially in states close to Delhi—Rajasthan, Madhya Pradesh and Chhattisgarh—from where more people would ordinarily be expected to join us; and also exams beginning on November 28.

P: Let me come back to the issues around which these mobilisations are happening. These still remain the minimum support price and loan waiver. What are the other things you are demanding apart from…

PS: There is more to that. The minimum support price and the loan waiver are the core of two bills that are being crafted by the All India Kisan Sangharsh Coordination Committee (AIKSCC), which must be passed. That is a demand.

---

*Organised by the All India Democratic Women's Association (AIDWA), the march was a protest against hate crimes and violence, fear, unemployment and hunger. The AIDWA cited the increasing incidence of violence against women—figures for 2015 and 2016 added up to 915 cases of kidnapping, sexual assault, dowry killings and domestic violence per day, while the conviction rate for such crimes stood at a mere 19 per cent, and 25 per cent in the case of rape.

P: Which came out of the mobilisation of 2017.*

PS: These bills must be passed and I believe a large number of political parties have signed on saying that they support this demand and will pass the bills. But there is a larger crisis—the agrarian crisis is also an agro-ecological one. It's a question of women's rights in farming. It has issues related to the mega water crisis. There is, apart from the loan waiver, a larger credit structure and public responsibility for that. There are questions of what kind of agriculture we want twenty to thirty years from now. And what about the pending issues of land reform?

The first of the Swaminathan Commission or National Commission on Farmers reports was submitted in December 2004. For fourteen years, those reports have lain with Parliament without drawing a single hour's discussion. Five reports, six volumes. But when it comes to a GST for the corporate world, a joint session of Parliament is called in no time and held at midnight with the president of India there. Surely, you can find some time for the farmers of your nation who have been in unending and ever-escalating crisis for twenty to twenty-five years now. And that should be the point of the special three-week session: pass the two bills, discuss the Swaminathan Committee report, discuss women's rights and entitlements and try passing a bill on that; discuss the water crisis and take a position on whether water is a fundamental right or a commodity; and let the victims of the crisis address Parliament and the nation.

P: Let's come to the organisation of the march because if we look at the Kisan Long March, a lengthy process took place three months before the actual event.

---

*June 2017 was when the first rumblings of large-scale protests by farmers were felt in Madhya Pradesh and Maharashtra, over the issues of loan waiver and crop pricing. In both states, specifically the Pune and Mandsaur regions, the protests began with leaders and organisations considered close to the BJP and Sangh, but quickly came to acquire an anti-government character.

PS: I think for two to three years before.

P: But the entire process took three to four months—assembling the logistics, convincing people to arrange for food and all that; so what's the plan when it comes to the Dilli Chalo march?

PS: There are several groups, well over a hundred groups involved here, and now with the middle classes coming in, the logistics are going to be very complicated, but then each group can look out for itself. The Delhi government—Mr Kejriwal's government—has promised the creation of toilets and stationing of ambulances, and will perhaps help with water also. Some members of that government, in their individual capacity, are trying to contribute to the food packets that are required. Maybe the Hawkers Federation and various others will all come in to provide everything at cost. Those kind of talks are going on, and we think this will happen.

P: So it's Doctors for Farmers, Students for Farmers. Have you also reached out to other political parties?

PS: The All India Kisan Sangharsh Coordination Committee has reached out to political parties and got them to sign on to the idea of the two bills. We, as Nation for Farmers, are not the organisers of the march, we are a solidarity group. We have created a petition to the president of India, calling for a special session of parliament; it's online, in different languages. We have a dedicated website, and anyone can go and sign the petition. There are also updates on where it is all to happen.

Now one of the things people keep asking me is how this is relevant to students. All over Maharashtra—in Aurangabad, Marathwada, Vidarbha, Nashik; also in Telangana, Mehboobnagar, Warangal—kids are dropping out of college and university as the drought bites in. Parents who are farmers have been bankrupted by the agrarian crisis of the last twenty years, and now the drought means they have no crop. There are dozens and dozens of kids in the universities of Pune, and it gets worse still in the privatised universities because kids who are unable to pay their hostel fees, their mess fees, their tuition fees, are in a complete dilemma, and demoralised over what to do. These cases are directly linked to the agrarian crisis. I find there is a great degree of sensitivity to that. I think you're also going to see the retired servicemen's groups which came out on September 5, they will also, in my opinion, be joining this march. The Pensioner Parishad will be joining the march, as well. In fact one of the things that I found in the last several years—I've been talking at the military colleges, the college of warfare in Hyderabad, the military colleges in Mhow and Delhi—is that army personnel are extremely sensitive to the agrarian crisis because your jawan is a kisan in uniform.

You'll find a very great and diverse spectrum of people involved, but it's important that this march, on November 29 and 30, be a beginning, not a culmination, and I find the momentum building up every day. People tell me we have formed this group in Secunderabad, or this group in Patna, I don't even know all the groups. It shows that there is some kind of ferment happening. We held a group meeting in Pune for Nation for Farmers. Veteran socialist Baba Adhav came and he told the crowd, I am very pleased that we are doing this, but he told me I will not forgive you if you stop this after November 30.*

P: You have said this is not going to be the end and there are programmes that will be held in the future also. What are those? If this does not work out, what are the next steps? And what's an appeal that you would like to end this interview with?

PS: I really want to appeal to all Newsclick readers, viewers, those who live in the National Capital Region, those who live nearby,

---

*Babasaheb Pandurang Adhav (b. 1930) is an anti-caste activist who has worked since Independence in his home-city of Pune to organise workers from the informal sector. Starting with a panchayat for hamals (porters), he went on to help auto drivers, rag pickers, domestic workers, construction labourers and hawkers to form collectives of their own and negotiate better terms of employment. After a strike in 1956 by hamals, followed by years of satyagraha, protest, and arrests, the Maharashtra legislature passed the Mathadi, Hamal and Other Manual Workers Act, 1969—the first law for the security of unorganised labour in independent India.

and those who don't live nearby but can come to Delhi, to join us. You know, we don't believe that any one march, or any one rally will yield a transformational result; it's a process. The farmers who marched to Mumbai had most of their demands accepted, and they still have to fight every day to see them implemented. So that's important to understand.

We think that simply holding a special session of Parliament on an issue concerning poor people will be a historic precedent. I don't expect that they will leap to do it, obviously. This Parliament will already be in session when the march happens, but we are demanding that every MP who claims to be pro-farmer should come and sign the petition for the special session. Let him or her march with the farmers towards the boat club, or wherever they stop. That's one thing. Second, I think what makes this different from the earlier marches is—you're broadening the spectrum to bring in the middle classes, the working class, a lot of people who don't go for rallies, political meetings, things like that. It's like what Baba Adhav said, I'll not forgive you if you stop on the 30th. Without much help from us, groups have formed, Patna has its Nation for Farmers. Bangalore convened three meetings and the last meeting that I attended made one of Karnataka's most famous progressive writers Baraguru Ramachandrappa the convener, in a very simple democratic process. What we do is, whoever comes for the convening meeting is part of the convening committee. They choose their convener, and none of us interferes there. So you'll get diverse groups and chapters in different places. There are many I don't know of. We are finding it hard to keep pace with them. Now the middle class begins talking to farmers and talking about farmers. With Students for Farmers, the WhatsApp groups are buzzing. And likewise in other professional and occupational groups.

In the last thirty years, if I asked a Supreme Court lawyer, or a well-known journalist, when did you last sit down and talk to a farmer or a labourer, there was an embarrassed, sheepish silence. I have found it so in every gathering of the middle class that I have spoken to on this subject. Reversing the atomisation that neo-liberal economic policy has brought—which has driven us very far away from the miseries of the countryside, the labourer, the farmer—creates a very different discourse where the words farmer, agrarian crisis, labourer, women's rights, all these start coming together. So we believe Nation for Farmers, will continue on the initiative of those who form new groups and there will be some universities, teachers, students that will be talking to farmers, about farmers, and thereby changing their own consciousness. This is not a culmination, it is a beginning. My appeal is, come there and you will leave with a different way of thinking.

First published in Newsclick, November 19, 2018

WHEN THE FARMERS GO MARCHING IN... We want to be in that number !

Orijit Sen, 2018

THE MOUNTAIN, FOREST AND STREAMS
ARE OUR GODS

Purusottam Thakur

The adivasis of the Niyamgiri hills of Odisha won a victory against mining in 2013, but the threats to their ancestral land remain. Rajkishor Sunani, poet and activist, sings of the people's land and the people's movement.

"From my childhood, I have been a rebel. I protest against injustice," says Rajkishor Sunani, a dalit poet, singer and activist from Karlagaon, a village around 110 kilometres from the Vedanta alumina refinery in Kalahandi district. "I joined the movement [against bauxite mining in the Niyamgiri hills] in 2002–03. I wrote songs to make people aware, and I travelled from village to village to spread the message of the movement," he says.

"At the time, my wife Leelabati and I lived in the villages here and sang songs," Rajkishor recalls. People would invite the couple into their homes and give them food and shelter. The Sunanis, modest cultivators in their own village, had no source of income and survived on the generosity of adivasis. "My wife and I also went to jail in 2004, for protesting against Vedanta. I was detained for three months and Leelabati for a month. Even today, the nexus between the government and [mining] companies continues to suppress people's movements," he says.

The Niyamgiri hills, which spread across Kalahandi and Rayagada districts in southwestern Odisha, are home to the Dongria Kondh (or Jharnia Kondh, as many of them call themselves)—a Particularly Vulnerable Tribal Group (PVTG), estimated to number only 8,000; other related adivasi groups live in around 100 villages in the region.

For long, the Dongria tribes have opposed a project by the government-owned Odisha Mining Corporation and Sterlite Industries (now Vedanta), a British multinational. The project proposed to mine their sacred hills for bauxite (used for making aluminium), for Vedanta's refinery in the state's Lanjigarh tehsil.

In 2013, the adivasis unanimously rejected the mining of their land through a Supreme-Court mandated referendum conducted in twelve villages around Niyamgiri. This movement was led by the Niyamgiri Suraksha Samiti, a collective of adivasis, and many activists like Rajkishor.

The Odisha government has since tried (so far without success) to overturn the referendum, and the refinery continues to operate with bauxite from other sources. The threats to the ancestral land of the adivasis remain on the horizon.

I met Rajkishor in 2018, at the annual post-harvest festival on the Niyamgiri plateau, near Anlabhata village. He had trekked across 6 kilometres of hilly terrain to get here. The festival is held from February 23 to 25 every year, and is dedicated to Niyam Raja (roughly, the King or Giver of Law). On the evening of the second day and the morning of the final day, when activists spoke about their experiences of people's movements, Rajkishor sang. When he started singing, more people gathered around.

He sings passionately, plays instruments like the dhap (a frame drum), and draws large crowds. Apart from the people's movement in Niyamgiri, he has written songs for other struggles too, including that in the Gandhamardhan hills of Bargarh district, against bauxite mining by the Bharat Aluminium Company (BALCO).

Now fifty-five, Rajkishor has been a singer-activist for over two decades. He is also a member of the Samajwadi Jan Parishad, a political party founded in 1995 by the socialist leader Kishen Pattnaik (1930–2004), which has supported people's movements in Niyamgiri and other villages of Odisha.

I ask him: what do you feel about the struggles you've been a part of? "If the world's environment is being conserved to any degree, it is only by such movements," he says. "Otherwise, everything would have been destroyed." And to make sure it isn't, he beats his dhap and sings of the beauty of the hills.

We will never leave the mountain, stream, forest and our home
We will not give up the struggle, even if we have to sacrifice our
    lives
Dear friends, we will not leave the struggle

The mountain, forest, and streams are our gods
The land is full of flowers and fruits that are like Kuber*
Dear friends, the mountain, forest, land and streams are our gods
The land, water, air, sky and fire are the devata

Our devata is the one "who always gives"—our god is our life
Dear friends, the mountain, forest, land and streams are our gods
It is our Bha-ga-ban: "bha" for bhoomi†, "ga" for gagan‡, "ba"
    for baayu§ and "na" for neer⁵

The land provides us with greenery, trees, fruits and roots
The sky provides the air, and gives the water of the stream
The water flows like mother's milk

Dear friends, we drink the milk of the motherland
You can stay alive after leaving your gods,
But we cannot live after leaving our god

Whether or not it is true, we don't know
How can you stay alive by giving up nature?

Oh dear one! This science is the truth
Dear friends! Please accept the truth
And discard untruths!
The mountain, land, forest and streams are our main deities

---

*The Hindu god of wealth

†land

‡sky

§air

⁵water

Our land is full of forest, fruits, roots and animals
We are neither Hindu nor Muslim nor Christian
We are the tribes and worshipers of nature
Dear friends, we are equal, man and woman
Dear friends, we enjoy freedom here

Dear friends, the government and the corporates suppress us
They're at one with each other
Dear friends, the mountain, land, forest and streams are our gods
We will save the forest, land, water, animals and people

If the environment is destroyed, all of us will be dead
We, the farmers, labourers and daily-wage workers, will all unite
We will drive away those who loot us, only then can we survive...

Dear friends, the mountain, land, forest and streams are our gods
Hey government! We will not be afraid of your lathis, bullets
    and jail
We will sacrifice for our motherland and not give up the struggle!
Wake up all the tribes and workers
If we are attacked, we, the children of the soil, will not remain
    silent
Our struggle will continue...

Dear friends! We wish to remain in peace—and be free!
Dear friends, we are fighting for our rights!
Dear friends, let the corporate government get out!
Dear friends, the mountain, land, forest and streams are our
    gods...

First published in PARI, April 20, 2018

ACKNOWLEDGEMENTS

This book is the result of many people's efforts. We would like to mention every writer, translator, cameraperson, video editor, transcriber and advisor, but such a list would probably fill up a book on its own. Special mention must be made, however, of the following: We thank the board and the editorial collective of the Indian Writers Forum: K. Satchidanandan, Romila Thapar, Indira Jaising, Anuradha Kapur, Shyam B. Menon, Ishita Mehta, Sreelakshmi KM, Abhilasha Chattopadhyay, Yogesh S., Daniya Rahman, Souradeep Roy and Sneha Chowdhury. We also thank, for their unstinted support, Pranjal, Prabir Purkayastha, Seema Mustafa, Harsh Mander, Teesta Setalvad, P. Sainath, Ashok Vajpeyi and Ravi Singh.

We are grateful for the work from the following sites committed to news and analyses of our citizens' lives:

- Newsclick <<https://www.newsclick.in/>>
- Indian Cultural Forum (ICF) <<http://indianculturalforum. in/>>
- Guftugu <<http://guftugu.in/>>
- The Citizen <<https://www.thecitizen.in/>>
- People's Archive of Rural India (PARI) <<https:// ruralindiaonline.org/>>
- Karwaan-e-Mohabbat <<https://karwanemohabbat.in/>>
- Citizens for Justice and Peace (CJP) <<https://cjp.org.in/>>
- The Leaflet, an imprint of the Lawyers Collective, <<https:// theleaflet.in/>>
- Café Dissensus <<https://cafedissensus.com/>>
- Sabrang India <<https://sabrangindia.in/>>
- The Wire <<https://thewire.in/>>
- Scroll.in <<https://scroll.in/>>
- The Hoot <<asu.thehoot.org>>
- Firstpost <<https://www.firstpost.com/>>

Most of all, we acknowledge those who shared stories of their daily lives of struggle and resistance with us, through videos, conversations and articles. This reader is about, for and by these citizens.

CONTRIBUTORS

Abhilasha Chattopadhyay is a research scholar pursuing a Ph.D. in Sociology from Ambedkar University, Delhi.

Abhishek Anicca is a poet, writer and disability rights activist based in Delhi.

Akhil Katyal's translation of Ravish Kumar's *Ishq Mein Shahar Hona* was brought out by Speaking Tiger as *A City Happens in Love*. His second book of poems *How Many Countries Does the Indus Cross* won the Editor's Choice Award of The (Great) Indian Poetry Collective. He teaches Creative Writing at Ambedkar University, Delhi.

Aman Khatri is an illustrator and graphic designer currently working for *Newsclick*.

Anil Sadgopal, an educationist and activist, was involved in setting up Eklavya, an NGO that works on education. Since 1994, Sadgopal has been professor of education in the University of Delhi. He has also been carrying out studies in education policy as Senior Fellow of the Nehru Memorial Museum and Library since 2001.

Ashok Vajpeyi is a well known Hindi poet, essayist and critic. He received the Sahitya Akademi Award in 1994 for his poetry collection *Kahin Nahin Wahin*. In 2015, he returned this award as a gesture of protest against increasing intolerance in the country. He is the Managing and Life Trustee of Raza Foundation, an arts and culture organization based in Delhi.

Aslah Vadakara is the Editor of Maktoob Media. He has a Masters degree in History from Nalanda University, Bihar, and a Diploma in Turkish from the University of Anadolu, Turkey. He has also been a trainee for three months at Al Jazeera English.

Bezwada Wilson is the national convenor of the Safai Karmachari Andolan (SKA), which works to eradicate manual scavenging. In 2016, Wilson received the Ramon Magsaysay Award for "his moral energy and prodigious skill in leading a grassroots movement to eradicate the degrading servitude of manual scavenging in India, reclaiming for the dalits the human dignity that is their natural birthright."

Bindu N. Doddahatti is a litigator with the Alternative Law Forum, Bangalore. She is currently working on making legal aid more accessible to under-trial prisoners, and religious and sexual minorities. She is also associated with various peoples movements working on the issues of caste, and gender.

Chaman Lal was professor of Hindi Translation at the Centre of Indian Languages in Jawaharlal Nehru University, New Delhi. He edited and translated Punjabi poet Pash's collection in Hindi; the collection won the Sahitya Akademi Translation Prize. He returned the award in 2015 to protest against growing intolerance in the country. He returned another award given to him by the Central Hindi Directorate for his Hindi translation of Surjit Patar's Punjabi poetry against the attack on JNU in 2016. He is also known for his books on Bhagat Singh.

Chandan Gowda teaches at the Azim Premji University, Bengaluru. He has recently translated UR Ananthamurthy's novel, *Bara,* and edited *The Way I See It: A Gauri Lankesh Reader* and *Theatres of Democracy: Selected Essays of Shiv Visvanathan.* A book of autobiographical interviews he did with UR Ananthamurthy entitled *A Life in the World* will be published later this year. He is presently completing a book on the cultural politics of development in old Mysore state and a fictional work on the legendary engineer, Sir M Visvesvaraya. He is also co-translating and editing *The Post Office of Abachooru,* a book of short stories by the Kannada writer Purnachandra Tejasvi.

Chandramohan S writes poetry in English. He is part of the P K Rosi foundation, a cultural collective named after the legendary actress that seeks to demarginalise dalit-bahujans. He is the author of several poetry collections, including *Warscape Verses,* and *Letters to Namdeo Dhasal,* which was shortlisted for the Srinivas Rayaprol Poetry Prize and the Harish Govind Memorial Prize. Chandramohan coordinates English poetry readings in collaboration with a subaltern cultural collective in Kerala. In 2016, *Outlook* Magazine listed him as one of the Dalit Achievers of the Year.

Chandrashekhar Azad 'Ravan' is a law graduate and co-founder of the Bhim Army or the Bhim Army Bharat Ekta Mission, an organisation which fights for the development of dalits and other marginalised sections.

Chinnaiah Jangam is an assistant professor at the Department of History, Carleton University, Ottawa, Canada. He holds a Ph.D. from the School of Oriental and African Studies, University of London and a postdoctoral Fellowship at the International Center for Advanced Studies, New York University (2005-6). He was awarded the Felix Fellowship for doctoral studies. His research interests include South Asian social and intellectual history, dalits and anti-caste epistemologies, race, gender and imperialism. His first book *Dalits and the Making of Modern India* was published by Oxford University Press in 2017.

Daniya Rahman is a member of the editorial collective of the Indian Writers' Forum. She holds a bachelor's degree in English Literature from the University of Delhi and a master's degree from Jawaharlal Nehru University, Delhi.

E.P. Unny is a well-known cartoonist. He has worked for a range of newspapers, including *The Hindu*, the *Sunday Mail*, and the *Economic Times*. He is currently the chief political cartoonist at the *Indian Express*. His most recent publication is *Business As Usual: Journeys of the Indian Express Cartoonist*. He received the Lifetime Achievement Award from the Indian Institute of Cartoonists in 2009.

Faakirah Irfan is a women rights activist and a stand-up poet. She writes on women's and mental health issues and has moderated workshops on issues like feminism, mental health, and childhood sexual abuse. Faakirah also manages an online women support group called "Maala" on SHEROES. She holds a bachelor's degree in Law from the Kashmir University.

Geeta Seshu is an independent journalist engaged in reporting and analysing issues pertaining to media and journalism such as freedom of expression, gender, media ethics, media ownership and working conditions of journalists. She began her career as a journalist in 1984 and has worked with several media organisations like the *Indian Express* and *The Hoot*. She was a senior research fellow at the Awa Wadia Archives for Women and is also a co-founder of the Free Speech Collective.

Ghanshyam Shah is a sociologist and the author of numerous books including *Social Movements in India*. He has taught at several universities including the Jawaharlal Nehru University, New Delhi. He was a national fellow at the Indian Council of Social Science Research, affiliated to the Centre for Social Studies, Surat.

Githa Hariharan has written several novels, short fiction and essays over the last three decades. Her highly acclaimed works include *The Thousand Faces of Night* which won the Commonwealth Writers' Prize for Best First Book in 1993, the short story collection *The Art of Dying*; the novels *The Ghosts of Vasu Master, When Dreams Travel, In Times of Siege, Fugitive Histories* and *I Have Become the Tide*; and the collection of essays *Almost Home, Cities and Other Places*. She has also written children's stories; and edited a collection of translated short fiction *A Southern Harvest*, and the essay collection *From India to Palestine, Essays in Solidarity*. For more on this Delhi-based author and her work, visit www.githahariharan.com.

Gulzar Bhat is a Srinagar based independent journalist reporting on conflict, human rights, politics and development. He writes for various local and national publications including *National Herald* and *The Hindu Business Line*.

Hafiz Ahmed was born in a Bengal-origin Assamese Muslim family in Barpeta district, Assam. A well-known writer and social activist, he was awarded the M. Elim Uddin Dewan Memorial Literary Award for his contribution to Assamese literature and the Swahid Alif Uddin Memorial Award for his struggle for the preservation of the rights of marginalized communities in Assam.

Harsh Mander is an activist who works with survivors of mass violence and hunger as well as homeless persons and street children. He is the director of the Centre for Equity Studies and is a special commissioner to the Supreme Court in the Right to Food case. He is associated with various social causes including issues of communal harmony, tribal, dalit and disabled persons' rights, and RTI among others.

Huchangi Prasad is a writer and activist. He currently teaches at the Government First Grade College, Davanagere, Karnataka.

Ishita Mehta is a member of the editorial collective of the Indian Writers' Forum. She holds a master's degree in German Translation and Interpretation from Jawaharlal Nehru University. She has previously worked at the Archives and Research Center for Ethnomusicology.

Jyoti Shinoli is a Mumbai-based journalist and a content coordinator at the *People's Archive of Rural India*. She has previously worked with news channels like *Mi Marathi* and *Maharashtra1*.

K. Satchidanandan is a widely translated Malayalam poet and a bilingual writer, translator, scholar, critic and editor. Satchidanandan has written sixty books in Malayalam, including twenty-one poetry collections and an equal number of translations of poetry, plays, essays and travelogues. He is the winner of thirty-five awards, prizes and honours, including four Kerala Sahitya Akademi awards (for poetry, drama, travel writing and criticism), three National Awards, the Friendship Medal from the government of Poland, a Knighthood of the Order of Merit from the government of Italy, and a Dante Medal from Italy.

K.P. Ramanunni is a Kerala based novelist and short story writer. He received the Kerala Sahitya Akademi Award for his first novel *Sufi Paranja Katha* (What the Sufi Said). He also received the Kendra Sahitya Akademi Award for his novel *Daivathinte Pusthakam*. His other works include *Charama Varshikam, Jeevithathinte Pusthakam, Vidhathavinte Chiri* and *Vendapettavante Kurish*.

Keki N. Daruwalla is an Indian poet and short story writer. He was awarded the Sahitya Akademi Award in 1984 for his poetry collection *The Keeper of the Dead*. In 2014, he was awarded Padma Shri, the fourth highest civilian award in India. He received and returned the Sahitya Akademi Award in October, 2015, as a gesture of protest against the Akademi for failing to speak out against ideological collectives that have used physical violence against authors.

Kureeppuzha Sreekumar is a noted Malayalam poet. His books of poetry include *Habibinte Dinakkurippukal, Sreekumarinte Dukkangal, Rahulan Urangunnilla, Amma Malayalam, Keezhaalan* and *Suicide Point*. He won the Best Poet Award in 1975 from the Kerala University, and the 1987 Vyloppilli Award for Malayalam poetry. In 2003, he received the Kerala Sahitya Akademi Sree Padmanabhaswamy Award for the best work in children's literature for his work *Penangunni*, which he refused as it is in the name of a savarna Hindu god. He represented India at an Afro-Indian conference and represented Kerala at the All India Poets Meet. In 2011, he won the Kerala Sahitya Akademi Award for *Keezhalan*.

Lal Singh Dil (1943-2007) was born into a dalit family in Ludhiana district. He was part of the Naxalite movement and was arrested by the police. Published in 1971, his first book of poetry is *Bahut Sare Suraj* (Many Suns). He then wrote his autobiography *Dastan*. His poems have been translated into Hindi, Urdu and English. A selection of his translations and memoirs, *Poet of the Revolution*, was published in English in 2012.

Lawrence Liang is a professor of law at Ambedkar University, Delhi. He is also a co-founder of the Alternative Law Forum.

M. Mohsin Alam Bhat is an assistant professor of law and runs the Centre for Public Interest Law at Jindal Global Law School, Haryana.

Mamata Pared is an aspiring journalist. She is pursuing a bachelor's degree in mass media from the Ramniranjan Jhunjhunwala College of Arts, Science and Commerce, Mumbai.

Manash Firaq Bhattacharjee is a poet, writer and political science scholar from JNU. He frequently writes for *The Wire*, and has contributed to *The New York Times*, *Al Jazeera*, *Los Angeles Review of Books*, *Guernica*, *The Hindu*, *Outlook*, and *EPW* among other publications. His book *Looking for the Nation: Towards Another Idea of India* has recently been published by the Speaking Tiger Books.

Meena Alexander was an award winning poet and scholar. Her works include a book of poetry *Atmospheric Embroidery* and an edited volume drawing on the works of Twentieth Century Indian writers in several languages, *Name me a Word: Indian Writers Reflect on Writing*.

Nandini Sundar is a professor of sociology at the Delhi School of Economics. Her publications include *The Burning Forest: India's War in Bastar*, an edited volume *The Scheduled Tribes and their India*, and *Civil Wars in South Asia: State, Sovereignty, Development*, co-edited with Aparna Sundar. She has worked towards the abolition of the notorious Salwa Judum. In 2010, Sundar was awarded the Infosys Prize for Social Sciences and the Ester Boserup Prize for Development Research in 2016.

Natasha Rather is a researcher with the Jammu & Kashmir Coalition of Civil Society (JKCCS) She has worked on issues of institutional and systematic sexual violence in Jammu and Kashmir. She is the co-author of the book *Do You Remember Kunan Poshpora?*, published in 2016 by Zubaan.

Nayantara Sahgal is the author of several fictional and non-fictional works, the first of which, *Prison and Chocolate Cake*, an autobiography, was published in 1954. Her works include classic novels such as *Rich Like Us*, *Plans for Departure*, *Lesser Breeds* and *When the Moon Shines* *by Day*. She has received the Sahitya Akademi Award, the Sinclair Prize and the Commonwealth Writers' Prize. She is a Member of the American Academy of Arts & Sciences. She has been awarded the Diploma of Honour from the International Order of Volunteers of Peace (Italy), and an Honorary Doctorate of Letters from the University of Leeds. She returned her Akademi Award in 2015 as a gesture of protest against the murder of three writers by vigilantes, and the Akademi's silence at the time. She has been a Vice President of the PUCL (People's Union for Civil Liberties) and is engaged in an ongoing protest against the assaults on freedom of expression and democratic rights.

Nikhil Wagle is the former editor of *Mahanagar* and *IBN Lokmat*. He began his career in 1977 with *Dinank*, a Marathi newsweekly and later became the editor-in-chief of *Dinank*. He also established the Marathi and Hindi newspaper *Mahanagar* in 1990. He served as the editor of the Marathi version of the newspaper, *Aapla Mahanagar*. He was attacked by Shiv Sena supporters for making critical comments on the Maharashtra legislators who were paying flattering tributes to a deceased MLA accused of having criminal connections. He was later imprisoned for his comments but refused to apologise to the legislators. He is currently a freelance reporter and works primarily on the nexus of crime and politics.

Nitesh Kumar works as a graphic designer for *Newsclick*.

Orijit Sen is a graphic artist, cartoonist, muralist and designer. He is the author of several works of graphic fiction and non-fiction including the graphic novel *River of Stories*. He is one of the founders of People Tree, a collaborative studio and store for artists, designers and craftspeople. Sen is also Mario Miranda Chair visiting professor at Goa University.

P. Mahamud is a well known political cartoonist who has worked with *Prajavani, Deccan Herald,* and *Vijayakarnataka.* He received the first Gauri Lankesh-PEN International Award in 2018.

P. Sainath is an Indian journalist and a photojournalist who focuses on social and economic inequality, rural affairs, poverty and the aftermath of globalisation in India. He is the Founder Editor of the *People's Archive of Rural India*. He was the Rural Affairs Editor at *The Hindu* till 2014. In June 2011, Sainath was conferred an Honorary Doctor of Letters degree (DLitt) by the University of Alberta. He is one of the few

Indians to receive the Ramon Magsaysay Award, which he accepted in 2007 in the category of Journalism, Literature and Creative Communication Arts.

Prabhat Patnaik is a professor emeritus at the Centre for Economic Studies and Planning, Jawaharlal Nehru University, Delhi. He is an Indian Marxist economist and a political commentator. He was the vice-chairman of the Planning Board of the Indian state of Kerala from June 2006 to May 2011. He specialises in macroeconomics and political economy and has written several books and articles on the same. His books include *Time, Inflation and Growth, Economics and Egalitarianism, Whatever Happened to Imperialism and Other Essays, Accumulation and Stability Under Capitalism* and *The Retreat to Unfreedom*. He is also the editor of Social Scientist, which under his stewardship, has become a highly effective vehicle for progressive ideas and research.

Prabir Purkayastha is the Editor of *Newsclick*, an online news site, President of Free Software Movement and a founder member of All India Peoples Science Network. He is an engineer and an activist.

Pranjal is a journalist and activist who works with *Newsclick*.

Purusottam Thakur is a 2015 PARI Fellow, and a freelance journalist, photographer and documentary filmmaker who reports from Chhattisgarh and Odisha. He also works for the Azim Premji Foundation.

Pushpamala N. has been called "the most entertaining artist-iconoclast of contemporary Indian art". She seeks to subvert the dominant discourse through her sharp and witty work as a photo and video performance artist, sculptor, writer, curator and provocateur. She lives in Bengaluru.

Ra Sh (Ravi Shanker N) is an Indian English poet from Palakkad, Kerala, whose collection *Architecture of Flesh* was published by Poetrywala, Mumbai, in December 2015, with an introduction by Meena Kandasamy. In 2018, his translation of 100 Malayali poets was published under the title *How to Translate an Earthworm?* by Dhauli Books.

Rajendra Chenni is a bilingual writer and activist. Formerly a professor of English at Kuvempu University, he is now the Director at the Manasa Centre for Cultural Studies, Shimoga.

Rebel Politik is a political cartoonist and illustrator. He uses his cartoons to look at the struggles of the people and the working-classes.

Salim Yusufji was a schoolteacher for fifteen years, and has previously edited *Ambedkar: The Attendant Details*, a selection of reminiscences by people in close proximity to B R Ambedkar.

Samyukta Shastri is the content co-ordinator at the *People's Archive of Rural India*. She has a bachelor's degree in Media Studies from the Symbiosis Centre for Media and Communication, Pune, and a master's degree in English Literature from SNDT Women's University, Mumbai.

Sanjukta Basu is a writer, photographer, and feminist scholar. She writes on women, politics, minority rights and other social issues. In 2009, she received the TED Fellowship for her blogging and digital activism. As a public speaker and trainer she has delivered talks / lectures at TEDx conferences, colleges, NGOs and conducted workshops on digital media and gender. Her bylines can be seen on *Firstpost, Huffington Post, Outlook, The Wire,* and *Daily O* among others. As part of the Karwan-e-Mohabbat collective led by Harsh Mander, she has travelled across India to document stories of hate crimes. Basu completed her BA LLB from the University of Delhi and is currently pursuing her Ph.D. in Women and Gender Studies.

Shalim M. Hussain is a poet, short-story writer, translator and filmmaker. His recent work has been focused on the syncretic culture of Assam.

Shanta Gokhale is a novelist, playwright, translator, cultural critic, columnist and theatre historian. She received the Sangeet Natak Akademi Award for her overall contribution to the performing arts in 2016. Some of her works include *The Theatre of Veenapani Chawla: Theory, Practice, Performance*; the novels *Tyā Varshī* and *Rita Welinkar* (Marathi); and the play *Avinash: the indestructible.*

Shashi Deshpande has written novels, short stories, essays and books for children over several decades. She has also translated several works from Kannada and Marathi into English. Her most recent work is a the literary memoir *Listen to Me.*

Shreya Roy Chowdhury is a Delhi-based journalist. She currently writes on education for *Scroll.in* and has previously written for *The Times of India.*

Somok Roy studies History at Ramjas College, University of Delhi. His research interests include early modern court cultures, the histories of desire and sexuality, and performance in Mughal India. Roy has trained in Hindustani classical music under Dr. Girija Devi of the Senia-Banaras tradition.

Soumyabrata Choudhury currently teaches at the School of Arts and Aesthetics, JNU . He has previously taught at CSSSC, Kolkata, and has been a fellow at CSDS, Delhi, and IIAS, Shimla. His book *Theatre, Number, Event: Three Studies on the Relationship of Sovereignty, Power and Truth* was published by IIAS, Shimla, in 2013. His latest book *Ambedkar and Other Immortals: An Untouchable Research Programme* was first published in 2015.

Sreelakshmi KM is a research scholar pursuing a Ph.D. in Linguistics from Jawaharlal Nehru University, Delhi.

Subodh Varma is currently working with *Newsclick*, after leaving mainstream print media. He writes on social and economic issues with a focus on evidence-based analysis. He has also worked with trade unions and other Left organisations.

Sumit kumar is a graphic designer and currently works with *Newsclick*.

Surajit Mazumdar is a professor at the Centre for Economic Studies and Planning, Jawaharlal Nehru University, Delhi. His areas of interest are political economy, Indian industrialisation, Indian corporate sector, and globalisation.

Surangya Kaur works as a journalist and video producer with *Newsclick*.

Sweta Daga is a Bangalore-based writer and photographer. She is working on several multimedia projects including fellowships with the *People's Archive of Rural India* and the Centre for Science and Environment.

Teesta Setalvad is a senior journalist, educationist and activist. She is co-editor of the monthly *Communalism Combat*, along with Javed Anand. Setalvad is involved with broadening the boundaries of history and social studies teaching through KHOJ, a programme for secular education, and has worked extensively on exclusion and communalisation in school curricula and textbooks. She has analysed and documented the communalisation of India's law and order machinery, and the rise of communal conflict in Gujarat since the early 1990s. Trained also in law, Setalvad was convenor of the Concerned Citizens Tribunal—Crimes Against Humanity, Gujarat 2002, headed by Justices V.R. Krishna Iyer, P.B. Sawant and Hosbet Suresh. She is also the secretary of Citizens for Justice and Peace (CJP), a civil rights group set up by her and other concerned citizens of Mumbai in April 2002.

Tejal Kanitkar is an assistant professor and the chairperson of the Centre for Climate Change and Sustainability Studies, School of Habitat Studies, Tata Institute of Social Sciences, Mumbai.

Tilak Tewari is a student of history and specialises in Medieval Studies. He has completed his graduation from the University of Delhi and post-graduation from Jawaharlal Nehru University, Delhi. He is currently working with the Indian National Trust for Art and Cultural Heritage as a research associate.

Uday Prakash is a contemporary Hindi poet, scholar, journalist, translator and short story writer. He was a recipient of the Sahitya Akademi Award for his collection of short stories *Mohan Das*. He returned the award in 2015 as a gesture of protest against the murder of scholar M M Kalburgi.

Vartika Rastogi is a part-time journalist and a student of English Literature at Hindu College, University of Delhi.

Vidhya is a research scholar in History specialising in Archaeology. She is one of the organisers of Women Against Sexual Violence and State Repression (WSS), a non-funded grassroot network of activists formed to address the intersections between sexual violence and state repression. Her writing focuses on people's movements across the country.

Vivan Eyben is a journalist working for *Newsclick*. He completed his law studies at the Christ University, Bengaluru.

Yogesh S is currently a journalist with *Newsclick* and is an independent researcher. He is also a former member of the editorial collective of the Indian Writers' Forum.

INDIA DISSENTS

3,000 Years of Difference, Doubt and Argument

Edited by Ashok Vajpeyi

Throughout Indian history, various individuals and groups have questioned, censured and debated authority—be it the state or empire, religious or political traditions, caste hierarchies, patriarchy, or even the idea of god. These dissenting voices have persisted despite all attempts made to silence them. They have inspired revolutions and uprisings, helped preserve individual dignity and freedom, and promoted tolerance and a plurality in thought and lifestyle. *India Dissents: 3,000 Years of Difference, Doubt and Argument* brings together some of these voices: collected in these pages are essays, letters, reports, poems, songs and calls to action—from texts ranging from the *Rig Veda* to Ambedkar's *Annihilation of Caste*; and by thinkers as varied as the Buddha, Akka Mahadevi, Lal Ded, Nanak, Ghalib, Tagore, Gandhi, Manto, Jayaprakash Narayan, Namdeo Dhasal, Mahasweta Devi, Medha Patkar and Amartya Sen. Their words embody the undying and essential spirit of debate and dissent in one of the world's most diverse, dynamic and ancient civilizations.

DISPOSSESSED

Stories from India's Margins

Ashwin Parulkar, Saba Sharma, Amod Shah,
Shikha Sethia, Rhea John, Anhad Imaan, Annie Baxi

In 2005, starving members of the Bhuiya clan in one of Bihar's poorest villages dug up a dead goat, cooked and ate it; sixteen people died within days, twelve of them children. Bengali-speaking Muslims who had moved to Rajasthan from West Bengal in the 1970s and '80s were summarily declared Bangladeshi terrorists in the aftermath of the 2008 Jaipur bomb blasts; they remain stateless in their own country. Landless Lodhas, members of an erstwhile 'Criminal Tribe', grapple even today with centuries of shame, prejudice and dispossession.

These stories—along with those of women with mental and physical disabilities in rural areas, homeless men in Yamuna Pushta in New Delhi, and patients in a leprosy colony in Orissa— reveal both stigma and support, harsh lives, an uncaring, corrupt state and moments of individual resilience.

Drawn from interviews and conversations as part of a study on destitution by the Centre for Equity Studies, *Dispossessed: Stories from India's Margins*, takes a wide-ranging view of what it means to be destitute, displaced and marginalized in contemporary India. Equally importantly, through these personal accounts of their research, the authors explore their own privileges in comparison. This is an important book that questions India's engagement with the people at its margins, and should be essential reading for all.

www.ingramcontent.com/pod-product-compliance
Lightning Source LLC
Chambersburg PA
CBHW050332270326
41926CB00016B/3418